*Web Writing*

# Web Writing

*Why and How for Liberal Arts Teaching and Learning*

Jack Dougherty and Tennyson O'Donnell, editors

*University of Michigan Press*
*Ann Arbor*

Published in the United States of America by
University of Michigan Press
Manufactured in the United States of America
Printed on acid-free paper

2018 2017 2016 2015 4 3 2 1

A CIP catalog record for this book is available from the British Library.

DOI: http://dx.doi.org/10.3998/dh.13396229.0001.001

ISBN 978-0-472-07282-8 (hardcover)
ISBN 978-0-472-05282-0 (pbk.)
ISBN 978-0-472-12135-9 (e-book)

This book was produced using PressBooks.com, and PDF rendering was done by PrinceXML.

## Dedication

*To all teachers who have patiently read, listened, commented on, and encouraged students in the writing process.*

*— J.D. and T.O.*

DIGITALCULTUREBOOKS, an imprint of the University of Michigan Press, is dedicated to publishing work in new media studies and the emerging field of digital humanities.

# Contents

# About this book

By arrangement with the University of Michigan Press, open-access digital editions of the book are freely available on the Trinity College ePress platform at http://epress.trincoll.edu/webwriting. Readers may view the web edition online, or freely download the PDF, ePUB, and Kindle (Mobi) editions. The Trinity College ePress platform also offers an extra Tutorials section with how-to guides for several digital writing tools mentioned in the text. This platform relies on two open-source WordPress plugins—Press-Books (by Hugh McGuire at Book Oven, Inc.) and PressBooks Textbook (by Brad Payne at BCCampus)—on a web server at TrinfoCafe.org (maintained by Carlos Espinosa).

In addition, the 2013 open peer review edition of the book manuscript is freely available from Trinity College at http://webwriting2013.trincoll.edu. This edition includes the open call for essay ideas, preliminary drafts, and over one thousand comments by readers of the manuscript. It relies on another open-source WordPress plugin, CommentPress Core (by Christian Wach at the Institute for the Future of the Book).

All web links to the final edition of this book were functional as of August 2014. Due to the changing nature of the Internet, all external links have been fully cited in the notes to assist readers of the print and digital editions. If a link is no longer active, search the web address using the "Way Back Machine" provided by the Internet Archive at https://archive.org/.

# Acknowledgements

Special thanks go to several people who nourished Web Writing in its early stages: The inaugural group of Center for Teaching and Learning Fellows who kindly provided feedback on the first draft (Kath Archer, Brett Barwick, Carol Clark, Luis Figueroa, Irene Papoulis, Joe Palladino), and several colleagues who offered early advice and encouragement, specifically Korey Jackson, Kristen Nawrotzki, colleagues at MediaCommons, and many THATCamp workshop participants. Carlos Espinosa at TrinfoCafe.org capably manages the server that hosts the CommentPress and PressBooks editions of this volume. Christian Wach developed the open-source CommentPress Core plugin (based on a previous version by Eddie Tejeda) and patiently answered several questions about customizing our child theme. Hugh McGuire and colleagues created the open-source PressBooks plugin, and Brad Payne coded the open-source PressBooks Textbook plugin and theme. Our logo was designed by Rita Law, manager of creative services at Trinity College. At Michigan Publishing, we thank editorial director Aaron McCullough and his colleagues Meredith Kahn, Christopher Dreyer, Kevin Hawkins, Jason Colman, Jillian Downey, and Tom Dwyer. We also appreciate the thoughtful commentary of the expert reviewers commissioned by the publisher—Barbara Fister, Jason Mittell, Amanda Seligman, and Kate Singer—as well as nearly seventy other readers who participated in the open peer review.

# Introduction

*Jack Dougherty and Tennyson O'Donnell*

## Why this book?

*Web Writing* reboots how we think about the Internet in higher education, with special attention paid to liberal arts teaching and learning. Our book carves out pedagogically pragmatic responses to contemporary debates that tend to be dominated by two extreme visions of technology. At one end, skeptics dismiss the web as an unwelcome intrusion into the college classroom, most frequently in the form of gadgets and platforms that distract students from the primary lesson or content. This perspective views Internet technology as a shallow substitute for true learning, yet rarely recognizes its potential to enhance what we value most about a liberal arts education: the intensified learning opportunities presented by writing across the curriculum. At the other extreme, proponents of massive online courses praise the benefits of large-scale video lectures and machine-driven assessments with the promise of opening up the college curriculum to all. Their view embraces the web as a tool to expand student enrollments while reducing instructional labor costs, yet rarely considers its consequences for highly-engaged student learning that we expect in small liberal arts colleges.

Prior to writing this book, much of our thinking was dominated by these two extreme positions. On one side, Nicholas Carr's *The Shallows: What the Internet is Doing to our Minds,* a Pulitzer Prize finalist, was selected by our liberal arts campus, Trinity College, as the required book for all first-year students in fall 2012.[1] A few months later on the other side, *The New York Times* declared 2012 to be "The Year of the MOOC," and its prominent opinion essayist Thomas Friedman announced that "nothing has more potential to enable us to reimagine higher education than the massive online course."[2] But neither of these extremes fit with our experiences as liberal arts educators who were experimenting with digital technologies to improve our students' writing. As a result, we decided to author our own book and invited others to join us in drafting chapters and openly peer reviewing the manuscript on the public web.

*Web Writing* seeks to bridge philosophical and practical questions that arise from the experiences of liberal arts educators who have stepped into the digital realm. What are the most—and least—compelling reasons for why we should integrate web writing into our curriculum? Which tools and teaching methods deepen—rather than distract from—thoughtful learning? How does student engagement and sense of community evolve when we share our drafts and commentary on the public web? To what extent does writing on the web enable our students to cross over divisive boundaries, and what new challenges does it create? The book's subtitle signals our desire to blend "why" questions with examples of "how" it can be done, presented in both print and digital formats.

As co-editors of this volume, we steer a middle course that argues for thoughtfully integrating web tools into a liberal arts education. Whether in persuasive essays, scientific reports, or creative expression, all academic disciplines value clear and compelling prose. The act of writing visually demonstrates our thought processes: how we respond to ideas that challenge our own thinking, consider alternative perspectives or counter-evidence, and create entirely new points of view. As college educators, we recognize that our students become more engaged in the writing process when they draft, share, and respond to writing with a community of peer readers who encourage and challenge them to revise muddled first drafts into more polished, thoughtful essays. Moreover, we now realize how a new generation of web-based writing tools—including wikis, Google Documents, WordPress, and others—can transform how our students author, edit, publish, and comment on texts in ways that advance, rather than distract from, our liberal arts mission. But exactly how college educators can make use of these tools in our classrooms is not simple, and requires both time and support from our institutions. Our motivation behind this book is to offer faculty a wide range of web-based writing examples across the liberal arts, to help all of us to rethink our current approaches and inspire us to innovate with our own students.

We did not design *Web Writing* as a theoretical study of composition, nor did we envision it merely as a high-tech user's guide. Instead, our book contributes to the scholarship of teaching. It aims to broaden the conversation among liberal arts faculty who actively engage with writing in their classrooms in multiple disciplines but need guidance on ways that web-based tools can contribute to our educational missions. We intentionally wrote the book in an accessible style that favors real classroom examples, avoids jargon, and appeals to our common interests as college educators who care about writing. The need for this book emerged during a faculty workshop series sponsored by the Center for Teaching and Learning at Trinity College that encouraged faculty to cross departmental boundaries and reflect on ways of improving our pedagogical practices across the campus. We formed a five-person advisory group to bring together ideas from our specializations in developmental psychology, digital humanities, educational studies, English literature, and rhetoric and composition. As a result, authors from fifteen colleges contributed chapters to the final edition that represent different approaches to web writing in the humanities, social sciences, and life sciences.

This book would not have been possible without the many scholars who previously created the field of digital writing and shaped our thinking about its possibilities. We drew inspiration from the expanding literature in rhetoric, technology, and pedagogy, including established journals such as *Kairos* and *Computers and Composition*, newer publications such as the *Journal of Interactive Technology and Pedagogy*, *Hybrid Pedagogy*, and *Writing Spaces*. We also benefitted from recent edited volumes such as *Hacking the Academy* and *Debates in the Digital Humanities*, organizations such as THATCamp and the Writing Across the Curriculum Clearinghouse, and the *ProfHacker* blog, co-founded by one of our advisory group members, Jason B. Jones.[3] During this process, we noticed that higher education lacks a comprehensive cross-disciplinary book on teaching digital writing that is comparable to titles authored for the K-12 sector by Troy Hicks and the National Writing Project.[4] In response, we chose to work with a leading scholarly open-access publisher to distribute our peer-reviewed book in two formats—print (for sale) and online (for free)—to maximize readership by college-level educators, their students, and anyone who wishes to learn about writing on the web.

## Why create this book on the web?

Since we could not find a book about web writing that met our needs as liberal arts educators, we decided to create one. We invited authors and readers to build it with us—in public—on the web. Our process began in spring 2013 with an open call for prospective contributors, who posted over forty one-paragraph chapter ideas for online discussion. Next, twenty-five authors submitted full drafts and agreed to our editorial and intellectual property policy, which preserved their copyright while publicly sharing the work under a Creative Commons license, and made clear that their contributions may not advance to the final volume. During the open peer review in fall 2013, seventy readers (including four expert reviewers commissioned by the publisher) generated over one thousand comments on our website, most of them quite substantive. We required all commenters to use their full names, but, to avoid deferential treatment, we did not identify which ones were the commissioned expert reviewers. Based on the editorial advisory group's judgment of reader feedback, we invited selected essays to be revised and resubmitted for the final manuscript. We collaborated with the University of Michigan Press and its umbrella organization, Michigan Publishing, on a contract that makes the final book available in print-on-demand (for sale) and open-access online (for free), with long-term electronic preservation through the HathiTrust Digital Library. Learn more about the process in the Tutorials section of the Trinity edition.[5]

As educators, our compelling reason for constructing this book online is because that's exactly what we ask our students to do when we assign them to share their writing with us and other readers. Every educator who requires students to post their words on a course learning management system (such as Moodle, Blackboard, etc.) or the open web should try the same experience by uploading their own writing for feedback from peers and the public. For many of us, our first experiences in publicly circulating drafts was equally terrifying and exhilarating. The process opened our eyes to how our writing changes when engaging with a broader audience, particularly one that talks back through comments that suggest new connections and sharpen our thinking. We hope that *Web Writing* will encourage more faculty to author and comment online, and that these experiences will transfer into richer forms of teaching and learning in their classrooms.

As scholars, we were driven by the idea of creating a book on the open web in order to improve the quality of our work through reader feedback and to expand the breadth of our audience with free access. We publicly shared each stage of *Web Writing* and welcomed input to guide editorial selections and contributors' revisions prior to its final publication. This "publish-then-filter" approach, as Clay Shirky and Kathleen Fitzpatrick have described it, is not without risks, particularly for authors whose work may receive negative comments, or not advance to the final volume. But the rewards are numerous: greater opportunities for developmental editing by experts and general readers, reduced social isolation of the solo academic writing process, and speedier time from concept to publication.[6] This "new" model of constructing an edited volume certainly beats the "old" way, where contributors typically submitted chapters solely to the editor, and rarely saw drafts by other authors until the book was finished, thereby missing the opportunity for valuable feedback to enhance their individual drafts and the volume as a whole. In particular, for those of us writing about digital influences on higher education, where rapid transformations outpace old-fashioned publication schedules (typically at least one or two years), sharing our texts online has the added benefit of timeliness.

Scholarly authors also benefit by publishing open-access, rather than locking our ideas behind a password or a pay-wall, because we expand the range of our audience, and with it, our academic reputations. While open-access means free to readers, it requires a rethinking of traditional financial arrangements.[7] Faculty can assign syllabus readings without increasing student textbook costs. Libraries can link publications to their online catalogues without paying intermediaries. Readers outside the gates of higher education can discover and instantly access our book through their web browsers without tuition bills. As part of this exchange, under our open-access book contract we do not expect print book sales to generate royalties for authors, but academics rarely made money from edited volumes in the past. The most significant change is institutional support. Trinity College supported this book by directly funding approximately $5,000 in pre-publication costs, and indirectly supporting additional technology learning and technical infrastructure costs. First, the Center for Teaching and Learning provided a $2,000 fellowship to the lead editor to conceptualize and draft initial essays for the book during a 2012-13 faculty seminar series. Second, the Center provided five $300 subventions to support outstanding essay proposals by non-tenure-track authors during the open call, plus $500 to Michigan Publishing to cover half the cost of commissioning four expert reviewers at $250 each during the open peer review. Third, the Trinity Institute for Interdisciplinary Studies awarded the editorial team a manuscript fellowship to sponsor a half-day seminar discussion with four guest readers from our campus and another from a nearby institution in fall 2013. To be sure, additional costs could be attributed to faculty and staff labor and web technology infrastructure that supported this book at Trinity, but these were already in place and would have been spent regardless of this particular book project. All of these pre-publication expenses enhanced the quality of the product yet were not linked to any promise of post-production sales revenue. Instead, the benefits that our institution reaps from its branding as a digital innovator in liberal arts pedagogy and scholarly publication is worth the relatively small dollar investment on this project.

## What's inside this book?

All of the chapters in *Web Writing* are essentially local stories about what worked (or could have worked better) in one instructor's classroom, or as a team of instructors at one campus or between two campuses. People who shared their stories of web writing responded to particular institutional missions, student needs, and from their own area of expertise. *Web Writing* does not attempt to convert the uninitiated to teaching online or prescribe a list of digital writing reforms. Instead, authors simply describe how and why they integrated web writing in their courses and allow readers to choose among various pedagogical ideas and learning experiences. None of the articles offer large-scale or programmatic writing initiatives with MOOC-sized student enrollments. Primarily, our book shines a bright light on individual innovations that stand in the long shadow of ideological debates.

Our contributors do not identify themselves solely as experts in the field of computers and composition, nor as theorists or technologists. We are everyday liberal arts educators who are trying their hand at digital innovations in order to help students write to learn and learn to write. They are committed to the concept that web writing offers a different experience of writing; even if the resulting content isn't remarkably different, instructors recognize the value of expanding the audience of readers (in and out of the classroom) during the writing and learning process. Most authors are at the early stages of trying out their ideas. As they sort out the process, they want to share what they have learned because it is fresh for them. The richness of the book is that it represents authors from 15 colleges across the liberal arts curriculum who demonstrate how they use writing in disciplines like biology, history and sociology and across platforms to improve student motivation and learning.

## Communities

Why should we teach our students to write on the web? Several contributors identified "communities" as a key theme, referring both to creating richer collaborations among students in the course, and to exchanging views with others beyond the classroom walls. In their co-authored essay, "Sister Classrooms: Blogging Across Disciplines and Campuses," Amanda Hagood and Carmel Price explain how student writing changed when they linked their two classes at different colleges through online writing about the environment. In "Indigenizing Wikipedia," Siobhan Senier describes what her students learned by attempting to write the stories of contemporary Native American authors into the popular encyclopedia, and the barriers they encountered by online editors. Michael O'Donnell evaluates his biology students' collective experience with an innovative approach to lab reports in "Science Writing, Wikis, and Collaborative Learning." Jim Trostle reflects on a class assignment and shares video excerpts of his students as they engaged in "Cooperative In-Class Writing with Google Docs." Finally, Jack Dougherty offers lessons he learned about community building in "Co-Writing, Peer Editing, and Publishing in the Cloud."

## Engagement

Several contributors advocate web writing because it increased student engagement, both with scholarship and civic life. Celeste Sharpe, Nate Sleeter, and Kelly Schrum explain "How We Learned to Drop the Quiz" with their innovative approach to teaching historical writing in online asynchronous courses. Leigh Wright tells her students to "Tweet Me A Story" and explains how incorporating social media into writing assignments taught them about journalism and screenwriting. In "Civic Engagement," Susan Grogan describes how her students created a Super PAC devoted to bringing political comedian Stephen Colbert to their campus, and began writing on the web about their roles in electoral politics. Jack Dougherty seeks to balance the competing values of "Public Writing and Student Privacy" and offers suggestions for college educators facing similar dilemmas. Jen Rajchel asks student web-authors to "Consider the Audience" when sharing their work online, especially as they navigate both public and private spheres. In "Creating the Reader-Viewer," Anita DeRouen reflects on the pedagogical and rhetorical challenges of engaging students to read, create, and assess multimodal web texts. Finally, Shawn Graham reveals how his students began writing history through video games in his essay, "Pulling Back the Curtain."

### Crossing Boundaries

For some educators, writing on the web raises the possibility of crossing boundaries, not only of race and culture, but also time and personal space. In their co-authored essay, Rochelle Rodrigo and Jennifer Kidd explain the process of "Getting Uncomfortable" with identity exploration in a multiclass blog, and their evaluation of its influence on student learning outcomes. Another digital pedagogy duo, Pete Coco and M. Gabriela Torres, outline their strategy for teaching "Curation in Writing," with building-and-breaking metaphors for student blogging on cultural anthropology. Alisea Williams McLeod reflects on the problems and possibilities of "Student Digital Research and Writing on Slavery," focusing on the experiences of students at a historically black college as they transcribed historical records of former slaves and their white masters during the Civil War era. Finally, Holly Oberle explores whether classroom technology affects international students differently than domestic ones in her essay, "Web Writing as Intercultural Dialogue."

### Citation and Annotation

When students author on the web, they invariably encounter other writers, which raises questions about the ways we learn to acknowledge and attribute other people's ideas. Christopher Hager recounts in "The Secondary Source Sitting Next to You" how students responded to a web assignment that required them to cite work by their peers. In "Web Writing and Citation: The Authority of Communities," Elizabeth Switaj explains how educators can draw on the logic of social referencing in online communities to help students recognize citation as a community practice. Laura Lisabeth explores how her students critiqued *The Elements of Style* writing guide in her essay, "Empowering Education with Social Annotation and Wikis." Despite everything the software industry has led us to believe, Jason B. Jones argues that "There Are No New Directions in Annotations," which explains why new tools of the trade should feel "radically familiar" in the liberal arts.

## Tutorials

This extra section features how-to guides for several web-based writing tools mentioned in the text. It appears only in the open-access Trinity College ePress edition of the book, which allows us to include more images and videos than the print edition, and to update them when desired.[8]

What is not in this book? During the open call phase of this book, we expressed interest in several ideas that did not result in fully developed chapters, which we identify here to encourage others to take up in future works.

No one defined the machine as the writing teacher. In other words, while many of our contributors used the web to connect authors and readers, none of them described using digital tools to directly instruct students or to evaluate their essays. This should not surprise us, given our skepticism about massive online learning in liberal arts education, but the absence of discussion about web-based writing tools deserves more attention. At a basic level, we wonder how college educators and their students make use of basic software tools designed to improve our prose, such as the ubiquitous spelling and grammar checkers. What have educators learned about implicitly assuming or explicitly teaching students how to use these in the writing process? Taking one step further, we are curious about what students learn about writing from web-based instructional resources, both inside and outside of the formal curriculum. A quick search of the popular

YouTube site can point learners to videos of writing instructors who sketch out different approaches to crafting introductions on a whiteboard, or a screencast of using a word-processor to create a "reverse outline" that reveals an essay's underlying structure.[9] Can these web resources effectively supplement our face-to-face writing instruction? Or at a more controversial level, can and will they replace us? Machine-scored essay evaluation is very contentious—and poorly understood—area of debate, which would benefit from the perspectives of liberal arts educators who can explain the artificial intelligence or who have first-hand experiences with these tools.[10]

On a related note, few contributors wrote directly about evidence. How do we really know if web-writing strategies will enhance our students' prose and identity as a community of authors? While this volume favors local stories of individual educators, we can see the value in moving our discussion beyond impressionistic accounts to social science experiments on the writing process. As we conceptualized this volume, an intriguing study by Ina Blau and Avmer Caspi caught our attention.[11] They compared collaborative student work on Google Documents across different conditions and found that suggesting revisions by inserting marginal comments (rather than directly editing a peer's text) positively influenced students' sense of ownership, responsibility, and perceived quality of writing outcomes. With further research, we might better understand how different forms of online collaboration might help or hinder different types of students (such as novice versus seasoned writers) or different aspects of writing (such as organization versus argumentation). But the key point is to demonstrate more systematic ways of evaluating pedagogical approaches on student outcomes. Even if we lack the time or training to conduct scientific studies, new digital tools allow us to more easily collect samples of student writing and to analyze contributions to multi-authored works.[12]

On a more personal level, no one explicitly wrote about sharing their "writing workflows" with students. Authors did not describe their steps from research and reflection to a fully written essay. No details were offered about the stages of brainstorming, note-taking, outlining, drafting, citing, editing, and revising process that take place on paper or a screen. The tools chosen for particular stages of work were not emphasized or discussed. Many of these invisible decisions could depend upon whether the writing is a solitary or collaborative act. When we consider that many of us have considered or adopted new tools in recent years, might our students (and colleagues) benefit from a more public discussion of different approaches to the writing process in the digital age? Or perhaps we should flip the question (and its assumption about who's teaching whom) to ask: how do students devise their own writing workflows, what sources influence them, and what does this tell us about teaching and learning with the web?[13]

There is a humorous saying in the software industry: "Eat your own dog food." It means that companies should use the same products that they sell to their customers. Building this book through the same tools and processes that our students might compose in has taught us valuable lessons that we are eager to explore with others. As we continue to weigh and measure the affordances that new technologies present to our pedagogical approaches in the liberal arts, we hope that readers of *Web Writing* feel a stronger sense of the exciting opportunities ahead.

On behalf of the *Web Writing* advisory group at Trinity College, Hartford, Connecticut

- Jack Dougherty, Associate Professor of Educational Studies
- Tennyson O'Donnell, Director of the Allan K. Smith Center for Writing and Rhetoric and Allan K. Smith Lecturer in English Composition
- Dina Anselmi, Associate Professor of Psychology and Co-Director of the Center for Teaching and Learning
- Christopher Hager, Associate Professor of English and Co-Director of the Center for Teaching and Learning
- Jason B. Jones, Director of Educational Technology

**How to cite:**

Jack Dougherty and Tennyson O'Donnell, eds., "Introduction," in *Web Writing: Why and How for Liberal Arts Teaching and Learning* (University of Michigan Press/Trinity College ePress edition, 2014), http://epress.trincoll.edu/webwriting/.

# Notes

1. Nicholas G. Carr, *The Shallows: What the Internet Is Doing to Our Brains* (New York: W.W. Norton, 2010); "Author Nicholas Carr Discusses the Benefits, Liabilities of the Internet," *Trinity College News & Events*, August 31, 2012, http://www.trincoll.edu/NewsEvents/NewsArticles/Pages/NicholasCarr.aspx.

2. Laura Pappano, "The Year of the MOOC: Massive Open Online Courses Are Multiplying at a Rapid Pace," *The New York Times*, November 2, 2012, sec. Education Life, http://www.nytimes.com/2012/11/04/education/edlife/massive-open-online-courses-are-multiplying-at-a-rapid-pace.html; Thomas Friedman's "Revolution Hits the Universities," *The New York Times*, January 26, 2013, sec. Opinion / Sunday Review, http://www.nytimes.com/2013/01/27/opinion/sunday/friedman-revolution-hits-the-universities.html. For a definitively non-*New York Times* review of this trend, see Audrey Watters, "The Year of the MOOC," *Hack Education*, December 3, 2012, http://hackeducation.com/2012/12/03/top-ed-tech-trends-of-2012-moocs/.

3. *Kairos: A Journal of Rhetoric, Technology, and Pedagogy*, http://kairos.technorhetoric.net/; *Computers and Composition Online*, http://www2.bgsu.edu/departments/english/cconline/; *Journal of Interactive Technology and Pedagogy*, http://jitp.commons.gc.cuny.edu/; *Hybrid Pedagogy*, http://www.hybridpedagogy.com/; *Writing Spaces: Readings on Writing* series, http://writingspaces.org/; *ProfHacker* blog in the *Chronicle of Higher Education*, http://chronicle.com/blogs/profhacker/; Daniel J. Cohen and Tom Scheinfeldt, eds., *Hacking the Academy: New Approaches to Scholarship and Teaching from Digital Humanities* (Ann Arbor, MI: University of Michigan Press, 2013), http://hdl.handle.net/2027/spo.12172434.0001.001; Matthew K. Gold, ed., *Debates in the Digital Humanities* (University of Minnesota Press, 2012), http://dhdebates.gc.cuny.edu/; The Humanities and Technology Camp (THATCamp), a series of unconferences coordinated by the Roy Rosenzweig Center for History and New Media, http://thatcamp.org; Writing Across the Curriculum Clearinghouse, Colorado State University, http://wac.colostate.edu/.

4. Troy Hicks, *The Digital Writing Workshop* (Portsmouth, NH: Heinemann, 2009), http://digitalwritingworkshop.wikispaces.com/; Dànielle Nicole DeVoss et al., *Because Digital Writing Matters: Improving Student Writing in Online and Multimedia Environments* (San Francisco: Jossey-Bass, 2010), http://www.nwp.org/cs/public/print/books/digitalwritingmatters; Troy Hicks, *Crafting Digital Writing: Composing Texts Across Media and Genres* (Portsmouth, NH: Heinemann, 2013), http://digitalwritingworkshop.wikispaces.com/Crafting_Digital_Writing.

5. See the open call, open peer review, and book contract in the "How this book evolved" section of *Web Writing*, Trinity College 2013 web edition, http://webwriting2013.trincoll.edu. Michigan Publishing, which is based and funded through the University of Michigan Library, "seeks to create innovative, sustainable structures for the broad dissemination and enduring preservation of the scholarly conversation... to ensure that the benefits of scholarship accrue to everyone." See "About Michigan Publishing," University of Michigan Library, 2013, http://www.publishing.umich.edu/about/. See HathiTrust Digital Library at

http://www.hathitrust.org/. See the Tutorials section in the Trinity College ePress edition of this book at http://epress.trincoll.edu/webwriting.

6. For a richer exposition of the "publish-then-filter" argument, see Clay Shirky, *Here Comes Everybody: The Power of Organizing Without Organizations* (New York: Penguin Press, 2008); Kathleen Fitzpatrick, *Planned Obsolescence: Publishing, Technology, and the Future of the Academy* (NYU Press, 2011), with open peer review draft (2009) at http://mediacommons.futureofthebook.org/mcpress/plannedobsolescence/; Kristen Nawrotzki and Jack Dougherty, "Introduction," *Writing History in the Digital Age* (Ann Arbor: University of Michigan Press, 2013), http://dx.doi.org/10.3998/dh.12230987.0001.001.

7. On the history and economics of different open-access publishing models, see Peter Suber, *Open Access* (Cambridge, Mass.: MIT Press, 2012), http://bit.ly/oa-book.

8. See Tutorials at http://epress.trincoll.edu/webwriting/part/tutorials.

9. See an expanded version of this paragraph in Jack Dougherty, "What Do Students Learn about Writing from YouTube?," *MediaCommons*, May 23, 2013, http://mediacommons.futureofthebook.org/question/what-does-use-digital-teaching-tools-look-classroom/response/what-do-students-learn-about-w.

10. As we prepared the public call for this book, nearly one thousand comments were posted in response to a news story on the edX MOOC by John Markoff, "New Test for Computers: Grading Essays at College Level," *The New York Times*, April 4, 2013, http://www.nytimes.com/2013/04/05/science/new-test-for-computers-grading-essays-at-college-level.html, which suggested that artificial intelligence tools can reliably evaluate student essays. Critics calling themselves Professionals Against Machine Scoring of Student Essays in High-Stakes Assessment have responded with a research-based petition drive, http://humanreaders.org/. Some computer scientists have attempted to reframe the debate by clarifying how computers can "describe" and "tabulate" texts, but not "read" them, such as Elijah Mayfield, "Six Ways the edX Announcement Gets Automated Essay Grading Wrong," *E-Literate*, April 8, 2013, http://mfeldstein.com/si-ways-the-edx-announcement-gets-automated-essay-grading-wrong. For a predecessor of this current debate, see Patricia Freitag Ericsson and Rich Haswell, eds., *Machine Scoring of Student Essays: Truth and Consequences* (Logan: Utah State University Press, 2006), http://muse.jhu.edu/books/9780874215366.

11. Ina Blau and Avner Caspi, "Sharing and Collaborating with Google Docs: The Influence of Psychological Ownership, Responsibility, and Student's Attitudes on Outcome Quality," in *Proceedings of the E-Learn 2009 World Conference on E-Learning in Corporate, Government, Healthcare, & Higher Education, Vancouver, Canada* (Chesapeake, VA: AACE, 2009), 3329–3335, http://www.openu.ac.il/research_center/download/Sharing_collaborating_Google_Docs.pdf.

12. An earlier version of this paragraph appeared in Dina Anselmi, "Peer Review on the Web: Show Me the Evidence," *MediaCommons*, May 22, 2013, http://mediacommons.futureofthebook.org/question/what-does-use-digital-teaching-tools-look-classroom/response/peer-review-web-show-me-eviden.

13. See more at idea 23, *Web Writing* call for essay ideas, Spring 2013, http://webwriting2013.trincoll.edu/how-this-book-evolved/ideas/.

*Communities*

# Sister Classrooms

*Blogging Across Disciplines and Campuses*

*Amanda Hagood and Carmel Price*

This volume speaks to contemporary debates about how best to integrate web tools into a critical element of the liberal arts curriculum: the theory and practice of writing. But any meaningful discussion of writing curriculum–regardless of the tools we use to teach it–ought to begin with an even more fundamental question: what do we *expect* of student writing?

All too often, the unexamined answer to that question is mastery. Traditional college writing assignments commonly ask students to demonstrate a command of both specific subject content and argumentation. (Perfect grammar would also be nice.) Multiply this expectation across the range of fields and writing assignments that a student is likely to encounter in her journey through higher education and you set a rather lofty goal: a student who can fluently speak the distinct dialects of half a dozen or more academic subjects, each with its distinct disciplinary vocabulary and grammar. This kind of expertise seems an appropriate goal for a student's major and minor subjects, but is discipline-specific writing, with all its particularities and palimpsests, really the best way to introduce non-majors to our fields?

Another common answer regarding writing expectations is academic integrity. And although it is critical for students to learn how to research and appropriately acknowledge the scholarly conversation around their subject matter, the form in which they must typically do so—the scholarly paper—does not necessarily reflect the process by which their learning actually occurs. In other words, traditional writing assignments allow only limited ways in which to acknowledge the community of learners that support a single student's intellectual development, privileging scholarly sources over the background of class discussions, Google searches, office hour chats, and study groups that helped to shape her ideas—especially in her early exposure to a subject. Moreover, when structured as a one-off assignment—to be viewed only by the instructor and perhaps a few peer reviewers—student writing also loses its potential value of making a meaningful contribution back to the learning community.

It is here—in the voice, the scope, and the process of student writing—that we believe class blogging presents a helpful way to rethink these goals, and the ways in which we might achieve them. As a collaborative class effort, intimately linked to the intellectual work we do in the classroom, a course blog can create a uniquely powerful learning community that invites students to learn *through* writing. Writing to a digitally-mediated audience of their peers allows students to re-articulate new ideas, test applications, link to related resources, and affirm or modify the ideas their peers bring forward. It allows them, in other words, to engage in the messy, immersive, referential, and uneven process of academic writing in a highly interactive environment. Through structured assignments, well integrated into classroom discussion, blogging can form a rich compliment to traditional writing assignments and, even more importantly, can help students become far more reflective about their learning.

*How* can blogs help us create more engaged and skillful student writers? Simply put, blogs can function as a staging ground for the practice of academic writing. As Kathleen Fitzpatrick argues, a blog is "not a *form*, but a *platform*—not a shape through which are extruded certain fixed kinds of material, but a stage on which material of many different varieties—different lengths, different time signatures, different modes of mediation—might be performed."[1] Like the course journals many of us have long assigned, blogs can provide students with the time and space to work through the materials they encounter both inside and outside the classroom: primary readings, secondary sources, news events, class discussions, and the personal associations and experiences they bring to the topic. Blogging platforms also add the ability to link directly to many of these sources (and the intellectual exercise of judging how and when to link). And, unlike course journals, blogs provide a means for transforming this scholarly monologue into a dialog through the readership and commentary of peers and, in some cases, wider audiences. A particularly insightful or articulate observation will often be recognized and acknowledged by a student's peers (or a watchful professor), and can even resurface in class discussion, as teachers and students connect the learning taking place in digital space to the progress of the course itself.[2] At its best, a class blog models the critical functions of the academic community—providing new information and synthesizing it through peer review—in a way that traditional assignments, with their more limited audience and impact, cannot easily do.

## Working Together: Two Models for Class Blogs

Our own experience with student blogging began as a larger experiment in which we placed students in Amanda Hagood's environmental literature course at Hendrix College (Conway, AR) in conversation with students in Carmel Price's environmental demography course at Furman University (Greenville, SC) via blogging and shared videoconference sessions.[3] In creating two interconnected courses—"sister classes," as we came to call them—our initial expectation was that students would use the relatively informal medium of blogging to discover and compare the very different approaches our two fields take to complex environmental issues. However, what we realized in watching their dialog unfold was that the exchange of content our class blogs facilitated was ultimately less important than the writing opportunity—the *blogging* itself—that the blogs presented.

We initially introduced the sister class concept to our students as part of a larger pedagogical mission as stated in the syllabus for both courses:

> Academic inquiry takes place in a living, evolving, and interconnected world and, in order to be meaningful, it must engage with that world: looking around to understand what local environments can teach us, while listening carefully to what those outside our context can tell us.[4]

With the extraordinary flexibility of the blog form in terms of both subject and scope, finding specific parameters for our students' writing was a challenge.[5]

## Hagood's Model

We took contrasting approaches to assigning and evaluating the blog posts.

For her class, composed primarily of literature majors and environmental studies majors, Hagood chose to take a relatively regimented approach that included a minimum number of posts and comments from each student. Working singly or in pairs, her seventeen pupils signed up to complete one weekly blog post covering any aspect of that week's course material. Students could choose whether to write a long essay-like post of at least 500 words, or a shorter discussion-oriented post that included carefully crafted questions for classmates to tackle as well as a closing synthesis of their colleagues' responses. Each student was also required to make a minimum number of comments, either on her own blog or on the sister class's blog, over the course of the semester. Posts and comments were evaluated for completeness and punctuality only, leaving each student free to make her own decisions about the style and content of her work. Students were also encouraged to make additional posts as they saw fit.

The resulting discussion was both surprisingly sophisticated and surprisingly varied (see Writing the Natural State course blog). Students in Hagood's course typically chose the longer format for their posts and produced everything ranging from a lively critique of a film the class screened, to a debate about the social construction of the natural world, to a poignant reflection on searching for the Ivory-Billed Woodpecker.[6] Many also made excellent use of images, external links, and stylistic variations that gave their posts added interest and personality—a particularly impressive feat given that few in the class had ever previously engaged in any kind of web writing. What most impressed Hagood about this collective student writing, however, was the way in which it consistently practiced the method and lexicon of literary criticism—in this case, consistently offering close readings of lines or scenes drawn from course texts to explore the differences between tragic and comic modes, the construction of subjectivity, and above all the many different representations of "nature" our texts presented.

The commentary that emerged from these posts, and also in response to the sister class's posts, was equally impressive. There were many instances of back-and-forth conversation between participants on several of the posts, suggesting that students were actively engaged in the intellectual interchange happening on the blog. Hagood also worked hard to integrate the blog through in-class discussion, both by highlighting especially interesting

**WRITING THE NATURAL STATE**

Syllabus    Readings    Assignments    Sister Class

**EXPLORING THE LITERATURE AND LANDSCAPES OF ARKANSAS**

**CATEGORIES**
FURTHER READING (13)
SISTER CLASS DISCUSSIONS (3)
UNCATEGORIZED (1)
WEEKLY FIELD REPORTS (13)

**ARCHIVES**
NOVEMBER 2012 (9)
OCTOBER 2012 (9)
SEPTEMBER 2012 (10)
AUGUST 2012 (2)

**SEARCH**
SEARCH FOR:
[          ] Search

**TOPICS**

**THINKING ABOUT BRINKLEY AND THE IVORY-BILLED WOODPECKER**
August 31, 2012, 6:01 pm
Filed under: Weekly Field Reports | Tags: Arkansas, endangered species, Ghost Bird, ivory-billed woodpecker, place

In high school, my science teacher's email ID was *ivorybilledwoodpecker*. So it's safe to say he was a bit of a fan of the "Good God Bird." In 2005, he led a group of students on a two-week expedition through Louisiana, around the historic location of the Singer Tract and down into the bayous. He wanted to find the ivory-billed woodpecker. They didn't, though they did find a swamp rat with a taste for Coffeemate.

This was after a team of researchers from Cornell University had taken several frames of blurry video of a possible ivory-bill in the Cache River

*Rachel's "Thinking of Brinkley and the Ivory-Billed Woodpecker," which makes great use of both images and links in her response to Hagood's class viewing of Scott Crocker's documentary film, "Ghost Bird."*

examples of student posts in class (and soliciting further comment from the group) and by adding her own comments to the blog when the conversation stalled or lost its way. Student assessments confirmed that blogging helped students to grasp and rearticulate new content, while giving them a greater sense of why their words matter.[7] One student observed that the blog "provided a different type of environment" in which "more people participated [and] everyone was able to think through their thoughts," and another student explained:

> The blog, in a sense, made me feel like I was contributing to something instead of operating within the school system: write a paper, paper graded, paper handed back and filed. This (course blog) is something that people, other people, could go on and see what this class was about, and how we, as individuals, think about certain issues.[8]

It was, after all, once a thriving roadside town, a stopping place for farmers and shipping companies. Some light research reveals the town was founded around the construction of a set of railway lines between Little Rock and Memphis in 1852, and that the settlement that would later be Brinkley was first called "Lick Skillet" which is, I have to say, a fantastically Arkansan name for a place. It was incorporated in 1872, and according to the town's official website, it has always been tied to the "transportation industry."

So there you have it. A little town like many other little towns, built where railways and highways converge. Those same railways and highways might well have carried wood to some Singer sewing machine factory, where it would be fashioned into cabinets, wood that might have fed or nested an ivory-bill, had it remained standing in the big, swampy woods of the Singer Tract. Maybe some of the trees cut

*Rachel links to Brinkley's city website to emphasize that fact that the town has always been dependent upon transportation infrastructure that primarily serves other cities. The website's banner describes the town's location as "Highway 40 between Memphis and Little Rock."*

## Price's Model

On the other hand, Price's model for the assignment, which varied significantly from Hagood's, encouraged students to take greater ownership over the content and pacing of their blog by pursuing topics of their own interest as the occasion arose. Because Price's class was designed to appeal to a wide range of students (including sociology and environmental science majors, and those fulfilling a general education requirement), she needed a blogging structure that was both flexible and responsive to class discussions. At the beginning of the course, Price suggested that her class elect one of its fifteen members to serve as a webmaster who would design and maintain the blog throughout the semester, and set aside fifteen percent of the total course grade to account for participation in the blog (in lieu of a more traditional attendance/participation grade). The class then chose to set a minimum of ten blog entries per student for the semester, with the webmaster only required to complete five, and Price revised the syllabus accordingly. Halfway through the class, however, the students asked her if they could reduce this self-imposed minimum and, in the interest of nurturing their sense of autonomy over the project, she obliged. In contrast to Hagood's guidelines, which confined students to a discussion of course readings for any given week, Price charged her students to write about any topics (relevant to the course) that provoked their interest, testing out the new sociological concepts and demographic skills they had learned against personal opinions, current events, and researched materials. In crafting their posts, they were encouraged to make use of data sets and other resources frequently drawn upon in sociological inquiry.

This arrangement allowed Price's students to cover topics as varied as the social impact of farm-to-school programs, the media's portrayal of human consumption and waste, and the FDA's ban on blood donations from homosexual men (see Population and Environment course blog).[9] Even more importantly, it allowed them to explore these topics in a low-stakes, interactive environment in which they were free to experiment with new concepts and draw in outside sources; many of the posts are well-researched with a list of works cited. Because these posts were issue-focused, rather than referencing particular moments in class discussion, students in Hagood's class felt much more at ease jumping into the conversation with their own comments and reflections. (Indeed, the majority of the intercampus blogging tended in this direction.) In one instance, one of Hagood's students even borrowed a resource discussed and linked on the sister class's blog—the EPA's Toxics Release Inventory—to prepare a presentation about one of her own class readings.[10]

At the semester's end, we each felt that our class blogs had increased student engagement and enriched student learning, albeit in different ways. And although we both anticipated even more interaction between the class blogs than we actually found, the idea of sister classmates as a friendly but challenging audience was still a major motivating factor in our students' writing.[11] Our richest instances of interactive writing were, in the end, clustered around the teleconference meetings we had scheduled for the beginning, middle, and end of the semester, particularly as we found ways to use the blog as a tool to prepare our students for these discussions. In fact, the palpable excitement that can be detected in the blogs on and around the topics we discussed in teleconference—in passages either addressed to the sister class or merely referencing it to the home class—suggests that the telepresence of peers added an additional incentive for students to explore and experiment with course material. And although teleconferencing may

# Reflection on "Dumping in Dixie"

Posted in Uncategorized. on Sunday, October 14th, 2012 by SOC 222 - Population and Environment

**Post by: Cristin Anthony**

In class on Wednesday, we spent time reviewing an excerpt from "Dumping in Dixie" by Robert Bullard. It caused me to wonder about the toxic releases in my hometown versus the toxic releases here in Greenville. I looked online at the National Library of Medicine, which provides information about all of the toxic releases in the United States. This information began to be provided by the government in 1986 as part of the Emergency Planning and Community Right to Know Act. In 1990, they expanded the inventory as part of the Pollution Prevention Act. (Read about it more here **http://toxmap.nlm.nih.gov/toxmap/faq/2009/08/what-is-the-toxics-release-inventory-tri.html**) What I found while I was doing my research was actually kind of surprising. In my hometown of

*Cristin Anthony's contribution to the "Population and Environment" class blog. Cristin's link to the EPA's Toxics Release Inventory, to search pollution sources in any part of the country, was later utilized by a student in Hagood's class in a presentation about environmental justice concerns near Hendrix College.*

not be appropriate for all class blogging situations, we did gain some useful insights in watching how it impacted our students' performance. Our findings suggest that the *social presence* of other learners in digitally mediated environments is key to web writing's power as a pedagogical tool.[12]

## The Next Step: From Learning to Teaching

When we first explored the idea of digitally linking our classes, we discovered a wonderful coincidence: we were both deeply influenced by the work of the great turn-of-the-century preservationist, John Muir. Price had learned of Muir's career, and his pivotal role in founding the Sierra Club, while doing conservation work in California. She was particularly fond of an inspiring passage in his 1908 essay "The Hetch Hetchy Valley"—calling for the city of San Francisco to suspend its plans to dam a canyon in the Yosemite National Park—in which Muir declares:

> Everybody needs beauty as well as bread, places to play in and pray in, where Nature may heal and cheer and give strength to body and soul. This natural beauty-hunger is displayed in poor folks' window-gardens made up of a few geranium slips in broken cups, as well as in the costly lily gardens of the rich, the thousands of spacious city parks and botanical gardens, and in our magnificent National parks.[13]

Hagood, on the other hand, had often used Muir in her classes to teach about literary Transcendentalism and its powerful effect on American visions of wilderness and nature. Building on our mutual enthusiasm, we planned an additional element for our classes that would bring our student writers face-to-face: a teleconference session in which we would discuss Muir's essay, considering both the rhetorical techniques employed in his argument and the sociological context in which he wrote. This live conversation, we reasoned, would allow us to explore the issues considered in "Hetch Hetchy" from two disciplinary angles, as well as strengthen the bonds of trust between our students.

At first the value of this conversation—particularly in this new digital context—was difficult for our students to grasp. Price's class, which was organized around the three primary components of population change (fertility, migration, and mortality), found the connection between Muir's essay and their study of populations unclear, while Hagood's students lacked the resources to delineate the social context that made Muir's words meaningful beyond their powerful rhetoric. However, these limitations began to erode as each class prepared for the meeting. Framing the Hetch Hetchy dam controversy in terms of population pressure from the growing city of San Francisco, Price had her students research census data from the turn of the century to share with their sister class. As they began to connect what they had learned about demographic transitions with the rapid growth of the population in California, the question of whether to build the dam became a great deal more complex—and a great deal more debatable. This was a turning point for the entire class. They began to realize that the demographic analysis skills they were learning could be connected to, and even shift their perceptions about, current and historic events, issues encountered in other courses, and even their personal experiences. What's more, in preparing and presenting their findings to Hagood's class, they got the chance to practice and demonstrate their new research skills, proving to be very capable teachers in the process.

Indeed the virtual discussion not only gave Hagood's students a better sense for why the dam might have been needed—an argument which Muir only glancingly addresses in the essay—but also helped them to ask their own discipline-specific questions in much more nuanced ways. In a blog post responding to the teleconference, two of Hagood's students noted that the strength of the essay lies in both the "rich, emotional imagery" that Muir employs to describe the Hetch Hetchy and the ruthless logic with which he attacks the opposition's claims that damming the valley will create a lake roughly equivalent to the current landscape in beauty and recreation-al opportunity. The two students noted that each type of argument has its own strengths:

> But, as the Furman class reminded us with their discussion of the demographic pressure of that era in the West, the intended audience was subject to a very different world-view than we have today. Which of Muir's persuasive techniques do you think were most appropriate for his twentieth century audience? Which of these techniques was most effective for you? Is there a discrepancy between the two?[14]

These questions, and the conversation that followed them, imply that with their sister class's assistance, Hagood's students were able to move beyond the fundamental question of how a text delivers its meaning and into higher levels of cultural analysis. Armed with the new perspective gained from their peers, they began to understand the important principle that words have different meanings in different social and historical contexts.

One fascinating characteristic of the blogosphere, even on the small scale in which we worked, is that topics will continue to resonate through posts, comments, and links, even as they filter down to the unrecorded spaces of everyday classroom conversation. In just such a way, our early conversa-tion about Muir and the Hetch Hetchy Valley continued to make an impact. Muir resurfaced in Price's class during the unit on immigration, when the

4.  ashley395 09.09.12 @ 4:05 am
Reply

The technique that most affected me personally was definitely
the aesthetics of the valley presented in the article. The way that
Muir is moved by the beauty of the valley moved me personally
and made me feel the personal connection that I know he must
have felt.
However, on page four when Muir begins to compare those
interested in damning the valley to Satan and money grubbing
farmers did nothing for his argument, in my opinion. In fact, I
thought it weakened his argument and made him seem almost
childish. With such a beautiful and eloquent way to describe a
valley, I felt that he ruined his description by being so dark.

5. julialee 09.11.12 @ 12:42 am
Reply

While I agree with Ashely concerning the weakening of Muir's
argument as he begins to embark upon the Satan comparison, I
do think we need to keep in my the history of the times. In
today's world (and especially Hendrix's world) readers' find this
parallelism appalling, but I think Muir's readers would have been

*Members of Hagood's class speculate about the impact of Muir's religious rhetoric on his turn-of-the-century audience.*

Sierra Club's deeply divided position on U.S. immigration policy became
a subject for discussion. Following the principles Muir drafted in essays
like "The Hetch Hetchy Valley," the club has long favored public policies
that protect the integrity of natural systems, which, given the important
relationship between the physical environment and human population, has
lead to much pressure on the Sierra Club to assume a stance on immigration. This debate provided Price an opportunity to take her class back to
Muir's essay, this time looking closely for rhetorical clues that help to shed
some light on what Muir might have said about population and immigration issues. Using the literary analysis skills gleaned from their sister class,

her students were able to complete this exercise and to understand how Muir's rhetoric continues to influence the Sierra Club immigration issue.

## Conclusion

Although our approaches to forging these intercampus connections varied with each classroom, our students showed a consistent desire for the intellectual community of their sister classes, suggesting that web writing, with its rich potential for collaborative learning, has an important role to play in improving learning outcomes for today's students. It is important to note that the idea of the network also powerfully shapes the demands of the business world and the practices of citizenship that our students will soon be called upon to fulfill. Teaching them to become responsible and valuable members of the learning community created by an interconnected class blog can play a small but significant part in preparing them for the challenges they will face after graduation, even as it creates a stimulating, supportive—and, dare we say, fun?—environment in which to learn and write.

Even as we discovered that the extended range and reciprocity of web writing makes it a wonderful tool for helping students learn the fundamentals of our fields, we also found ourselves, after the fact, wondering what we might have done to build on these capacities. Both of our courses, for instance, required more conventional, discipline specific writing assignments, including a literary analysis and a media analysis; one untapped possibility would have been to interlink our sister class project with the drafting and revision processes for these assignments. In some cases, there was a clear thematic or topical link between the writing students produced for blogs and their formal assignments, suggesting that blogging played an important role in preparing students to assume the critical perspective these assignments required. But bringing these connections into the open—by having students, for instance, exchange a draft of a key assignment with students in their sister class—might help them further interrogate the disciplinary assumptions that structure what scholarship looks like in each field. A similar exchange could be facilitated via the videoconference platform, too, if students in each class were required to discuss a given topic—say, for instance, environmental justice—with their sister class students by preparing and delivering a lesson on a key concept or method needed to understand that topic.

In the end, perhaps one of the most fascinating and productive dimensions that the blogs added to our courses, both separately and collectively, was a new sense of awareness. As witnessed by their evaluations, our students truly began to think of themselves as a learning community reflected in, and enriched by, the virtual environments of our own tiny blogosphere. One student recounted:

> I feel that our discussions online usually took conversation beyond that of the classroom. Further, it provided a different type of environment in which to express ideas…more people participated, and everyone was able to think through their thoughts, resulting in well-articulated comments.

As gratifying as it may be to hear students conceding that their own learning was positively effected by a new assignment, what is truly striking about this reflection is that the writer's observations focus mainly on *group* behaviors—capacities to think, articulate, and participate that have been enhanced by the availability of this relatively free writing platform—suggesting that the student has begun to understand herself as functioning within a diverse community of learners. As one student so eloquently stated in her anonymous evaluation: "It was especially interesting in that the other class brought perspectives rooted in English/Literature, while we held sociological mindsets, but in the end we were all approaching similar conclusions through different lenses."

*About the authors: Amanda Hagood directs the Blended Learning Initiative of the Associated Colleges of the South. Carmel Price is an Assistant Professor of Sociology in the Department of Behavioral Sciences at the University of Michigan – Dearborn. They created the project described above while serving as Mellon Environmental Fellows at Hendrix College and Furman University respectively, 2011-2013.*

How to cite this chapter:

Amanda Hagood and Carmel Price, "Sister Classrooms: Blogging Across

Disciplines and Classrooms," in *Web Writing: Why and How for Liberal Arts Teaching and Learning*, ed. Jack Dougherty and Tennyson O'Donnell (University of Michigan Press/Trinity College ePress edition, 2014), http://epress.trincoll.edu/webwriting/chapter/hagood-price.

*See an earlier version of this essay with open peer review comments.*[15]

# Notes

1. Our project was generously supported by two Blended Teaching and Learning grants from the Associated Colleges of the South. For more information about the project, you may access our final grant reports on their Blended Learning Initiative webpage, Winter 2012, http://www.colleges.org/blended_learning/funded_proposals.html#w2012.

2. Kathleen Fitzpatrick, "Networking the Field," *Planned Obsolescence* blog, January 10, 2012, http://www.plannedobsolescence.net/blog/networking-the-field/.

3. The momentum a class blog can create derives in part from the fact that it reinforces the social structures that are inherently a part of learning in a class. Participants in student blogs will often substitute interpersonal behaviors such as nodding or raising eyebrows with verbal equivalents such as "I agree with [Sandy]'s comment" or "I think [Mark] is making a different point." Students will also use inclusive language, for instance "As we've already discussed," to keep track of or redirect the discussion, suggesting a shared learning experience, a shared endeavor. Garrison suggests that, "Reaching beyond transmission of information and establishing a collaborative community of inquiry is essential if students are to make any sense of the often incomprehensible avalanche of information characterizing much of the educational process and society today." D. Randy Garrison, Terry Anderson, and Walter Archer, "Critical Inquiry in a Text-Based Environment: Computer Conferencing in Higher Education," *The Internet and Higher Education* 2:2-3 (2000): 95, http://dx.doi.org/10.1016/S1096-7516(00)00016-6.

4. Joint statement in course syllabi by Amanda Hagood, "English 395: Writing the Natural State: Exploring the Literature and Landscapes of Arkansas," Hendrix College, Fall 2012, http://naturalstate.edublogs.org/syllabus/; Carmel Price, "Sociology 222: Population and Environment," Furman University, Fall 2012, http://popandev.edublogs.org/.

5. We chose Edublogs to host our class blogs because it provides generous storage space for course materials and media, easy-to-build pages that can be connected to the blog, and a wide range of page styles and widgets that can be incorporated into the blog for a truly pleasing appearance. Moreover, once we had created Edublog identities for each of our students, it was very simple for them to log in and contribute to one another's blogs. Another advantage of using this education-oriented blog service here is that it allows you to track the number of comments and posts made by each of your student users.

6. A particularly fine example of student writing is Rachel Thomas's "Thinking about Brinkley and the Ivory-Billed Woodpecker," *Writing The Natural State* course blog, August 31, 2012, http://naturalstate.edublogs.org/tag/ivory-billed-woodpecker/, which was especially meaningful for the many Arkansans in the class. The Ivory-Bill, which was long believed to be extinct, was allegedly sighted in the Big Woods of Arkansas in 2004, generating national attention for the state. See James Gorman, "Is Ivory-Billed Woodpecker Alive? A Debate Emerges," *The New York Times*, March 16, 2006, sec. Science, http://www.nytimes.com/2006/03/16/science/16cnd-bird.html.

7. We conducted pre- and post-assessments to evaluate the unique components of our project; readers may access the assessments in their entirety
through Hagood's and Price's respective final grant reports for the Associated Colleges of the South, http://www.colleges.org/blended_learning/funded_proposals.html#w2012.

8. Anonymous student assessment, Writing the Natural State, Hendrix College, Fall 2012.

9. "Population and Environment" course blog, Furman University, http://popandev.edublogs.org/.

10. U.S. Department of Environmental Protection, "Toxics Release Inventory (TRI) Program," http://www2.epa.gov/toxics-release-inventory-tri-program.

11. Some online audiences, however, can be challenging in unproductive ways. While there is always a danger that student work will attract negative attention or even abusive commentary from a public audience, this risk can be translated into a useful opportunity to teach students about privacy concerns and strategies. We were transparent with our classes about the precautions we had taken in framing the assignment--such as creating usernames that partially disguised students' identities and using an "unlisted" privacy setting for our course blogs--and we tried to help students understand the possible implications of publishing any material online. Conversations about personal privacy and FERPA policies need to be a part of any student blogging project, and we recommend that educators provide multiple opportunities for students to "opt out" of publicly publishing their work, keeping suitable alternatives at the ready.

12. Garrison, "Critical Inquiry," p. 89, believes that this *social presence*—which he defines as "the ability of participants in the Community of Inquiry to project their personal characteristics into the community, thereby presenting themselves to the other participants as 'real people'"—is a key factor in the creation of successful online learning communities, along with the "cognitive presence" of individual students and the "teaching presence" of the instructor.

13. John Muir, "The Hetch Hetchy Valley," *Sierra Club Bulletin* 6:4 (January 1908), http://www.sierraclub.org/ca/hetchhetchy/hetch_hetchy_muir_scb_1908.html.

14. "Persuasion Through the Ages," *Writing the Natural State* course blog, September 6, 2012, http://naturalstate.edublogs.org/2012/09/06/persuasion-through-the-ages/.

15. Hagood and Price, "Sister Classrooms: Blogging Across Disciplines and Campuses," in *Web Writing* (Open peer review edition, Fall 2013), http://webwriting2013.trincoll.edu/communities/hagood-price-2013/.

# Indigenizing Wikipedia

*Student Accountability to Native American Authors on the World's Largest Encyclopedia*

*Siobhan Senier*

In Spring 2013 I had my students write for Wikipedia. This is by no means an original idea, but the specific assignment was somewhat novel: in a senior class on 21st Century Native American Literature, each student was to write a biography of a living Native American author (one not yet represented on the site), consulting with that author to craft an entry that met both the author's and Wikipedia's standards.[1] It has been awhile since I have had students quite so motivated and invested in a writing assignment. The process was not without difficulties: we sometimes ran afoul of Wikipedia's problematic "notability" standard. However, students still gained new skills and a much better grasp of the professional writing process. The Native authors were gratified to be represented on Wikipedia and often helpful in pointing us to further sources. And I got to enjoy the pedagogical role of facilitator, rather than gatekeeper, while helping to improve Wikipedia's representation of indigenous literature and, hopefully, contributing to efforts to reshape its demographics.

Contrary to popular belief, it is not the case that "anybody" can put "anything" on Wikipedia. The site has clearly articulated rules that, in the interest of recruiting new writers, it boils down to 5 "pillars":

> 1. Wikipedia is an encyclopedia that disallows primary research and opinions (an important contrast to some academic encyclopedias);
> 2. It is written from a "neutral point of view" (NPOV);
> 3. It is free content that anyone can edit, use, modify and distribute;

4. Editors (contributors) should treat each other with respect and civility;

5. Wikipedia does not have firm rules (its guidelines are subject to contributor debate).[2]

Every hour, thousands of volunteer Wikipedians (with varying levels of editorial power) vet the site, accepting or rejecting articles, cleaning them up to meet basic editorial standards, and flagging them (e.g., "This article is a stub. You can help Wikipedia by expanding it" or "The neutrality of this article is disputed").[3] There are robots to root out common errors and trolling; and a "three-revert" rule to shut down edit wars (with some entries, like Osama bin Laden's, on lockdown).[4] As any thoughtful person who has used the site knows, Wikipedia is not unproblematic. It does contain errors and some frankly appalling prose. It has troubling imbalances in coverage, which can be traced to troubling imbalances in its demographics. It is not, however, the unscrupulous free-for-all that some people imagine.[5]

Wikipedia encourages School and University Projects, offering online tutorials and other support for teachers and students; hundreds of courses, all over the world, have signed up.[6] Several such experiments have been described in the volume *Writing History in the Digital Age*. Amanda Seligman uses Wikipedia in a methods course to teach undergraduates about tertiary sources; Shawn Graham had a freshman seminar edit a single entry, on the Ottawa Valley.[7] In these case studies, historians use Wikipedia to reflect on their profession's standards vis-a-vis the practices of popular and crowd-sourced history.

But, in that volume, only Martha Saxton tackles the more global problem: "to the extent that popular judgment determines what history gets produced in this format, the significance of women's role in it and gender as a discourse or a method of analysis are likely to be devalued."[8] I, too, was concerned about Wikipedia's failures in coverage—specifically its lack of representation of Native American authors, and even more specifically, its lack of representation of authors based in New England, though that last failure is not unique to Wikipedia.[9] Before Spring 2013, the site included only three Native authors from this region: eighteenth-century Mohegan minister Samson Occom, nineteenth-century Pequot minister William Apess, and contemporary Abenaki poet Joseph Bruchac).[10] This trifecta, repeated in many anthologies and a good deal of literary scholarship, perpetuates the misconception that Native people in New England assimilated early on and survive only as isolated "remnants" today.

Coincidentally, in that same spring, academics were joining the movement to revise Wikipedia from within.[11]Moya Z. Bailey, a blogger well known in Digital Humanities circles, used the Twitter hashtag #toofew (for "Feminists Engage Wikipedia") to recruit new writers and editors.[12] She set March 15, 2013, as a day for people to gather (face to face as well as virtually) to edit the site in conjunction with some of the edit-a-thons run by THATCamp.[13] The event had a Wikipedia meetup page, where people could sign in and propose content; and it was announced broadly on *The Chronicle of Higher Education*, HASTAC, and even Al Jazeera, where Bailey called for Wikipedia to "better reflect the diversity of our living." [14] Since March 15, the editing initiatives have continued, including Adeline Koh and Roopika Risam's "Rewriting Wikipedia Project."[15] Such projects are responding to increasingly visible reports (including the Wikimedia Foundation's own editor surveys) indicating that only about 10 percent of contributors are women.[16] They are also scrutinizing Wikipedia's purportedly "objective" criteria. As Koh and Risam argue, these criteria depend on "the weight of already-existing knowledge, knowledge which postcolonial studies writers have systematically argued is racially and culturally charged. To subscribe to [Wikipedia's criteria] uncritically has the effect of reproducing uneven social forms of privilege against groups that deserve to be represented." As my students found, when it comes to Native American authors, Wikipedia's "notability" benchmark is particularly bothersome.[17]

\*\*\*

"Native American Literature in the 21st Century" enrolled thirty senior and junior English majors (a couple from Journalism, one from History). I had planned from the beginning to have students write for a site I manage, called *Writing of Indigenous New England*. But after #toofew inspired me to try my hand at adding a brief entry (on Abenaki poet Cheryl Savageau), I began to see the pedagogical possibilities of asking students to post their author profiles on Wikipedia first.[18]

Professorial maligning of Wikipedia aside, I do not know too many who *truly* require their students to abide by standards as rigorous as those of Wikipedia, whatever we might wish or claim. This was an enormous surprise for me as well as my students, and I have colleagues who still refuse to believe it. But the students found there was simply no way to grade-grub or plea-bargain their way out of the site's very basic writing standards. If they committed mechanical errors, an anonymous editor would correct those. If they committed too many, an editor could take their article down altogether, or at least flag it ("This article could benefit from an improvement in writing style"). If their research was thin, they would be mortified to find some 17-year-old in Turkey declaring their article a "stub," or someone with a silly handle nominating their work for deletion altogether. In the end, one of this assignment's greatest boons was that students came to see me the way I'd always seen myself—as the facilitator, not the bad guy. They were in closer and more frequent contact with me about their drafts than any students I can remember, seeming unusually accountable and motivated.

Part of this was undoubtedly due to Wikipedia's publicity and immediacy. It can take me days to reply to students' blog posts, a week to return their essays; but a Wikipedia editor might respond in as little as 20 minutes. In addition to the speed, students relished the opportunity to be part of something bigger. One said, "I often feel that I am just taking, taking, taking from the Internet and rarely being a contributor. Now I can put something up online that is credible, academic, and a contribution to the World Wide Web."[19] The opportunity to collaborate with a Native author also undoubtedly helped; in our case, the authors generally responded positively to the students' work with most of their suggestions being for further resources.

I gave students a clear sequence of steps, spread out over 3-4 weeks:

1. Sign up for an author.[20]

2. Sign up for a Wikipedia account, and take the tutorials.[21]

3. Begin drafting your article in your sandbox, and send me the link.[22]

4. After I approve your draft, send the link to the Native author who is your subject for feedback.[23]

5. "Create" the article.[24]

I was fortunate to teach in a digital lab, so we devoted several class periods to reviewing what makes an article "stick" in Wikipedia as well as to writing and editing. Many students, at least at my public university, still lack basic web literacy—signing up for accounts, following tutorials—and most were grievously intimidated by the prospect of using markup (which Wikipedia has since made optional). The assignment was thus an empowering one for our English majors, showing them that they can master more "tech" skills than they realized. Moreover, writing for Wikipedia is a powerful lesson in the professional writing *process*. Some graduating seniors, who had grown rather accustomed to writing their essays the night before their deadlines and squeaking through with Bs or Cs, found that procrastinating was simply impossible in this platform. Some students consequentially found their articles proposed for deletion, and did poorly on the assignment, because they skipped some of the interim, low-stakes (yet critically important) parts of the assignment designed to keep them researching, writing and revising.

Proposed deletion is not the only interesting thing that happened during this class experiment; but it was, for students, the scariest thing, and it is probably the thing that reveals the most about the politics of "indigenizing" Wikipedia. Some of my students who wrote, by my estimation, very good articles nevertheless had their work proposed for deletion on the grounds that their subjects did not meet Wikipedia's "notability" criterion. To be considered "notable" enough to pass muster with Wikipedia, a subject must demonstratively receive "significant coverage" in "reliable, published [secondary] sources." Wikipedians favor newspaper and magazine articles, along with scholarly books and journals. But "reliability," of course, is slippery: even in the academic realm, telling our students that university presses are "better" than "the Internet" isn't teaching them critical thinking. As my students delved further into their topics and began actually consulting with Native writers and historians and reading tribal websites, they found what historian Roy Rosenzweig once said so succinctly: "the general panic about students' use of Internet sources is overblown. You can find bad history in the library."[25] Still, a Wikipedia entry that references only tribal websites will likely be struck down on grounds of "non-notability."

Two journalism majors, who previously had been only modestly engaged with course content up to that point, were suddenly on fire at 2 a.m. when their article on Narragansett journalist John Christian Hopkins was proposed for deletion:[26]

---

John Christian Hopkins ( edit | talk | history | links | watch | logs | views ) – (View log · Stats)

(*Find sources:* "John Christian Hopkins" – news · newspapers · books · scholar · JSTOR · free images)

non notable author, awards are not major, lacks coverage about Hopkins in independent reliable sources. mix of primary, local puff and non reliable sources. I found nothing better. duffbeerforme (talk) 13:25, 17 April 2013 (UTC)

---

*Excerpt from "Talk" page on John Christian Hopkins entry in Wikipedia, 2013.*

Aside from the mortification of being called out by someone called "duffbeerforme," these students were invested and wanted that article to stick. They had ample opportunity to improve their piece: as indicated in Wikipedia's fifth "pillar," editors try to operate by consensus, rather than outright votes. In the debate that ensued, "Vizjim" pointed to institutional biases against Native intellectual sovereignty, a concept that eluded "duffbeerforme":[27]

- **Keep**. I know this argument isn't always popular, but numbers matter when discussing Native American writers. Hopkins is significant because he is one of very few Narragansett writers, and one of very few opinion columnists from any tribe at the time his career began, as noted in Sage's Encyclopedia of Journalism [3] @ (p. 320). Wikipedia criteria are usually good but can distort the argument when it comes to very small tribal nations (Narragansett have less than 3000 members). Vizjim (talk) 11:44, 18 April 2013 (UTC)
    - It's not a popular argument because it is fundamentaly flawed. Being Native American is not part of any Wikipedia notability policy, he is judged the same as others. I am one of the few Wikipedia editors from my street, does that make me notable? No. Sage just has a passing mention, nothing indepth. We don't treat small tribal nations as something different, would you apply the same argument to a town of less than 3000? To a street of less than 3000? duffbeerforme (talk) 12:19, 22 April 2013 (UTC)
        - No, because those are not tribal nations with tribal sovereignty. Vizjim (talk) 11:46, 24 April 2013 (UTC)

*Additional excerpt from "Talk" page on John Christian Hopkins entry in Wikipedia, 2013.*

By participating in such forums, students engaged in *real* conversations about *real* matters affecting Native people, while getting practical experience in convincing readers that their topic matters–not least by improving their research and writing. The Hopkins debate was finally closed for lack of consensus, and (at least as of this writing) the article remains live.

Few things on Wikipedia are permanent, so I told the students it wasn't the end of the world if their articles were flagged or proposed for deletion. (Wikipedia also archives every change, though I always counsel students to back up their own work multiple times, in multiple formats.) I granted favorable grades to those who conducted their research scrupulously and polished their drafts assiduously, no matter the outcome among Wikipedians. Perhaps the most vexing "notability" debate came over the article on Trace DeMeyer, an award-winning journalist from *The Pequot Times* and *Indian Country Today* who has published a memoir, an anthology about Indian out-adoptees, and a book of poetry, among other works.[28] But here's the rub: her books are mainly self-published, and she has received little coverage by sources not already affiliated with her. At the end of the semester, and well after the student writer had graduated, this article—as well researched as any of those our class produced—had still been declined. Some weeks later the discussion was revived and, as with the John Christian Hopkins article, the DeMeyer piece was allowed to stand for lack of editorial consensus:

Wikipedians are justifiably concerned about individuals (and other entities, from garage bands to corporations) attempting to use the site for promotional purposes. But these editorial debates over Native American public figures allow students to see that this concern can also have racial and political overtones. At least in the DeMeyer case, some editors appear sensitive to the proposition that "notability" itself is not an apolitical concept. And here was another powerful lesson for students: editors are sometimes not objective, or informed, or even that smart. They carry their own agendas no matter how "neutral" they may claim or try to be.

DeMeyer was one of a handful of Native authors whom I was able to bring into my class (others emailed or Skyped with the students). By the time she visited, students had some insight into the forces that keep indigenous literature and indigenous issues invisible. Settler colonial society, of which the United States is undeniably one, has in fact to do a great deal of work to keep those issues invisible. Spring 2013 was the heyday of #IdleNoMore and the Violence Against Women Act, indigenous issues that received only

**Trace DeMeyer**  [edit]

Trace DeMeyer ( edit | talk | history | links | watch | logs | views ) – (View log · Stats)

(*Find sources:* "Trace DeMeyer" – news · newspapers · books · scholar · JSTOR · free images)

Non-notable author, page recently accepted from AfC. The non-fiction works are in 12 libraries total according to [http://www.worldcat.org/title/two-worlds-lost-children-of-the-indian-adoption-projects /oclc/812289694&referer=brief_results ⊡

- **Weak Delete** Article is clearly promotional with no reputable secondary sources. Evidence of notability seems to rest on the awards which IMHO do not meet the standards of WP:AUTHOR and WP:ANYBIO. -Ad Orientem (talk) 19:15, 4 June 2013 (UTC)

  Note: This debate has been included in the list of United States of America-related deletion discussions. · Gene93k (talk) 00:45, 5 June 2013 (UTC)

  Note: This debate has been included in the list of Poetry-related deletion discussions. · Gene93k (talk) 00:45, 5 June 2013 (UTC)

  Note: This debate has been included in the list of Authors-related deletion discussions. · Gene93k (talk) 00:45, 5 June 2013 (UTC)

- **Strong keep**. At least you're being honest enough to write IMHO (In my honest opinion) above, because that's all it honestly is - your opinion. Just because something is not at all notable to you, doesn't mean it isn't notable to other readers. And just because it isn't at all notable to YOU, doesn't mean there is no room for it on wikipedia. Til Eulenspiegel /talk/ 13:27, 5 June 2013 (UTC)

- **Delete**. Notability is not established. Search results yield only self-published websites and social media hits. -Uyvsdi (talk) 03:26, 6 June 2013 (UTC)Uyvsdi

- **Keep** Important within a small community for a specific population that is already heavily marginalized. Has indeed written articles and personal details into works like Origins USA.[1] ⊡ The claims of awards from Native American Journalists Association need to be confirmed, but this would seem to meet GNG if they could be sourced. It will take some time, but the notability claim is there. ChrisGualtieri (talk) 14:20, 8 June 2013 (UTC)

*Excerpt from "Talk" page on Trace DeMeyer entry in Wikipedia, 2013.*

modest coverage in "notable" sources like *The New York Times*.[29] When I required students to follow these issues on Twitter, they found huge numbers of Native American people (indeed, images of huge Native American *crowds*), using social media, fighting for sovereignty, speaking their languages, protecting their traditional homelands, and *writing*. But to find those, of course, they had to bother to look.

Wikipedia's "notability" standard thus mimics the centrifugal force exercised by literary canons, even within such ostensibly canon-busting fields as Native American literary studies. "Notability" purports to be relatively neutral, while the academic term "significance" purports to be more authoritative or considered. But in either case, indigenous histories, aesthetics and values are too often erased. This was a critical lesson of "21st Century Native American Literature." Our class started with novels by Sherman Alexie and Louise Erdrich, who have published with major houses; moved on to Craig Womack's beautiful novel, *Drowning in Fire,* published by a university press; then to a poetry chapbook by Mihku Paul—part of the "Native New England Authors" series at Bowman Books, a Native publishing venture run by Joseph Bruchac and his son Jesse; and finally to a self-published memoir by Wampanoag elder Joan Tavares Avant.[30] I wanted students to think about the politics of Native publishing, to engage with the concerns articulated by Native scholars over non-Native aesthetic assumptions and mainstream publishing demands. These writers have shown that the texts that garner the most critical and commercial success are those that most closely mimic Western literary aesthetics; tribal authors who express tribally-specific values in tribally-specific forms are often dismissed as "too political" or "too hard to follow."[31] At the end of our Alexie-to-Avant trajectory, most students were fully prepared to appreciate lesser-known Native writers from New England. But the argument made by Vizjim—that "numbers matter," and that tribal sovereignty is a reality worth respecting—is still a hard sell on Wikipedia.

Crowdsourced knowledge presents itself as contingent, as always subject to further input and revision. Wikipedia changes to reflect not only changing facts, like shifting national borders; it has the potential, at least, to reflect shifting intellectual paradigms. In this respect, wikis are not unlike oral traditions, which in Native communities still carry enormous weight, even—interestingly—when it comes to preserving and transmitting *literary* history. There are writers who are revered within their tribes and beyond, whose work is read and recited at public events, who are honored at community gatherings, and yet they have yet to attract attention from university-based scholars or mainstream publishers.[32] Wikipedia offers one space in which writers with the skills, access and time can mediate between Native authors and powerful editors to improve the representation of Native culture and history. When I call this an exercise in student "accountability," I mean something more than just our accountability as Wikipedia users to improve the site; and more still than our accountability, as inhabitants of settler colonial societies, to recognize indigenous space and presence. I mean our accountability to indigenous people's own ideas of "notability" and value: that we vet projects with them beforehand, that we consult actively with them as we try to represent their point of view, and perhaps even (most difficult for academics) that we decline to publish if the work doesn't meet with their approval. It's too early to know whether my students' articles will have the longevity or grow to the length of Wikipedia entries on more canonical writers like Alexie and Edrich. Sustaining and stewarding them might be a project for a future class.

*About the author: Siobhan Senier is Associate Professor of English at the University of New Hampshire, and editor of* Dawnland Voices: Writing from Indigenous New England *(University of Nebraska Press, 2014) as well as* Writing of Indigenous New England. *She can be found on Twitter @ssenier, and in the blogosphere at http://indiginewenglandlit.wordpress.com/author/ssenier/.*

## How to cite:

Siobhan Senier, "Indigenizing Wikipedia: Student Accountability to Native American Authors on the World's Largest Encyclopedia," in *Web Writing: Why and How for Liberal Arts Teaching and Learning*, ed. Jack Dougherty and Tennyson O'Donnell (University of Michigan Press/Trinity College ePress edition, 2014), http://epress.trincoll.edu/webwriting/chapter/senier.

*See an earlier version of this essay with open peer review comments.*[33]

# Notes

1. Quite a few people have written or spoken about teaching with Wikipedia, most of them historians, including T. Mills Kelly, who has famously had his students write some hoaxes on the site (Yoni Appelbaum, "How the Professor Who Fooled Wikipedia Got Caught by Reddit," *The Atlantic*, May 15, 2012, http://www.theatlantic.com/technology/archive/2012/05/how-the-professor-who-fooled-wikipedia-got-caught-by-reddit/257134/). For a discussion of pedagogical uses of Wikipedia in the context of college composition, see Robert E. Cummings, *Lazy Virtues: Teaching Writing in the Age of Wikipedia* (Vanderbilt University Press, 2009).

2. "Wikipedia: Five Pillars," http://en.wikipedia.org/wiki/Wikipedia:Five_pillars.

3. "Wikipedia:Administrators," http://en.wikipedia.org/w/index.php?title=Wikipedia:Administrators&oldid=567726235.

4. "Wikipedia:Protection Policy," http://en.wikipedia.org/w/index.php?title=Wikipedia:Protection_policy&oldid=567197436.

5. For an engaging history of Wikipedia, see Andrew Lih, *The Wikipedia Revolution: How a Bunch of Nobodies Created the World's Greatest Encyclopedia* (New York: Hyperion, 2009).

6. "Wikipedia:School and University Projects," http://en.wikipedia.org/w/index.php?title=Wikipedia:School_and_university_projects&oldid=565127934.

7. Amanda Seligman, "Teaching Wikipedia Without Apologies," http://writinghistory.trincoll.edu/teach/seligman-2012-spring/; Shawn Graham, "The Wikiblitz: A Wikipedia Editing Assignment in A First Year Undergraduate Class," http://writinghistory.trincoll.edu/crowdsourcing/graham-2012-spring/. See also Adrea Lawrence, "Learning How to Write Analog and Digital History," http://writinghistory.trincoll.edu/teach/lawrence-2012-spring/.

8. Martha Saxton, "Wikipedia and Women's History: A Classroom Experience," http://writinghistory.trincoll.edu/crowdsourcing/saxton-etal-2012-spring/.

9. For a readable intro to "vanishing Indian" myths in this region, see Jean M. O'Brien, *Firsting and Lasting: Writing Indians Out of Existence in New England* (Minneapolis: University of Minnesota Press, 2010).

10. "Samson Occom," http://en.wikipedia.org/w/index.php?title=Samson_Occom&oldid=566410109."William Apess," http://en.wikipedia.org/w/index.php?title=William_Apess&oldid=564492835; "Joseph Bruchac," http://en.wikipedia.org/w/index.php?title=Joseph_Bruchac&oldid=559919036.

11. I thank the late Adrianne Wadewitz for pointing out that these efforts were already years underway, pioneered by groups like WikiChix.

12. Moya Z. Bailey, "Patriarchy Proves the Point of #tooFEW," *Moya Bailey*, accessed May 5, 2013, http://moyabailey.com/2013/02/26/toofew-feminists-engage-wikipedia-315-11-3-est/.

13. The Humanities and Technology "unconference," which trains scholars and students in a variety of digital tools and practices, including Wikipedia editing.

14. "Wikipedia:Meetup/Feminists Engage Wikipedia," http://en.wikipedia.org/w/index.php?title=Wikipedia:Meetup/Feminists_Engage_Wikipedia&oldid=548328074; Adeline Koh, "Tips for Participating in #TooFEW: Feminist People of Color Wikipedia Edit-a-Thon Today, 11am-3pm EST! - ProfHacker," *The Chronicle of Higher Education*, March 15, 2013; Fiona Barnett, "#tooFEW - Feminists Engage Wikipedia | HASTAC," *HASTAC: Humanities, Arts, Science, and Technology Advanced Collaboratory*, March 11, 2013, http://hastac.org/blogs/fionab/2013/03/11/toofew-feminists-engage-wikipedia; Adrianne Wadewitz, "Who Speaks for the Women of Wikipedia? Not the Women of Wikipedia. | HASTAC," *HASTAC: Humanities, Arts, Science, and Technology Advanced Collaboratory*, April 30, 2013, http://hastac.org/blogs/wadewitz/2013/04/30/who-speaks-women-wikipedia-not-women-wikipedia."#tooFEW Feminists Engage Wikipedia," *Al Jazeera*, March 7, 2013, The Stream, http://stream.aljazeera.com/story/201303072321-0022594.

15. Adeline Koh and Roopika Risam, "The Rewriting Wikipedia Project," *Postcolonial Digital Humanities*, accessed May 5, 2013, http://dhpoco.org/rewriting-wikipedia/.

16. Ayush Khanna, "Nine Out of Ten Wikipedians Continue to Be Men: Editor Survey," *Wikimedia Foundation Global Blog*, April 27, 2012, http://blog.wikimedia.org/2012/04/27/nine-out-of-ten-wikipedians-continue-to-be-men/.Nathalie Collida and Andreas Kolbe, "Wikipedia's Culture of Sexism – It's Not Just for Novelists. | Wikipediocracy," accessed May 9, 2013, http://wikipediocracy.com/2013/04/29/wikipedias-culture-of-sexism-its-not-just-for-novelists/.

17. "Wikipedia:Notability," http://en.wikipedia.org/w/index.php?title=Wikipedia:Notability&oldid=562817535.

18. "Cheryl Savageau," http://en.wikipedia.org/w/index.php?title=Cheryl_Savageau&oldid=561288574.

19. *ENG 739: American Indian Lit in the C21* (private class blog), April 21, 2013.

20. I had a list of 30 Native American authors: I was personally acquainted with each author and had previously secured their permission to participate. That was critical for this project.

21. "Wikipedia:Student Tutorial," *Simple English Wikipedia, the Free Encyclopedia*, July 3, 2013, http://simple.wikipedia.org/w/index.php?title=Wikipedia:Student_tutorial&oldid=4482547.

22. "Wikipedia:Sandbox," *Wikipedia, the Free Encyclopedia*, http://en.wikipedia.org/w/index.php?title=Wikipedia:Sandbox&oldid=567952638.

23. Most of the authors in this particular assignment were relatively hands-off; when they did participate, it was usually to supply further resources.

24. There *are* strategies for ensuring that articles will succeed in Wikipedia. See Adeline Koh and Roopika Risam, "How to Create Wikipedia Entries That Will Stick," *Postcolonial Digital Humanities*, accessed August 10, 2013, http://dhpoco.org/rewriting-wikipedia/how-to-create-wikipedia-entries-that-will-stick/.

25. Roy Rosenzweig, "Can History Be Open Source? Wikipedia and the Future of the Past," *Journal of American History* 93, no. 1 (June 2006): 117–46.

26. "John Christian Hopkins," http://en.wikipedia.org/w/index.php?title=John_Christian_Hopkins&oldid=564987519.

27. "Wikipedia:Articles for deletion/John Christian Hopkins," http://en.wikipedia.org/w/index.php?title=Wikipedia:Articles_for_deletion/John_Christian_Hopkins&oldid=552213787. I did weigh in during this debate; in a departure from usual Wikipedia practice I chose not to remain anonymous, so I was up front about my role. The site's discussion system is actually *not* an easy one to game, despite the publicity lavished on cases like Sarah Palin's Tea Party supporters. And it *can* work surprisingly well: see, for instance, the talk page for the #tooFEW event, where editors who complained about a "special interest group intent on using Wikipedia to spread propaganda" and the "unreliability" of the "whole feminism movement" were quickly overruled by the community. In the interest of full disclosure I should add that, having "met" Vizjim through Wikipedia's talk pages, I have since begun to collaborate with him on another essay about Native American literature on the site.

28. "Trace DeMeyer," http://en.wikipedia.org/w/index.php?title=Trace_DeMeyer&oldid=562418785.

29. A respectable introduction to Idle No More can be found, indeed, on Wikipedia: http://en.wikipedia.org/wiki/Idle_No_More. *The New York Times* did include a powerful op-ed on VAWA by Ojibwe novelist Louise Erdrich: http://www.nytimes.com/2013/02/27/opinion/native-americans-and-the-violence-against-women-act.html?_r=0.

30. Sherman Alexie, *The Absolutely True Diary of a Part-time Indian* (New York: Little, Brown and Co., 2009); Louise Erdrich, *The Round House* (New York, NY: Harper, 2012). Craig S Womack, *Drowning in Fire* (Tucson: University of Arizona Press, 2001); Mihku Paul, *20th Century Powwow Playland* (Greenfield Center, N.Y.: Bowman Books, 2012); Joan Tavares Avant, *People of the First Light: Wisdoms of a Mashpee Wampanoag Elder* (West Barnstable, MA: West Barnstable Press, 2010).

31. See especially the essay, "The American Indian Fiction Writers: Cosmopolitanism, Nationalism, the Third World, and First Nation Sovereignty" in Elizabeth Cook-Lynn, *Why I Can't Read Wallace Stegner and Other Essays: A Tribal Voice* (Madison: University of Wisconsin Press, 1996), 78-98.

32. Some of these writers, covered by our class, include "Joan Tavares Avant," http://en.wikipedia.org/w/index.php?title=Joan_Tavares_Avant&oldid=554359537; "Linda Coombs," http://en.wikipedia.org/w/index.php?title=Linda_Coombs&oldid=554559711; "Loren Spears," http://en.wikipedia.org/w/index.php?title=Loren_Spears&oldid=561285183; "Stephanie Fielding," http://en.wikipedia.org/w/index.php?title=Stephanie_Fielding&oldid=567070076; "Donna Caruso," http://en.wikipedia.org/w/index.php?title=Donna_Caruso&oldid=554839719; "Donna M. Loring," http://en.wikipedia.org/w/index.php?title=Donna_M._Loring&oldid=559588552; "Charles Norman Shay," http://en.wikipedia.org/w/index.php?title=Charles_Norman_Shay&oldid=560376795; "Mihku Paul," http://en.wikipedia.org/w/index.php?title=Mihku_Paul&oldid=564203851; "Melissa Tantaquidgeon Zobel," http://en.wikipedia.org/w/index.php?title=Melissa_Tantaquidgeon_Zobel&oldid=554555368  and "Larry Spotted Crow Mann," http://en.wikipedia.org/w/index.php?title=Larry_Spotted_Crow_Mann&oldid=565962268.

33. Senier, "Indigenizing Wikipedia," in *Web Writing* (Open peer review edition, Fall 2013), http://webwriting2013.trincoll.edu/communities/senier-2013/.

# Science Writing, Wikis, and Collaborative Learning

*Michael O'Donnell*

Laboratory experiences play a central role in science education. Calls for reform in science education have re-emphasized the very goals that we strive for when developing laboratory curricula: inquiry-based research experiences that develop students' science process and communication skills.[1] Despite creating inquiry-based experiences for students in introductory biology laboratories, I was dissatisfied with student outcomes (i.e., lab reports) and their assessment. I was dismayed that some students leaned heavily on their more engaged lab partners during the design and execution of an experiment, used data others had worked hard to generate, and then wrote a decent lab report that nevertheless showed little scientific creativity. Conversely, students who may have fully engaged in the experiment had trouble writing a decent report.

Educators who utilize labs strive to create lab experiences that expose students to the process of science as realistically as possible. We embrace the pedagogy of collaborative learning and stress that science itself is a collaborative endeavor, but then what do we do? After having students design and carry out experiments in a group, and perhaps analyze results in a group, we make them go their separate ways to write a lab report. That's not how science is done; it's very hard to find primary articles in the research literature written by one author. We have students collaborate for part of the science process and then send them into solitary confinement to finish the process. They end up spending more time writing in isolation than they did collaborating on data collection. Perhaps this is one reason why students hate lab reports so much, as shown by the popular "I Hate Lab Reports" Facebook page.[2]

## Collaborative Writing

Students often do not understand the purpose of the lab report; they see it as a summary of the experiment that reports the "right answer" for a grade. Instead, we need to emphasize science writing as an important part of the collaborative process of science and present lab reports as an authentic learning activity that allows for a deep engagement with the material. Collaborative writing provides opportunities for peer instruction that promote critical thinking, enhance decision-making skills, and deepened understanding of the scientific concepts being studied. However, when students have submitted group lab reports in the past, one person predictably ends up doing the bulk of the work. I could never determine who meaningfully contributed to the finished product. That was a major sticking point – how do I evaluate the contribution and participation of each group member?

This need to assess individual contributions moved me to examine online collaborative writing tools such as GoogleDocs and wikis that store every version of the document. Instructors can compare document versions (using the history log) and therefore identify, verify, and evaluate individual student contributions. Educators have recently started to use wikis to support collaborative learning.[3] Educational use of wikis in the sciences has been relatively rare, and usually involved with class notes, but Elliott and Fraiman report on chemistry classes using web-based collaborative lab reports. [4]

Since I rely heavily on our institutional learning management system (Moodle) in the laboratory course, I felt it would be better to use a tool within Moodle itself, so I had students in our second-semester introductory biology course use Moodle's wiki module for collaborative writing of laboratory reports. This introductory class is a large-enrollment team-taught course for beginning science majors. Each semester of this course has 70-90 students, who enroll in one lecture section taught by two faculty, and also one of four laboratory sections (about 18-24 students each) taught by two other faculty.

The wiki platform allows all students in the group (and the instructor) to track every change made to the document, compare different versions side-by-side, and assess individual student contributions to the group report, as shown below.

COMPARING VERSION 6 WITH VERSION 10

| Version 6 View Restore | Version 10 View |
|---|---|
| 13 October 2010, 8:20 PM | 18 October 2010, 12:03 AM |
| The purpose of this experiment was to investigate the effect of temperature on the efficiency or initial rate of SDH activity and determine whether there is an optimal temperature for this enzyme. In contrast to the hypothesis, increasing the temperature decreased the initial rate at which the enzyme oxidized the reaction, as seen in Figure (INSERT NUMBER). This result is supported by research done by Bernstein et al. because their data also shows that increasing temperature decreases the rate of enzymatic activity. It was expected for higher temperatures to result in higher rates of enzyme activity because molecules of the substrate move at greater speeds at high temperatures than lower temperatures. This increased movement increases the likelihood that the substrate will come | The purpose of this experiment was to investigate the effect of temperature on the efficiency of succinate dehydrogenase (SDH), which was measured by initial rate of SDH activity, and determine whether there is an optimal temperature for this enzyme (here maybe say an optimal temperature at which this enzyme functions or something along those lines). It was expected for higher temperatures to result in higher rates of enzyme activity because molecules of the substrate move faster at high temperatures than at low temperatures. This increased movement increases the likelihood that the substrate will come in contact with the enzyme and bind to its active site. However, at a certain temperature the bonds maintaining the tertiary protein structure of the enzyme break and |

*The wiki platform allows students and the instructor to track individual contributions to a group report and compare different versions side-by-side.*

## Implementation

Wikis were set up so that each group sees and edits only their own lab report, following the typical structure and format, with clearly defined student roles. For each report, students wrote different sections (Intro, Methods, Results, Discussion are all separate wiki "pages"), and then all students contributed peer review comments on all sections. The original author of each section used those comments to write a final version. One student served as "Principal Investigator" (PI) to check style between sections and finalize the report. Roles were rotated for subsequent reports, so each student wrote every section and also served as a PI. See table below.

Students were told that both their writing and their reviews of other students' writing would be assessed. This forces students to reflect upon the quality of their contribution as they review and comment on their peers' writing.[5] I graded each section of the report (based upon a rubric shared with students) and evaluated contributions made by each student. Each contribution received a score of 0 (not useful), 1 (somewhat useful), or 2 (good, useful comment). Nancovska Serbec et al. note that the quality of contributions rather than the quantity is important in assessing student wiki work.[6] I had students submit a "Team Member Assessment" after every report so I had peer grades for each student. Students' grades were determined by a combination of: (1) the grade on the section they wrote, (2) their "contribution factor," which is their contribution score relative to the group's average contribution score, (3) their peer review grades assigned by other group members, and (4) the grade on the completed full report.[7]

| Wiki Section | Draft | Reviews | Final Draft |
| --- | --- | --- | --- |
| Title | Group effort | Everyone | Group effort |
| Abstract | Group effort | Everyone | Group effort |
| Introduction | Student A | Everyone | Student A |
| Methods | Student B | Everyone | Student B |
| Results | Student B | Everyone | Student B |
| Discussion | Student C | Everyone | Student C |
| Literature Cited | Group effort | Everyone | Group effort |
| Overall (PI) | Student A | | |

One of the typical benefits of collaborative work using wikis was the peer-to-peer learning in the comments.[8] More experienced and confident students would guide less experienced students in their writing and understanding of concepts, often pointing out requirements from the rubric or from the writing guidelines that were missed. In some cases, less experienced students would see the working habits and thought processes of the successful students resulting in a helpful lesson that lasted much longer than the writing assignment. Successful students benefited by practicing and teaching skills needed to critically evaluate writing. Lundstrom and Baker report that peer reviewers receive a benefit towards their own writing by evaluating others' writing at the level of content and organization.[9] This multi-level feedback was common, as reviewers helped with underlying science concepts and the organizational rules for scientific papers.

## Assessment and Discussion

To assess the impact of collaborative writing with wikis, I compared the two years of the course with group wiki writing to the two years prior without group writing. Though quality of lab reports (grade on completed reports) improved, student performance in lab (final lab grades) was not affected by collaborative writing with wikis. Before using wikis, lab grades generally reflected grades on individual reports. With collaborative wiki reports, lab grades now reflected students' writing plus their contributions to the group's final product.

Student perceptions of the course and of their gains from wiki writing were affected. There was a shift toward a more positive perception (chi-square test for independence; all $P<0.05$). In this positive shift, more students agreed that (1) the amount of work during lab sessions was appropriate to the time available, (2) the total workload for lab was appropriate, (3) the lab handout readings were clear, and (4) students had opportunities for extra help. The first two perceptions are not surprising; with students writing only part of a report instead of a whole report, they should feel that the workload is lessened. I do not think students perceive the time spent commenting on the work of peers is as onerous as the time spent writing reports. The last two perceptions were unexpected (clear lab handouts and opportunities for extra help). At first glance they don't seem to be related to group writing. However, since peers were always on hand (via the web) to answer questions or make comments on each other's work, students felt less abandoned during the learning process. No matter the reasons for this shift in perception, any such positive shift can increase student engagement.[10]

Students' perceptions of group reports relative to individual reports were also positive. The majority (62-75%) of students reported that, compared to writing individual reports (as they did in the previous semester's introductory course), writing group reports: (1) helped their understanding of the concepts presented, (2) helped improve their scientific writing, (3) helped them think about the strengths and weaknesses of their writing, and (4) helped increase confidence in their ability to write scientifically.

Student responses to open-ended questions were similarly positive. Typical responses expressed the beneficial aspects of peer learning and the less stressful workload:

> "It made effective use of my time during the year. The lab reports offered a chance to more fully investigate the labs we conducted without the effort of writing a whole lab report. At the same time we were

able to learn how to write better because of the feedback from our group and also by observing other's work."

"It helped foster a greater understanding of the course material. It was helpful to discuss topics in a group and listen to other peoples ideas."

"I felt it was much more helpful to only have one section to focus on as opposed to an entire lab report. It took a lot of stress off."

Typical negative responses were related to group members not doing their fair share within a reasonable time:

"Using the wiki was fine but I hated having group projects. I felt like my grade in this class suffered because of my group members and their inefficiency to get their work done."

"Not all group members contributed equally or put in their best effort into the report so more work was left with some individuals."

## Conclusion

The teaching laboratory is a collaborative learning environment where students work together to design and implement experiments. This collaborative environment usually ends when the laboratory session ends. Collaborative lab reports allowed students to more closely mimic the process of science, and the wiki environment allowed student research teams to discuss and report on experimental findings outside of lab time. This use of wikis allows for the reflection needed in constructivist learning, as students continue constructing their own knowledge through interactions with other students during report writing. By using peer reviews and group discussion in the wikis, the focus is not only on the content of the finished lab report, but also on science writing as a creative and iterative process.

Students reported improved attitudes about learning science, and a decreased workload with collaborative wiki writing. For the instructors involved, assessing individual contributions in addition to student writing was no more time consuming than grading four times as many individual reports, and it was more enjoyable reading one-quarter as many higher-quality reports. Even though student grades in lab were not improved by group wiki writing, the beneficial effects of positive student perception toward such a large introductory science course should not be ignored. It would be interesting to look at whether collaborative writing influences retention in the sciences, as experiences in introductory science courses are important in determining whether students continue in science, and how they view science and its connection to their everyday lives. [11]

*About the author: Michael O'Donnell is a Principal Lecturer and Laboratory Coordinator in the Department of Biology at Trinity College, Connecticut. His teaching philosophy is to get students to be active participants in the creative process of science.*

How to cite this chapter:

Michael O'Donnell, "Science Writing, Wikis, and Collaborative Learning," in *Web Writing: Why and How for Liberal Arts Teaching and Learning*, ed. Jack Dougherty and Tennyson O'Donnell (University of Michigan Press/Trinity College ePress edition, 2014), http://epress.trincoll.edu/webwriting/chapter/odonnell.

*See an earlier version of this essay with open peer review comments.*[12]

# Notes

1. National Research Council, *Inquiry and the National Science Education Standards: A Guide for Teaching and Learning* (The National Academies Press, 2000), http://www.nap.edu/catalog.php?record_id=9596.

2. "I Hate Lab Reports" Facebook page screenshot, circa 2011, uploaded by author to http://epress.trincoll.edu/webwriting/wp-content/uploads/sites/12/2014/03/ODonnell-M-Facebook-IHateLabReports.png.

3. Kevin Parker and Joseph Chao, "Wiki as a Teaching Tool," *Interdisciplinary Journal of E-Learning and Learning Objects* 3, no. 1 (2007): 57–72, http://editlib.org/p/44798.

4. Edward W. Elliott and Ana Fraiman, "Using Chem-Wiki To Increase Student Collaboration through Online Lab Reporting," *Journal of Chemical Education* 87, no. 1 (January 1, 2010): 54–56, http://dx.doi.org/10.1021/ed800022b.

5. Xavier de Pedro Puente, "New Method Using Wikis and Forums to Evaluate Individual Contributions in Cooperative Work While Promoting Experiential Learning:: Results from

Preliminary Experience," in *Proceedings of the 2007 International Symposium on Wikis*, WikiSym '07 (New York, NY, USA: ACM, 2007), 87–92, http://doi.acm.org/10.1145/1296951.1296961.

6. I.N. Šerbec, M. Strnad, and J. Rugelj, "Assessment of Wiki-supported Collaborative Learning in Higher Education," in *2010 9th International Conference on Information Technology Based Higher Education and Training (ITHET)*, 2010, 79–85, http://dx.doi.org/10.1109/ITHET.2010.5480060.

7. See author's supplementary teaching materials: the "General Rubric for Reports" is included in students' lab manuals and used for all writing assignments, http://epress.trincoll.edu/webwriting/?attachment_id=829; the "Team Member Assessment" was posted to Moodle as an online assignment, http://epress.trincoll.edu/webwriting/?attachment_id=830; the "Plant Hormone Grade Sheet" is specifically used to grade that lab's writing assignment, http://epress.trincoll.edu/webwriting/?attachment_id=828, and is patterned on LabWrite's Excel rubrics, available from http://www.ncsu.edu/labwrite/.

8. Screenshot of peer-to-peer learning in wiki comments, uploaded by author to http://epress.trincoll.edu/webwriting/?attachment_id=76.

9. Kristi Lundstrom and Wendy Baker, "To Give is Better Than to Receive: The Benefits of Peer Review to the Reviewer's Own Writing," *Journal of Second Language Writing* 18 (2009):30-43.

10. David L. Neumann and Michelle Hood, "The Effects of Using a Wiki on Student Engagement and Learning of Report Writing Skills in a University Statistics Course," *Australasian Journal of Educational Technology* 25, no. 3 (2009): 382–398, http://www.ascilite.org.au/ajet/ajet25/neumann.html.

11. This essay was originally delivered at a conference presentation, and the slides are available at Michael O'Donnell, "Science Writing, Wikis, and Collaborative Learning" (presented at the Teaching Millenials in the New Millennium, Center for Teaching and Learning conference, Trinity College, Hartford CT, April 2011), http://digitalrepository.trincoll.edu/millennials/5.

12. Michael O'Donnell, "Science Writing, Wikis, and Collaborative Learning," in *Web Writing* (Open peer review edition, Fall 2013), http://webwriting2013.trincoll.edu/communities/modonnell-2013/.

# Cooperative In-Class Writing with Google Docs

*Jim Trostle*

How can we help contemporary college students employ their multi-tasking and tech-savvy skills while pursuing the more venerable scholarly goals of discussion and documentation? Based on my own experience of research collaboration with my peers, I offer one possible strategy: cooperative writing using Google Documents. For more than a decade I have been part of an interdisciplinary and international team studying the effects of social change upon human health. Given the size and complexity of our topic, our papers tend to have multiple authors. The form of our collaboration evolved from multiple iterations of documents sent around on e-mail, to phone conversations and face-to-face meetings where each researcher had a computer window open to the same document. Later we made manuscript changes page by page using the Microsoft Word "Track Changes" feature. Our collaboration on research documents moved forward in 2008 when we began to use Google Docs to post documents to the web to facilitate exchanges. In 2011 we had four co-authors in a seminar room at the University of Michigan, all simultaneously editing and viewing changes on the same document. This last step offered the precedent for my classroom experiment.

The process was exhilarating. Google Docs editing is efficient (we avoided at least a few rounds of consecutive edits), but more importantly it offered our research team the opportunity to shape our ideas publicly instead of privately. One of us would claim, "We need a sentence here to introduce this next idea." Another would reply, "How about this one?" while simultaneously writing a draft sentence. And a third might silently follow along with a cursor just behind the author's new words, cleaning up. I felt sometimes like we were elephants on parade, dropping words behind us, with the sweeper tidying up at the end. But the joys of the exercise were that we were all authors and all readers and all editors; false starts and new beginnings could take place before our (collective) eyes.

## A Classroom Experiment with Google Docs

In the spring of 2013 I decided to test this public editing approach with my Introduction to Anthropology course at Trinity College. While Google Docs had been a great tool for research collaboration with my peers, I had a lot of questions about how the experience of using it would translate for students in the classroom. Forty students were enrolled in the course, half freshmen, a quarter sophomores, and the rest juniors and seniors. It was late in the semester, and we were doing a small unit on digital culture. Would public writing in groups during class stimulate or burden discussion? Would public writing produce a usable document or trash? Would a document represent a group or one highly motivated individual? Was this a reasonable way to help students prepare for a final exam, produce useful study materials, and give them some experience with new digital technologies?

In order to answer these questions, I developed an exercise using Google Docs as a platform for students to complete the activity. Before class, I emailed a set of five questions to all students, each with a web link to a publicly accessible Google Document, which appeared as follows:

> Anthro 201 Questions for GoogleDoc exercise: One numbered question (Q1-Q5) per group, plus one for all. But don't work on this til the class starts please. You don't yet know what group you'll be in, and we'll need to review the "rules of the game" together. (Not to mention seeing whether the experiment works!) — Jim

> Q.1: We've spent a good part of the second half of this semester reading and thinking about how anthropology is adapting so that it can study people and objects in motion. Give at least two examples of this, with your own evaluation of how successful anthropology has been in this study. Link to Google Doc Q.1.[1]

> Q.2: Fairly early in the course we discussed the importance of words and vocabulary in conveying certain cultural messages and in preserving culture through time (remember the *Duden*?). Pick two different words and make this argument about each one. The words should come from the course readings or from issues we have discussed in the course. Link to Google Doc Q.2.[2]

Q.3 Throughout the semester I have been arguing that culture provides a set of specific adaptive advantages to specific ecological environments (mountains, desert, islands, altitude, land quality, etc.). Choose two environments, choose one or two specific cultural adaptations to those environments, and make the argument. Link to Google Doc Q.3.[3]

Q.4 We have read and discussed many examples of anthropologists getting things wrong (at least at first) and learning from their errors. Give two examples of works we read that analyzed fieldwork experiences in this way, and discuss how the authors made sense (or learned something) from their mistakes. Link to Google Doc Q.4.[4]

Q.5 We have read and discussed many contemporary examples of how culture at once constrains us and frees us. Many of these examples were within the domain of social stratification. Choose two types of social stratification and discuss how culture constrains and frees human behavior related to that stratification. Link to Google Doc Q.5.[5]

Q.All. Here we are at the end of the semester. I've been asking you to write questions for each reading all semester long. Here's your last chance: What is the most important question about anthropological knowledge or research that you have at this point? Link to Google Doc Q.All.[6]

Students were told that they would be asked to construct their answers jointly during class, and advised that these answers would remain available to all as part of their preparation for the final exam. (The questions were explicitly described as similar in form, though not in content, to some of the essay questions on the final.)

At the beginning of class I spent about 10 minutes explaining steps and goals, noting that they would be working in five groups of seven to eight students each:

1. Groups were organized by counting off by five, assigned their question, and chairs were rearranged (5 minutes).

2. Students opened their particular question on Google Docs. (It immediately became apparent that no more than four or five people in each group, 20-25 in all, could keep a reliable internet connection to the document and move easily around in it. I

therefore asked members of each group to take turns writing or editing.)

3. Students first discussed how to answer the question (5 minutes), then began to do so with concurrent discussion and writing (30 minutes). I sometimes circulated among groups to answer questions during this time.

4. Each group's final product was reviewed on-screen with the whole class, and clarifying questions were asked of the authors of each document (10 minutes).

5. I led a discussion of the exercise to get student feedback (10 minutes).

## Technical Issues

I asked every student to bring a laptop to class to complete this particular assignment. I worried that our electrical or bandwidth use might overwhelm the classroom, so I brought multiple extension cords and checked with our academic computing staff in advance to assess the system load. They thought it might be slow but were not completely sure.

In order to document and learn from the exercise, I placed a video camera on a tripod at the front of the classroom to record discussion groups or projected images of the questions posted on Google Docs, and explained the camera's purpose to the students.

Note in the videos that the student roles vary and switch, and with some conversing while others are composing and editing their common text. These behaviors change through time, and they are visible in the first video clip above of the early stage of classroom discussion, as well as the second video clip of the projected writing from one of the group's emerging documents, and the third video clip of writing-in-progress across all five group documents.[7]

*Video frame from early stage of classroom discussion during the writing exercise.*

## In the Classroom

During the document discussion/writing period I flipped among the different documents on the screen at the front of the room. This gave all the students a sense of how other group's documents were taking shape. Nonetheless, different groups made different types of documents – some produced finished essays, some discussion points and references, and other groups created a document with some of both.

The class discussion itself sounded and looked a bit muted compared to prior small group discussions without computers present. After the initial flurry of excited exchanges, participation slowed. I think this is because some students in each group were focused on writing instead of speaking, and vice versa. The conversation dynamic may also have been different because students were dividing their attention between the developing document on the computer screen in front of them and to students who were speaking, and because some were unable to post or edit because of bandwidth constraints. (The video camera at the front of the classroom plus the single document projected on the classroom screen also were distracting.) Overall the quality of the writing seemed better than that produced by multiple iterations among multiple authors in a cooperative group. It was

certainly faster. A major difference from other web-based writing processes (such as blogs, wikis, or discussion threads) is that student discussion and
documentation are happening simultaneously, with each ideally helping to
focus the other.

I did not attempt to grade student participation either as authors or discus-
sants during this exercise. My objective was to improve the review process
for the final, not to create a proto-final itself. Google Docs is not an ideal platform for assessing individual contributions and changes to a group
document, though it can be used for this purpose (see other essays in this
section for comparison). In the future, were I to assign groups to document
their discussions out of the classroom in this fashion, I would be inclined to
emphasize that I wanted to see evidence that all had contributed to the final
document, and would show them the Google Docs features that allows this
to take place.

## Student Feedback

Our evaluation discussion in the last 10 minutes of class showed strong
support for the exercise. Students felt it was a novel way to collaborate
with their peers and said things like "making you write stuff down, at least
in bullet points, and seeing it on a page, is helpful." They thought it was
an effective way to review material in groups, and a valuable way to prepare for writing final exam essays. They were slightly frustrated by the slow
connection speed, saying it reduced their engagement in the exercise, and
suggested that when I do this exercise again that I should use a college computer lab rather than a classroom. Most seemed happy with the group size
of around six to seven per group.

## Conclusion

In 2002, anthropologists reviewing literature on the study of digital culture
argued that, "Despite early assessments of the revolutionary nature of the
Internet and the enormous transformations it would bring about, the
changes have been less dramatic and more embedded in existing practices
and power relations of everyday life."[8] In contrast, in 2008 an anthropologist named Michael Wesch argued that web-based platforms like YouTube

"allow us to connect in ways we never have before." He said this in a video called "An anthropological introduction to YouTube" that five years later has been downloaded almost two million times.[9] Using Google Docs to facilitate face-to-face discussion in the classroom would seem to support both of these positions. Classrooms, and face-to-face interaction, are still central points of learning. New technology, like Google Docs, allows group discussion to be accompanied and documented by group writing, leading to new forms of group conversation, attention to text production, and learning in the classroom. The experiment is certainly one I will repeat, and it is readily adaptable for use by others.

*About the author: Jim Trostle is a Professor of Anthropology at Trinity College, CT.*

### How to cite:

Jim Trostle, "Cooperative In-Class Writing with Google Docs," in *Web Writing: Why and How for Liberal Arts Teaching and Learning*, ed. Jack Dougherty and Tennyson O'Donnell (University of Michigan Press/Trinity College ePress edition, 2014), http://epress.trincoll.edu/webwriting/chapter/trostle.

## Notes

1. Anthro 201 link to Google Document for Question 1, https://docs.google.com/document/d/118L2AJZtu55BKo56fmYS37CBXV1v6yRHJmans-kMtng/edit?usp=sharing.

2. Anthro 201 link to Google Document for Question 2, https://docs.google.com/document/d/1QSwz63Fjcd4OSblJgwqs4NT0drVvSU4lmmEvYXzxUto/edit?usp=sharing.

3. Anthro 201 link to Google Document for Question 3, https://docs.google.com/document/d/1g_5PXzE0FHAjFcM3NYQ1VkoMBF57is5pMcQO_L23Bec/edit?usp=sharing.

4. Anthro 201 link to Google Document for Question 4, https://docs.google.com/document/d/1VXvHNnuZQ6uhBsyNv9IXBvgIsbAcF82XI0xrd8Ffr38/edit?usp=sharing.

5. Anthro 201 link to Google Document for Question 5, https://docs.google.com/document/d/1IbaMKX2ULzPIRjlZFOy0ojfnt8_GVe4HpJjxi5o5xLM/edit?usp=sharing.

6. Anthro 201 link to Google Document for Question for All, https://docs.google.com/document/d/1b6rf7s3MbkT1BhUmnzUOsCsjwnVVL3j1cqfn3s6TWOM/edit?usp=sharing.

7. Jim Trostle, three Anthropology 201 Spring 2013 video clips for "Cooperative In-Class Writing with Google Docs" essay, uploaded to Vimeo: https://vimeo.com/87185460, https://vimeo.com/87186785, and https://vimeo.com/87185461.

8. Samuel M. Wilson and Leighton C. Peterson, "The Anthropology of Online Communities," *Annual Review of Anthropology* 31 (January 1, 2002): 449–467, http://www.jstor.org/stable/4132888.

9. Michael Wesch, "An Anthropological Introduction to YouTube," (Video of presentation at the Library of Congress, 2008), http://youtu.be/TPAO-lZ4_hU.

# Co-Writing, Peer Editing, and Publishing in the Cloud

*Jack Dougherty*

Most of today's college professors came into the profession, or adjusted more than a decade ago, using conventional word processing tools. The most common writing implement on campuses today is Microsoft Word, which prevailed over competitors such as WordStar, WordPerfect, and MacWrite during the 1980s and 1990s. Word can be a wonderful tool, and I still rely on it when drafting much of my single-author scholarship. But in 2010 I began to realize how most of my student writing assignments were framed by what Word could (and could not) do. Asking my students to co-write an essay, or simultaneously peer review each other's work, or publish directly to the web was not easy, because our primary word processor was not designed for these tasks. The tool limited how I taught writing.

For years I told myself that *it's the writing that matters, not the technology,* which was a comfortable philosophical stance. But a recent wave of net-worked writing tools—such as Google Docs, WordPress, and others—have nudged many of us to rethink our practices and to look for better ways of integrating meaningful writing into a liberal arts education. In some ways, newer technologies have challenged our traditional norms about what kinds of writing matter. In a twist on the philosophical puzzle about the sound of a tree falling in the forest, I began to ask myself: if a student writes a paper, and the professor is the only one who reads it, is it meaningful writing? Stated another way, if the broader purpose of expository or persuasive writing is to exchange ideas and consider alternate views and evidence, then liberal arts faculty should strive to create more authentic writing assignments that connect authors with audiences beyond the individual instructor.

If that mission sounds overwhelming, you are not alone. Many college faculty consider ourselves unofficial teachers of writing, even as we embrace the importance of writing without having had specialized training in helping students to enhance their prose. We claim to know good student writing when we see it, but few of us have a formal background in fields such as rhetoric and composition. Moreover, keeping pace with the dizzying array of new tools is difficult, because we lack the crucial ingredient—time—to sort out which technologies will help or hinder our teaching. Therefore, it is no surprise that many faculty simply rely upon the traditional word processors we have used for a decade or more. In light of these real-world constraints, this essay offers some simple strategies for teaching with web-based writing tools, and argues that harnessing the inherent power of communities—both inside and outside of our classrooms—can make the writing process more authentic and meaningful for liberal arts education.

## Choosing the 'Write' Tools

When faculty colleagues ask for advice on this topic, I encourage them to focus primarily on their goals for student learning, and secondly, on the most appropriate tools for achieving those aims. Ask yourself: *What do I want my students to learn through writing?* Then work backwards to figure out the answer to: *What are the most appropriate strategies, tools, and social interactions to achieve my goal?* In my case, I began to transform historical essay assignments (when the sole audience was only the instructor) into public history written for a broader audience on a statewide website. My decisions about writing platforms were driven by learning objectives. I admired several colleagues whose students had authored essays on Wikipedia, but my assignments did not lend themselves to encyclopedia entries and I wanted students to feel a strong sense of ownership of their work through a byline. Rather than Wikis, I leaned toward a web publishing platform such as WordPress. Then I discovered that WordPress was not ideal for stages of developmental writing, where authors need feedback on early drafts from multiple readers. As a result, I paired two tools—Google Docs and WordPress—to enhance the writing process for my liberal arts students as described below. See the Tutorials section of the Trinity College edition to learn how to choose writing tools to match your learning goals.[1]

## Collaborative Writing in the Cloud

Long before the web, innovative faculty began teaching collaborative writing techniques as a challenge to the tradition of solitary authoring. The transition from typewriters to word processors made this technique easier to teach, as students could independently author text and assign one team member to merge it into one document, or collaborate on writing one document by passing it back and forth. Several faculty took co-authoring one step further with wiki tools, which allow multiple users to edit the same web-based document (as shown by Michael O'Donnell and others in this volume).

But the writing tool that dropped my jaw—and reawakened the pedagogical side of my brain— was Google Documents, which enabled multiple users to edit the same web document and view collaborators as they typed changes in *real time*, in contrast to the delayed view of editing in wikis. Looking back to May of 2009, I originally understood that users could upload and share files on Google Docs but did not fully grasp its multi-authoring features until 2010 at my first THATCamp (The Humanities and Technology Camp), where session organizers shared links to Google Documents for multiple participants to simultaneously share notes. If you have never seen a crowd-sourced document in action, see the second and third video clips in Jim Trostle's chapter in this volume.[2]

Five years after the public release of Google Docs, educators continue to invent new ways of incorporating this writing tool into their liberal arts classrooms, building on a shared sense of community to enhance learning. Some focus on creating *one collaborative document* by multiple authors, such as when two or more people co-write an essay or pool together their notes.[3] Others use Google Docs to highlight *variations of the same text* by different authors, such as Brandon Walsh's "Writing Out Loud" activity. While writers usually try out alternate versions of a sentence in the privacy of our own minds or our notebooks, Walsh models how to make this editing process more visible and tangible for the entire class. "We usually turn to the exercise when a student feels a particular sentence is not working but cannot articulate why," he explains. By pasting the original sentence into a Google Doc template and sharing editing privileges with the class, individual students can quickly suggest a range of possible rewrites, then discuss the merits of different approaches as a group. From Walsh's perspective, this shared micro-editing process "allows you to abstract writing principles from the actual process of revision rather than the other way around."[4]

Both pedagogical approaches share a common vision of drawing upon the wisdom of the crowd: the belief that knowledge created collectively is richer than what individuals produce in isolation. Google Docs (and other collaborative authoring tools) can help transform the writing process from a solitary exercise into a community-oriented learning experience, which fits better with the broader purpose of teaching writing in a liberal arts context. When my Trinity colleagues and I first conceptualized Web Writing in fall 2012, we experimented with a simple crowd-writing exercise to clarify what our intended audience expected from the volume. At a faculty workshop, I began by asking participants to respond individually (on a paper handout) to this prompt: *As a prospective reader, what would you like to see in this book? What topics or questions should be addressed? What kind of digital resources would be valuable to you?* After individuals penned their responses, they moved into small groups to share and compare their hand-written notes. Next, each group was provided with a laptop or tablet to type their selected comments into a publicly shared Google Document.[5] For many faculty in the room, this was their first experience with real-time co-writing in Google Docs. The exercise pushed them to consider new questions: Should they hold back from placing untested ideas on a public document where others can read them? Should they claim ownership of words they typed into a group document by adding their individual names? While the answers will vary depending on the objective of the writing exercise, the best way for faculty to recognize these issues is to step into the role of the student writer and experience what collaborative writing feels like, with an eye toward enhancing liberal arts learning.

## Peer Editing in the Cloud

Like collaborative writing, many faculty integrated peer editing into their writing instruction years ago. Prior to digital technology, we asked students to exchange papers with one another. When shared networks became more common in the early 1990s, faculty at my campus and elsewhere created electronic folders of word-processor documents and set privileges to allow students to view and comment on each others' drafts, to build a stronger community of writers.[6] Beginning in the late 1990s, many of us began using Learning Management Systems (at my campus, Blackboard, and then open-source Moodle) to allow the exchange of writing and commentary inside our classrooms.

But I began to rethink my peer editing process in 2012 and adopted the Google Docs platform to support simultaneous commenting with multiple readers, both inside and outside of our classroom. Clarissa Ceglio, an editor at ConnecticutHistory.org, and I collaborated on designing a public history digital essay assignment for my mid-level undergraduate seminar students to interpret past episodes of discrimination and civil rights to present-day audiences. As an experienced writing instructor, she visited our seminar to coach students on the expectations for this online publication, then gener-ously agreed to participate long-distance in our peer editing process. This was not a collaborative writing assignment, as each student was respon-sible for authoring an individual essay on a selected topic. But we relied on Google Docs for multiple readers to insert comments in the margins of online drafts during our tight turn-around period, especially for Ceglio, who did not have access to our campus computer network. Furthermore, since texts are easily imported and exported out of Google Docs, students were allowed to compose their drafts in their preferred word processor. See the Tutorials section of the Trinity College edition to learn how to organize peer editing with Google Docs.[7]

When my students and I first tried peer editing with Google Docs in 2012, the mechanics worked well but I failed to provide sufficient guidance on how to thoughtfully comment on a classmate's writing. Students did not fully understand the difference between broad and narrow comments, nor the ideal placement of each type on the page, and several writers reported feeling overwhelmed when trying to sort through the feedback. To address this concern the following year, I provided evaluation criteria and instruct-ed each student to paste it at the top of their Google Doc draft. I hoped that placing the criteria at the top would encourage readers to write general comments at the top of the page, and narrower, line-specific items below. Laying out the evaluation guidelines before the assignment, with a visible reminder for students to refer to during the peer editing process, provides a common vocabulary for judging what makes "good writing" for each assignment.[8] In the current version of this public history writing assignment, there are four criteria:

1) Does the essay open with a compelling argument or story that explains the significance of the topic to Connecticut history? Does it inspire readers to think in new ways?
2) Are the claims supported with appropriate evidence and reasoning? Is the historical research accurate and balanced, with full source citations?
3) Does the writing style engage broad audiences, and provide sufficient background for those unfamiliar with the topic? Is the text well organized and grammatically correct?
4) [For draft 2 only:] Are digital elements (such as links, images, and videos) thoughtfully integrated into the web essay, and properly credited?

While not all student reviewers followed my advice on posting broader comments at the top (some found this to be cognitively challenging), the placement of the evaluation criteria at the top of the page helped me and my collaborator to communicate more clearly, and we agreed that the comments posted in the second year were more focused than those posted in the first year.[9]

Overall, the Google Docs peer editing platform works far better than alternatives I have used in the past, particularly emailing Word documents back-and-forth (aka "attachment hell"). Like any collaborative assignment, the organization requires an initial time investment by the instructor, but those costs are far outweighed by the added benefits of commenting to develop each other's writing and building a stronger community of authors and readers, both inside and outside the classroom.

## Publishing in the Cloud

After the hard work of drafting, peer editing, developmental editing, and revising, it is a relatively simple step to teach my students to publish their work to the public web as a means to connect with broader communities of readers. For the public history assignment above, all students were required to post their drafts on our seminar's website (based on guidelines in my

Public Writing and Student Privacy chapter in this volume), and those who revised even further were invited to publish on the ConnecticutHistory.org site. My college supports a self-hosted multi-site installation of the open-source WordPress.org tool, which I essentially use as a public Learning Management System to share my syllabus and student posts, while private items such as student grades and contact information remain separate and individually password-protected. Faculty at other campuses have impressed me by setting up their own course sites that operate on other free blogging platforms. With any of these tools, most students quickly learn the basics of how to post their first essay to the public web. During my third year of teaching a writing intensive course with WordPress, my first-year seminar of seventeen students learned how to publish in seven minutes. I also created a four-minute video screencast as a supplemental resource for students to view at their own pace. See Tutorials in the Trinity College edition to learn how to publish on a course site with WordPress.[10]

Without question, I have invested additional time as an instructor to select and learn more about the most appropriate writing tools for my liberal arts classes, but the payoffs have become clearer over time. When I used a conventional Learning Management System (such as BlackBoard or Moodle), all of the intellectual energy I spent on my teaching—designing syllabi, crafting learning resources, commenting on student drafts—was locked inside a password-protected box, making it very difficult to share with others (or even my students after they had finished the course). Now, on an open-access WordPress platform, all of this work is publicly accessible, attached to my name, and linked to my reputation. Based on anecdotal comments from professional colleagues and my personal web statistics, thousands of people have discovered and apparently found value in my open-access teaching resources, probably more than have read my scholarship. Sharing my teaching on the web reaches far outside my classroom, connecting my students and me with communities of readers who we may never meet face-to-face.

Listening to students reflect on their experiences of publishing on the web reminds me of the reasons why we devote so much time to writing in the liberal arts. In a short video with students who participated in the ConnecticutHistory.org public history assignment, "I struggle with writing" was one of the most common themes, even among those who persisted and appeared in the final publication. Academic writing can intensify this feeling because it is typically done in isolation. Even though my students wrote *individual* essays, they identified this process as *collaborative* work because they supported each other through its stages with publicly visible peer editing. Furthermore, they wrote essays for an audience larger than one professor. "I really felt more like a contributor, like a colleague, rather than just a student handing in an assignment," explained Amanda Gurren. "We felt like we were working with people, rather than for them." Seeing each others' work appear on the ConnecticutHistory.org website, and hearing how a student in another class cited it, proved that they had contributed to the education of someone other than themselves. While many of us have taught long enough to remember hearing students express similar emotions on pre-Internet assignments, it is also clear that web writing—with a broader purpose—has a rich potential to connect us and engage us with broader communities.[11]

*About the author: Jack Dougherty is an associate professor of educational studies at Trinity College in Hartford, Connecticut, who tweets about web writing at @DoughertyJack.*

### How to cite:

Jack Dougherty, "Co-Writing, Peer Editing, and Publishing in the Cloud," in *Web Writing: Why and How for Liberal Arts Teaching and Learning*, ed. Jack Dougherty and Tennyson O'Donnell (University of Michigan Press/Trinity College ePress edition, 2014), http://epress.trincoll.edu/webwriting/chapter/dougherty-cowriting.

*See an earlier version of this essay with open peer review comments.*[12]

## Notes

1. The Tutorials section is freely available online at http://epress.trincoll.edu/webwriting/part/tutorials/.

2. Jim Trostle, Jim Trostle, three Anthropology 201 Spring 2013 video clips for "Cooperative In-Class Writing with Google Docs" essay, uploaded to Vimeo: https://vimeo.com/87185460, https://vimeo.com/87186785, and https://vimeo.com/87185461.

3. George Williams, "GoogleDocs and Collaboration in the Classroom," The Chronicle of Higher Education, ProfHacker, June 14, 2011, http://chronicle.com/blogs/profhacker/googledocs-and-collaboration-in-the-classroom/34075; Jesse Stommel, "Theorizing Google Docs: 10 Tips for Navigating Online Collaboration," Hybrid Pedagogy, May 14, 2012, http://www.hybridpedagogy.com/Journal/files/10_Tips_for_Google_Docs.html. For shared note-taking with other tools, see Jason B. Jones, "Class Notes Assignment," Professor Jones's Wiki, 2009, http://jbj.pbworks.com/w/page/13150225/Class-Notes-Assignment; Kris Shaffer, "Collaborative Note-taking in Class," September 16, 2013, http://kris.shaffermusic.com/2013/09/collaborative-note-taking-in-class/.

4. Brandon Walsh, "Writing Out Loud: Google Docs for Live Writing, Revision, and Discussion," September 25, 2013, http://bmw9t.github.io/blog/2013/09/25/writing-out-loud/.

5. Jack Dougherty, "Web Writing: A Guide for Teaching and Learning," Trinity Center for Teaching and Learning faculty workshop, September 2012, http://bit.ly/WebWritingIdeas.

6. At Trinity College, my Writing Program colleagues began experimenting with shared network folders for portfolios and peer editing in 1991, as described by Beverly C. Wall and Robert F. Peltier, "'Going Public' with Electronic Portfolios: Audience, Community, and the Terms of Student Ownership," Computers and Composition 13, no. 2 (1996): 207–217, http://dx.doi.org/10.1016/S8755-4615(96)90010-9. At the same time, my high school faculty colleagues and I also created shared network folders for peer editing in our tenth grade curriculum: Keith Corpus, Jack Dougherty, and Jeff Reardon, "Newark Studies: Relevancy is Key to Interdisciplinary Curriculum for Improving Writing Skills," THE Journal: Technological Horizons in Education 19, no. 4 (October 1991): 44–47, http://dl.acm.org/citation.cfm?id=121244.121259.

7. Jack Dougherty and Clarissa Ceglio, "Assignment: Compose Web Essay for ConnecticutHistory.org," Cities, Suburbs, and Schools seminar, Trinity College, Fall 2013, http://commons.trincoll.edu/cssp/seminar/assignments/connecticut-history-entry/; CTHumanities, *ConnecticutHistory.org*, http://connecticuthistory.org. The online Tutorials section of Web Writing is freely available at http://epress.trincoll.edu/webwriting/part/tutorials/.

8. See also Heidi A. McKee and Dànielle Nicole DeVoss, eds., Digital Writing Assessment and Evaluation (Logan, UT: Computer and Composition Digital Press/Utah State University Press, 2013), http://ccdigitalpress.org/dwae/.

9. Screenshot of typical fall 2013 Google Doc comments, uploaded to http://epress.trincoll.edu/webwriting/?attachment_id=924, from Emily Meehan, draft of "How Racist Actions of Housing Committees Shaped the Demographic of Hartford Today," Fall 2013, https://docs.google.com/document/d/15IxYNRGDSe4UMGlvbrhzPocRRljaDsQ-C9TZy7lNo_A/edit; screenshot of typical fall 2013 Google Doc comments, uploaded to http://epress.trincoll.edu/webwriting/?attachment_id=923, from Amanda Gurren, draft of "Project Concern: City-Suburb Integration Program," Fall 2012, https://docs.google.com/document/d/1-sd_2t5JPCLOD9kkWaVo8x30A_Ah9hg7IHPY03HqBtc/edit, both from my Cities Suburbs & Schools seminar, Trinity College.

10. Jack Dougherty, "How to Post on Trinity Commons WordPress v3.5," YouTube video 2013, http://youtu.be/fzfPG9k__hs. See online Tutorials at http://epress.trincoll.edu/webwriting/part/tutorials/.

11. CTHprograms, *Make Life Collaborative*, YouTube video 2013, http://youtu.be/NuWg9Jrkrpw. See published student essays at "Trinity College Students Call Attention to Histories of Inequality," *ConnecticutHistory.org*, http://connecticuthistory.org/trinity-college-students-call-attention-to-histories-of-inequality/.

12. Dougherty, "Collaborative Writing, Peer Review, and Publishing in the Cloud," in *Web Writing* (Open peer review edition, Fall 2013), http://webwriting2013.trincoll.edu/communities/dougherty-collaborative-2013/.

*Engagement*

# How We Learned to Drop the Quiz

*Writing in Online Asynchronous Courses*

*Celeste Tường Vy Sharpe, Nate Sleeter, and Kelly Schrum*

*Directions: Select the correct answer for the following question.*

1. Why are multiple-choice quizzes a common assessment tool in online courses, even with topics that require more complex and nuanced thinking?

- A. Instructors love to write them.
- B. Taking such tests is an enriching experience for the student.
- C. Multiple-choice quizzes are the best way to assess understanding of complex topics.
- D. None of the above.

Pencils down.

What follows is the story of how we decided to embrace the implications of the above question for *Hidden in Plain Sight* and *Virginia Studies*, two online courses designed for practicing K-12 teachers.[1] While we make no broad claims about the general utility of multiple-choice quizzes, for our purpose of teaching historical thinking[2] we concluded that an emphasis on iterative writing exercises better suited our pedagogical goals. The opportunities for course participants to revisit and revise their interpretations over the span of a module and the course as a whole allowed for a stronger focus on the process of historical thinking over rote memorization. Accordingly, we dropped the multiple-choice quizzes. The difficulty and frustration with writing good multiple-choice questions needs little documentation, but participant responses also played a central role in the decision.

Several years ago, the Roy Rosenzweig Center for History and New Media at George Mason University, with funding from the Virginia Department

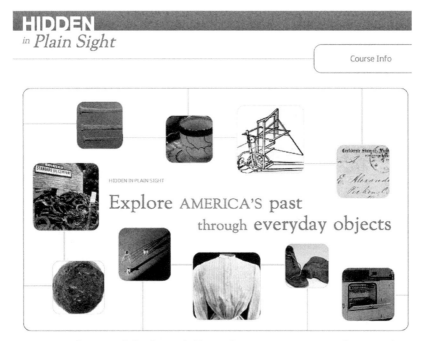

HIDDEN
*in* Plain Sight

Course Info

HIDDEN IN PLAIN SIGHT

Explore AMERICA'S past
through everyday objects

*Practice historical thinking skills and discover new ways to learn and
teach about American history in this self-paced online course.*

*"Hidden in Plain Sight" course website, Roy Rosenzweig Center for History and New Media.*

of Education, designed *Hidden in Plain Sight* and *Virginia Studies* to provide
quality online professional development focused specifically on history
education. We started by asking ourselves a series of questions:

- What did we want teachers who completed the courses to learn?
- How could we model historical thinking in an online
  environment?
- How could we make the courses engaging?
- How could we incorporate writing into the process?
- How could we frame the feedback on writing in a way that
  encouraged teachers to engage deeply with primary sources and

historical analysis, as well as with strategies for teaching both in the classroom?

- And perhaps most important, how could we measure progress and assess growth in the ability to think critically about the past and to teach historical thinking in the classroom?

We structured the content and navigation in *Hidden in Plain Sight* and *Virginia Studies* with these questions in mind. Each course begins with an introduction to historical thinking followed by a series of content modules. Each module opens with an object, such as an 18th-century homespun coat or a can of instant coffee, presented without label or context. Participants are asked to form a hypothesis based on close observation—taking note of the details of the object—before drawing conclusions. They are also prompted to think about the object in historical context, drawing on their own knowledge to hypothesize how the object fits within American or Virginia history, respectively. Participants then proceed to *Resources* to learn more about the object and its historical context. Materials in this section include maps, prints, posters, handbills, personal letters, songs, and diary entries, with accompanying text or video providing historical interpretations and models for analyzing sources.

Initially, after exploring *Resources*, participants completed a multiple-choice quiz to assess comprehension. After the quiz, participants were asked to review their initial hypothesis, which appeared on the screen, and to *Rethink* their conclusions by writing a revised hypothesis. Participants then applied their newly acquired skills and content in *Classroom Connection*, where they developed an activity for their own classrooms drawing on the resources of the module and the lessons learned. They could then view and comment on the submissions of others on the final wrap-up page.

We originally included the multiple-choice quiz for several reasons: to assess basic learning, to ensure that course participants read through all of the materials in the module, and to provide immediate feedback at a specific point in the process. We created it with some ambivalence, a feeling that deepened during the development and pilot testing phases as technical, functional, and pedagogical questions arose. Should teachers, for example, be allowed to take the quiz more than once? Should they be allowed to return to *Resources* while taking the quiz? Doing so could allow for deeper learning and encourage course users to spend more time with the sources. At the same time, it might lead some to skip to the quiz and then look through *Resources* for specific answers to the questions, allowing the quiz to define the learning experience. Another set of questions loomed even larger: did the quiz questions support the overall objectives of the course? Did they facilitate historical analysis and critical thinking? Did they allow the course instructors to see growth in thinking?

Another drawback of including a quiz emerged while teaching the course. Participants put far more weight on the meaning and value of the quiz than we did as instructors. Despite extensive, personalized feedback on written responses, we received regular emails expressing concern about quiz scores. This was especially notable because most participants took the course for professional development credit and not for graduate credit. One teacher, whose written responses were exemplary, emailed the instructors to reassure us that, "I read the stuff, really," and to ask "[will] quiz scores affect our recertification?" Another who clearly demonstrated learning throughout the course felt "embarrassed" by less than perfect quiz results.

This concern was by no means unique, as participants communicated similar worries each time the courses were offered. Some asked to retake the quiz. In response to the number and tenor of the requests for retakes, we reformatted the course settings to allow participants to take the quizzes multiple times. Some students decided to take the quiz repeatedly until they achieved a perfect score. Given that the goal of these courses is not the retention of facts, but the development of historical thinking skills and their application in the classroom, the attention and mental energy that course participants devoted to the multiple choice quizzes was concerning.

In contrast, the writing assignments (*Hypothesis, Rethink,* and *Classroom Connection*) proved very successful at engaging participants in historical thinking. Individuals taking the course demonstrated growth, often significant growth, in their ability to engage with primary sources, analyze historical contexts, develop their own interpretations, and integrate strategies for teaching students to do the same. They built on experiences from the first module, improving their ability to hypothesize about the context and meaning of the initial object. Perhaps equally important, the written submissions provided discrete evidence of this growth in thinking, growth that did not necessarily correlate with quiz results. While the emphasis on writing and providing detailed feedback necessitates a considerable workload — two graduate students working twenty hours per week can administer a semester course to 100 participants — we have found it a worthwhile investment in light of the demonstrable results.

The *Hypothesis-Rethink-Classroom Connection-Feedback* arc of each module provides an opportunity for iterative learning, for course users to rehash and strengthen their written interpretations over the course of the module. We see this combination of writing assignments as central to encouraging historical thinking in an asynchronous learning environment: since teachers taking the course have the chance to revisit, amend, and expand on their hypotheses based on additional information and evidence, much of the pressure to write the one "right" answer is lifted. Growth is encouraged and rewarded. In addition, these educators are engaging in the same exercises that they often pose for their students—and the same processes that historians use regularly.

## Hypothesis

The first writing activity in each module involves forming a hypothesis on the historical significance of an everyday object—an important first step in the iterative writing process that is central to these courses. Handmade nails, a suffragette's dress, and a split-rail fence are a few examples. Participants are prompted to frame their hypotheses in response to two questions: "What do you notice about this object?" and "How might this object connect to broader themes in American (or Virginia) history?" Knowing that some may hesitate to give detailed responses, afraid of not saying the "right thing," course instructors frequently encourage participants to take risks and use the hypothesis for observing and brainstorming. As one instructor wrote, the hypothesis is "a space to speculate and include your thoughts on the objects and their connection to broader histories—and also where there's no such thing as a wrong answer."

In response to an image of a World War II-era tin can, for example, one participant noted its age and appearance and then hypothesized that the can was used by American soldiers during the war.[3] To answer the question about the object's broader historical significance, the participant suggested that the can was related to "either the challenges of mobilizing an army and the growing military technology, or just the industrialization of agriculture and modern society." After submitting the hypothesis, course participants view the module's primary sources and commentary by historians before revisiting their original hypothesis in a written assignment entitled *Rethink*.

## Rethink

*Rethinks* are structured writings prompted by two primary questions. The first question asks course participants how the module's object and resources have influenced their thinking on the historical themes or topic. In the porcelain module in *Hidden in Plain Sight*, for example, the first question is "How does porcelain connect to broader themes in 18th-century history? Use specific examples." The second question prompts an analysis of the materials presented in the module: What sources or points of view are missing? What is emphasized (or not)? How does the module connect to prior knowledge of the subject? In the case of the porcelain cup, the second question asks, "What additional information (not included in this module) would you want to know before making an argument about the causes of the American Revolution?"[4]

A quality *Rethink* connects the *Resources* to the relevant themes and historical context, and engages meaningfully with the interpretations presented. For example, one participant of *Virginia Studies* discussed how the fence module enriched her perspective on the relationship between geography and history:

> The fence symbolizes ownership and settlement. The shape and materials show how the settlers tried to control their environment. They used natural resources, wood, to build the fence and by building it they were taking ownership of the land, a concept that was different from the native peoples. The fence is an important part of Virginia's history. It shows us that when the settlers arrived they were planning

on staying here. Building fences began the process of transforming the landscape of Virginia. I thought it was interesting that all the modules were pieces of the Virginia Studies curriculum, which most teachers teach from a viewpoint of history. Yet, each module used geography as the starting point. . . Virginia's history might be better understood and engaging to students if you use the themes of geography—location, environment, landscape, human-environment as a starting point for instruction.

The *Rethink* provides a formal opportunity for course participants to revisit their initial thoughts on a historical object, and to synthesize and interpret the arguments and information learned while exploring the module resources. It encourages thoughtful engagement with the material and with historical thinking through a structured writing exercise rather than the rote recounting of historical facts. In feedback, instructors help course users expand on their responses, often by posing questions to prompt more critical analysis and the further development of connections made in their reflections. In response to a thoughtful *Rethink* on the porcelain module that discussed relationships between the tea cup and 18th-century themes of political representation, revolution, and mercantilism, the instructor encouraged the teacher to explore the consumer and political culture angle, including colonist decisions to purchase (or not purchase) imported goods as an expression of political beliefs and the decisions of American merchants who simultaneously faced public pressure to refuse imports or face lost revenue from boycotts.

## Classroom Connection

After submitting the *Rethink*, course users move to *Classroom Connection* and are asked to apply what they have learned in the module by creating an activity for students. Unlike the more structured *Rethink*, *Classroom Connection* is an unstructured writing activity. The emphasis is on developing an inventive, practical activity based on the module's content and historical thinking through primary sources. Similar to the previous writing assignment, course instructors provide feedback. In addition, participating teachers also receive feedback in *Classroom Connection* from each other in the form of comments on activity ideas.

In a module on the Triangle Shirtwaist Fire, for example, one teacher's *Classroom Connection* asked students to investigate workplace safety in local businesses. Students compared federal (U.S. Occupational Safety and Health Administration, OSHA) and local regulations with photographs and documents from the 19th-century, before such laws were created. By studying workplace safety and regulation over time, students could examine the Triangle Shirtwaist Fire in its historical context. The teacher posed thoughtful questions for students, including the benefits and drawbacks of extensive safety regulations for businesses and workers. They then investigated the causes and development of specific regulations and policies.

Participating teachers are often highly motivated to incorporate primary sources into their classroom activities but sometimes struggle to connect primary source analysis with the larger historical narrative. The quizzes did not effectively address this gap, whereas the written *Classroom Connections* in each module raised these issues to the surface and provided the opportunity for thoughtful feedback.

The Virginia Studies module on the colonial period, for example, features a source that many participants incorporate into classroom connections: a letter written by an indentured servant named Richard Frethorne describing the harsh conditions of servitude and labor.[5] One teacher developed an activity in which students would read this moving letter and then write their own letter from the viewpoint of an indentured servant. Through feedback on *Classroom Connection* submissions, the instructor encouraged the teacher to incorporate other sources and direct the lesson to a larger historical question, suggesting that the teacher use advertisements designed to lure individuals to the new world. Promises by the Virginia Company could be contrasted with stories of hardship in Virginia, asking students to consider what the colonies might represent to prospective colonists and why they might choose to come despite rumors of hardship from individuals such as Frethorne. This teacher's writing offered an opportunity to provide specific feedback on how historical evidence can help students understand the choices made by those in the past (e.g., why individuals would choose to become indentured servants in 17th-century Virginia) and address larger historical questions, such as how the Virginia colony grew in population despite a high mortality rate.

## Conclusion

The team teaching these courses met regularly during pilot testing and the first iterations of each course. At each meeting, we improved functionality, revised content based on feedback, and adjusted the structure of the course. We compared evaluations, student work, and instructor experiences and discussed strategies for improving the courses for future iterations. The decision to eliminate the quiz evolved out of these conversations and reflections.

The act of writing and, perhaps most importantly, the cycle of *Hypothesis-Rethink-Classroom Connection-Feedback*, encouraged participants to go beyond descriptive history and to think of new ways to engage students in learning about the past. Through writing, receiving feedback, and revising initial hypotheses, participants made insightful connections between sources and history, showed growth in their understanding of historical thinking, and applied new knowledge to their classrooms in creative ways.

The courses' approach to writing has also inspired participants to use a similar hypothesis-rethink model using historical objects with their own students. Several participants have asked about the technological aspect with interest in adding more online work to their classrooms. Some have even reported sharing their own work and feedback received in the course with their students to model their own learning process as well as to demonstrate the benefits of iterative writing for learning. Success on the quiz did not demonstrate the same growth, and often did not correlate with a significant development of historical thinking skills across modules.

Removing the quiz from *Hidden in Plain Sight* and *Virginia Studies*, however, eliminates the benefits of automatic grading and instant feedback. This is a somewhat daunting prospect for an asynchronous online course where participants can work through modules entirely at their own pace. At the same time, through trial and error, we learned that omitting the quiz allows us to keep the focus of the courses on the original goals—developing and assessing historical thinking—and to focus all of the instructional time on the structured and unstructured writing of participants. Feedback is comprehensive, ongoing, and focused on each individual's work and progress. This regular engagement with instructors has proven to be a key feature of the course's success as indicated by course evaluations. We have found it a worthwhile investment in light of the demonstrable results.

Course evaluations have been overwhelmingly positive. Ninety-eight percent of participants either agreed or strongly agreed that they learned history content, teaching strategies, and tools for analyzing and teaching with primary sources while taking the course. One hundred percent reported that the course structure stimulated their thinking, and that they would recommend the course to a colleague. Individuals who completed the courses described them as "thought provoking," "very user friendly and engaging," "meaningful," and "eye opening." One teacher noted, "This course really helps you understand the STORY behind the standard." Formal and informal interactions among course instructors and participants throughout each semester via assignment submissions, comments, and emails confirmed the value of writing in the online course. On the same post-course surveys, the feedback on the quiz was far more equivocal, and in fact stood out as the only feature of the course that did not receive uniformly positive reviews.

The structure and emphasis on writing in these courses allows us to assess not only whether participants are retaining content (the original point of the quiz), but also whether they are engaging with that content in meaningful ways. We are exploring ways to apply this focus on deeper understanding and critical learning to other online, asynchronous courses in place of the emphasis on rote learning and discrete facts that plague many of the current open-enrollment, online educational offerings.

From our perspective, the online asynchronous model has much to recommend it. Courses such as *Hidden in Plain Sight* and *Virginia Studies* are available to individuals whose location or work-life schedules make attending a traditional in-person course impossible. In addition, these courses have the potential to reach large numbers of students, and demonstrate that writing assignments, both structured and unstructured, can be effectively incorporated into an online learning environment. The completion rates for these courses have been encouraging as well: over 90% of participants who begin the courses go on to complete them. Currently these courses are offered on a semester model, but they could allow for continuous enrollment, significantly increasing the number of participants each year.

It is this potential for online learning—the opportunity to provide meaningful learning experiences while reaching a broad audience—that provides the core focus for our reflections on and modifications to the course. While online learning never has been and never will be a panacea, in this context, *Hidden in Plain Sight* and *Virginia Studies* offer exciting possibilities for liberal arts education beyond selecting quiz answer bubbles labeled A, B, C, or D.

*About the authors: Celeste Tường Vy Sharpe is a PhD candidate in history and art history at George Mason University. She works as a graduate research assistant at the Roy Rosenzweig Center for History and New Media, and a teaching assistant for the online courses Hidden in Plain Sight and Virginia Studies. Nate Sleeter is a PhD candidate in history at George Mason University and graduate research assistant at the Roy Rosenzweig Center for History and New Media. He works as a teaching assistant for the online courses Virginia Studies and Hidden in Plain Sight. Kelly Schrum is the director of educational projects at the Roy Rosenzweig Center for History and New Media and an associate professor in the Higher Education Program and the Department of History and Art History at George Mason University. She has worked for more than a decade to create innovative, open digital resources and tools for teaching and learning, including Teachinghistory.org and History Matters.*

## How to cite:

Celeste Tường Vy Sharpe, Nate Sleeter, and Kelly Schrum, "How We Learned to Drop the Quiz: Writing in Online Asynchronous Courses," in *Web Writing: Why and How for Liberal Arts Teaching and Learning*, ed. Jack Dougherty and Tennyson O'Donnell (University of Michigan Press/Trinity College ePress edition, 2014), http://epress.trincoll.edu/webwriting/chapter/sharpe-sleeter-schrum.

*See an earlier version of this essay with open peer review comments.*[6]

# Notes

1. *Hidden in Plain Sight* course website, http://edchnm.gmu.edu/hidden and *Virginia Studies: Thinking Historically about Virginia* course website, http://edchnm.gmu.edu/virginiastudies, created by the Roy Rosenzweig Center for History and New Media, George Mason University.

2. We define historical thinking as the complex process of analysis, reading, and writing necessary to understand the past. For an expanded definition, see "What is Historical Thinking?" *Teaching History.org*, http://teachinghistory.org/historical-thinking-intro.

3. Field ration, U.S. Army K ration Nescafe tin can, early 1940s, image from Oshkosh Public Museum, Wisconsin, http://www.oshkoshmuseum.org/Virtual/exhibit6/e60535b.htm.

4. "Rethink: Porcelain Module," *Hidden in Plain Sight*, screenshot uploaded to http://epress.trincoll.edu/webwriting/?attachment_id=894.

5. "'Our Plantation Is Very Weak': The Experiences of an Indentured Servant in Virginia, 1623," *History Matters: The U.S. Survey Course on the Web*, George Mason University, http://historymatters.gmu.edu/d/6475.

6. Sharpe, Sleeter, and Schrum, "How We Learned to Drop the Quiz," in *Web Writing* (Open peer review edition, Fall 2013), http://webwriting2013.trincoll.edu/rethinking/sharpe-sleeter-schrum-2013/.

# Tweet Me A Story

*Leigh Wright*

When most people think about Twitter, two things come to mind: short bursts of information containing a link to news sources and promotions or the drivel of TMI (too much information) of celebrities and the public. Twitter and social media curation tools, though, when used deliberately can be an effective means of social communication and an effective means of teaching concise writing with a creative twist for pedagogical purposes. Using only 140 characters forces the writer to focus. Every character matters.

## What is Twitter?

Although Twitter is a social media application, it is considered microblogging. The service boasted more than 140 million users by March 2012.[1] Microblogging descended from Short Message Service (aka texting), Internet Relay Chat, and Instant Messaging.[2] Users post 140 characters to answer the prompt "What's happening" and tweets may have a hashtag (ex: #JMC194) or a label to help followers keep up with a conversation. The @ symbol is used as a means of identification or the user's Twitter handle. RT signifies a retweet, or simply passing the message along as one would by handing someone a newspaper article, and MT signifies a modified tweet. Ryan Cordell offers an extensive, but easy to follow, Twitter user's guide on *ProfHacker*.[3] The example below illustrates how to use the @ mention and two hashtags for a tweet concerning a class and a campus event:[4]

Twitter's ease of use has made it an easy tool for journalists and public relations practitioners as well as the general public. Oriella PR Network surveyed journalists in 14 countries and found 59 percent use Twitter, up from 47 percent in 2012.[5] The app allows reporters to quickly take notes while attending an event or send a burst of information along with a photo or video to their followers.

**Leigh Landini Wright**
@leighlwright

I'm looking forward to grading my
@murraystateuniv #JMC294 first
Videolicious projects about
#MurrayStateACS. Fun stories.

↩ Reply  ♺ Retweet  ★ Favorite  ••• More

6:53 AM - 17 Apr 2014

*Sample tweet by the author.*

## Classroom Uses

As a journalism professor, I strive to find ways to connect the current practice of digital and social media journalism to my classes. As a former journalist, I know the world of reporting still has the same skills I learned
decades ago, but I have observed how reporters use social media tools to
supplement the traditional methods. I have used Twitter to teach students
how to write concisely, how to think quickly, and how to take the social
media conversation, weave it with their own narration and craft a social
media story on a digital platform.

When beginning journalism students start to write leads, or the introductions, to their stories, they use every fact. They assume that the standard
introduction of a freshman composition essay, where they typically outline
three points with a strong thesis statement, will work for a news story.
However, newspaper editors want leads of 35 words or less.[6]

During the lead-writing exercises, I provide students with a list of facts.
We start with the summary lead, which tells readers the who, what, where,
when, why and how of the story, but it may not use all those elements.[7]
Although I tell them not to use every piece of information listed, inevitably,
several try. When I noticed several students struggling with the conciseness

of lead writing, I tested a social media tool they used while they were supposedly listening to my lectures: Twitter.

"But it's only 140 characters," one student complained.

"That's exactly why I want you to use it," I explained. "You have to focus on the key point for a good tweet."

A sample lead writing exercise might look something like this:[8]

- *Who: Backwoods State University*
- *What: planning to build two new residence halls at a cost of $4 million, funds come from state bonds and private fundraising campaigns.*
- *Where: at the northeast corner of campus on Walnut Drive*
- *Why: aging residence halls, 10 percent increase in enrollment*
- *How: Board of Trustees approved the construction and ground will be broken Monday, Sept. 2.*

A beginning writer tends to tell the reader first about the new residence halls, the reason behind it, the cost, and the groundbreaking. A seasoned journalist might write the lead like this: Backwoods State University will build two new residence halls on Walnut Drive. (12 words) Or: Backwoods State University will break ground Monday for two new residence halls located on Walnut Drive. (16 words) The writer then would use the other information (the cost, the reasons behind it and the date of the groundbreaking) in the nut graph, or the paragraph that states the reason for the story in the second to fifth paragraph.[9]

I found an example of a wordy summary news lead: "The 5th Circuit Court of Appeals has stayed the execution of Robert James Campbell, 41, on the grounds that he did not have a 'fair opportunity' to argue his IQ is too low, just two weeks after Oklahoma botched the lethal injection of a death row inmate who was seen writhing and moaning before he eventually died 43 minutes later."[10]

The 60-word lead could be shortened: A federal court has halted the execution of an intellectually disabled Texas man hours before he was scheduled to die.

News writers must employ an economy of words to snare their readers. The well-crafted lead achieves this goal with 20 words. The extra information from the lengthy lead could be used later in the story. I distribute sample leads from national news outlets and then show examples of how tweeting can improve wordy leads.[11]

As with the traditional lead writing exercise, I gave them nuggets of information. They had to condense it into a tweet for their lead. However, unlike the Twitter conversations they might have with friends, they had to use proper grammar, spelling, and punctuation. They were not allowed to abbreviate anything into what I call "text-speak" and they had to use Associated Press style, the style manual for journalists. Thus, rather than using a number for a digit under 10, they must write it out. They also may not use an abbreviation for a school or government agency on first reference unless the AP guidelines suggest otherwise. My rules on grammar and AP style reinforce the teaching of the style manual while emphasizing conciseness. To enhance the point, the lead-writing tweets must be completed on a deadline in class, similar to a real-world situation. We work together on the first tweet lead and then they work individually. So that I could group the conversation for purposes of illustrating it on the projector screen, I gave them a class hashtag (#JMC194). The tweets appeared in real-time, and we discussed why one lead worked and another did not work. The exercise helped them to see that Twitter can be used for journalistic writing.

Since using the lead-writing exercise with beginning journalism students, I have asked my students to maintain a professional account for Twitter. Although students often have a personal Twitter account, the professional account separates their personal and professional lives and forces them to maintain a body of social media writing that can be shown to potential employers. As a best practice, I now require my students to sign a permission form that will allow their social media writing to be published inside and outside the classroom.[12]

## Live Tweeting

Once my writing students are familiar with how to use Twitter effectively, I challenge them with a series of live-tweeting exercises. At the beginning of the semester in a 200-level class, I distribute a scavenger hunt list of questions, ask them to look for clues on campus and interview people as they tweet.[13] To facilitate the discussion, I set up a class hashtag (#wright294). The 10-character hashtag also requires students to write concisely. Several students snapped photos to tweet as they unraveled my clues about the university's history and unique landmarks.[14]

For a second exercise in the same class, students were asked to attend either the men's or women's basketball game and tweet. The exercise challenged them to take notes electronically and tweet on deadline.[15] As with other assignments, I set up a class hashtag (#RacerNation) and offered suggestions of people with whom they could interact via Twitter. The selected tweeters had a connection to the athletic team, either as journalists, bloggers or members of the media athletics relations department, and their tweets served as the model. I required a minimum of 12 tweets, but some students exceeded the limit before halftime.

Of course, I had not anticipated that some students would not like basketball or even know the rules. One student developed a snarky tone as he tweeted about the odd chants and cheers. For instance, he heard the fans cheering "Leggo" instead of the more formal "Let's Go" and he used the "Leggo" chant as a funny tweet about not understanding the basketball faithful. Those tweets actually enlivened the class feed and provided another angle to a traditional sports story. Another student turned her attention away from the game and live-tweeted about the variety of school color fashions.

I taught the same 200-level class in Spring 2013. This time, their live-tweeting assignment involved the Presidential Lecture Series featuring filmmaker Spike Lee. Prior to his visit, I asked my students to research Lee and formulate questions they might ask. Several days before the lecture, I played a video of a graduation speech and asked the students to live-tweet during class to enforce concise writing. As a best practice, if a student chose to use his personal account, I asked him to tweet a warning to his followers.[16] One student tweeted, "Disregard. Working on a class assignment. This is about to get weird."

During the class period before Lee's lecture, I distributed the assignment sheet that listed the requirements.[17] For future Presidential Lectures, I will require a minimum of 20 tweets as I found that my better students quickly completed the 12-tweet requirement.

Five of my seven students tweeted on their phones or laptops, but two experienced issues with technology and the wireless or cellular networks. They took notes and then tweeted immediately after the lecture.

In my opinion, the exercise runs better if the professor attends the event, tweets alongside the students for modeling and encouragement, and sets clear expectations about the number and type of tweets required. I marked several tweets as "favorites" and retweeted several others to my followers for encouragement. The assignment was both difficult and enjoyable to grade because each student found his own style of writing an effective tweet. Tweeting is not like solving a math problem.

No two students tweeted the same quote or wrote in the same tone. Some adopted a reportorial tone while others took a conversational or engaging tone in which they offered observations and sought interactivity. The students who were already involved with the campus newspaper were able to correctly capture Lee's direct quotations, and the students who had not yet experienced live note-taking struggled. Exercises like live-tweeting can help them to build the confidence needed to take notes quickly. Plus, with crowd-sourcing, if a student incorrectly tweets a quote, someone in the Twittersphere will point it out.

Although they are tweeting as reporters, they can also offer what might be called "color commentary" about their surroundings. Reporters often engage in observation for soft news and feature stories. Details make a story more interesting. Social media also allows for a more informal tone, and reporters can show their followers glimpses of their personality through a tweet. For instance, if the reporter has admired the speaker's work, he can tweet about his excitement to finally meet the speaker. Followers of the news outlet's account will appreciate that the reporter is a human and not a robot.

One student tweeted so effectively about Spike Lee's lecture that a stranger on Twitter praised his reporting. He replied that he was working on a class assignment, listed the class hashtag and directed his new follower to my Twitter handle so that I would see the interaction.

## Building A Story with Class Tweets

Once my students completed the live-tweeting assignment, I asked them to compile their tweets as well as those from the university public relations staff, fellow students, the regional media, and the community. Those tweets were woven together using a social media curation site known as Storify.[18] Founder Burt Herman worked as an Associated Press foreign correspondent for ten years and started Storify as a way to merge what worked well (a narrative story) with traditional journalism using social media tools like Twitter, Facebook, Flickr, YouTube, and web links. Herman defines curation to journalists as, "It's really like what you guys have always done. It's taking a lot of information, pulling out the relevant parts of it, giving it context, and telling a story. That's important to remember." He also said reporters need to take social media and incorporate it into their reporting.[19]

Unfortunately, some news organizations have not truly embraced the creativity of Storify. A cursory scan of the Storify home page in August 2013 showed several media outlets with "stories" that were merely a collection of tweets in chronological order.[20] However, Storify lends itself to the art of actually crafting a story that utilizes digital social media elements and can then be presented with multimedia and social media to tell a richer story.

To build their story, I asked my students to first write a headline of four to eight words that summarized their story and would catch a reader's attention. The headline helps with search engine optimization or the keywords that will boost a piece's rank in Google News.[21] The headline reinforces my admonition to write concisely and cleverly. Next, they had to write a lead that would engage with the reader and give their audience a sense of the story's purpose. I allowed them to choose the type of journalistic writing style for their Storify, whether they followed the traditional inverted pyramid of the most important information coming first and narrowing to the least important or writing the story in the *Wall Street Journal* style, which features an anecdotal lead followed by facts. Most students chose the inverted pyramid because it is the easiest to write and organize.

As with any form of writing, the writer must determine how to best organize and present his story in the social media curation form. The drag-and-drop functionality allows the user to change his mind before publishing. Storify auto-saves the story, but the user must hit the "publish" button before it is uploaded online, and the owners of the tweets and other social media elements that are used may receive a notification if the writer chooses. It simulates the traditional writing experience where the writer revises the work, adds paragraphs, subtracts dialogue or eliminates scenes.

The students reported that they enjoyed the challenge of live-tweeting and then submitting a digital story on deadline. One student chose to lead with a photograph to tell the story chronologically while another student chose the more traditional approach with a summary lead and the inverted pyramid. Storify allowed the students to experiment with their own emerging writing style and immediately share it. Since Storify is not well known to the public, the students only garnered 20 views.

Examples:

- Spike Lee Rocks Lovett Stage
- Spike Lee Invades Murray State
- Lecturer Spikes Thought at Murray State[22]

Not only do I use Storify as a teaching tool, I use it for my own digital writing. I combined tweets, Instagram, Vine and websites and wove them with my own reporting notes during a Scripps Howard Foundation/Association of Education in Journalism and Mass Communication Social Media Externship at the Scripps Treasure Coast Newspapers in July 2013.[23]

## Applications to other Writing Disciplines

Twitter and Storify are not limited in the use of teaching writing to the style found in a journalism classroom. Both social media tools allow students to develop their voices and their style. A student might experiment with a creative style for an English class but need to develop a more authoritative style for a history or political science class. One style does not fit every situation.

A political science professor could ask students to curate the tweets from a debate or lecture and have the students write analysis in the text boxes. By choosing those elements and placing them in a certain order, the student would have to support his or her argument.

A history professor could find social and digital media that discusses a particular historical event or time period. If scholars had debated on Twitter about the commemoration of a Civil War battle, the students could use those social media elements in support of their position about historical accuracy of re-enactments. Or the professor could assign students to research a public figure and tweet his findings. Those results could then be wrapped into a Storify with narration and other social and digital media elements. The result might take the form of a digital term paper.

Creative writing professors could ask their students to take on personas of their characters and tweet dialogue or description. The student then could choose elements of dialogue and build a scene based on several characters but weave in transitions.

I used this type of exercise in a scriptwriting class where students wrote a short script. Most lacked experience writing dialogue or a scene for creative writing. I divided the students into groups of three to four, and I provided them with enough background information to begin writing a scene. They were assigned a corresponding hashtag (ex: #JMC336town or #JMC336bball), but I allowed them to come up with the characters' names and backgrounds before they began to tweet the dialogue and description.

Students had to immerse themselves in their character and tweet. The result was a stream of dialogue punctuated with details and rich descriptions of the character's actions. Much like live-tweeting an event for a journalistic purpose, students did not know what would happen next. The exercise forced them to immediately tweet a line of succinct dialogue or description. I monitored the groups and encouraged them to write quickly rather than waiting for perfection. Several students froze with the pressure, but their peers encouraged them to see where the story led. Students could either use their smart phones or computers, and the majority said it was easier to tweet from their phone than it was to sit in front of a computer as they were already accustomed to thinking quickly with texting.

For example, students were assigned a scenario in which a young lawyer moves into a small town and envisions a peaceful life filled with hunting, fishing, and golfing. He finds that the small town has a dirty secret: a corporation wants to buy the mineral rights for an oil and gas operation, but the corporation has connections to the Mafia. I asked them to develop three to five characters and write the dialogue that showed conflict between the lawyer and clients by using the hashtag #JMC336town.[24]

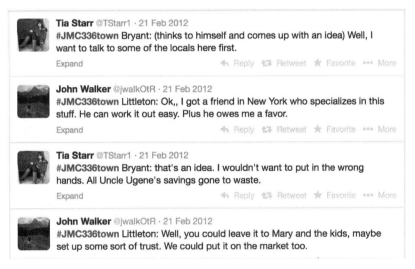

*Students in a scriptwriting class at Murray State University wrote dialogue for a class assignment on Twitter. The exercise forced them to think creatively and quickly.*

Although I did not choose to do so, the tweets then could be combined with other elements such as websites or photos in Storify, and with the narration, the student could build a scene in real-time and find an audience that might offer suggestions as they wrote. One could think of this exercise as digital crowd-sourcing meeting serial fiction.

Harriett Beecher Stowe's classic *Uncle Tom's Cabin*, written initially as a story about "How A Man became A Thing," found an audience as serialized fiction in the *National Era* from June 5, 1851 to April 1, 1852. Editor Gamaliel Bailey published a letter in the June 1866 *Atlantic Monthly* that addressed the sudden rise of Stowe's work. "Of the hundreds of letters received weekly, renewing subscriptions or sending new ones, there was one scarcely that did not contain some cordial reference to Uncle Tom."[25]

What would have happened if Ernest Hemingway and F. Scott Fitzgerald had experienced the digital social media publishing world as a way to test their works in the public eye rather than their brief forays into serial fiction? Fitzgerald sold the serial rights to his second novel, *The Beautiful and Damned*, which helped him with "understanding of subsidiary publication as a prime opportunity to remain before the public eye."[26] Contemporary authors such as Stephen King, Tom Wolfe and Patricia Cornwell published pieces of their larger works in magazines, harkening references to the practice of 19th century literary serial fiction.[27] Imagine if they turned to social media tools to test their market.

Some authors use social media as a way to develop their writing voice and build their audience. Author Jennifer Weiner asserts that Twitter helps authors build connections if they don't have a public relations staff. Her advice for prospective tweeters: "Whatever it is, polish it, edit it, give it the same attention that anything else you were going to publish is going to get. Make it funny, make it trenchant, make it pithy and relevant and smart, and the followers will come."[28]

As long as social media continues to permeate society, we, as teachers of writing, will need to continue to find interesting ways to make the writing process relevant and useful to digital natives. By using these tools, we can embrace the twist of technology while giving students the tools to develop their voice, tone, and unique writing style. Anne Trubek, Writer-in-Residence at Oberlin College, wrote in 2011 how Twitter transformed both her writing and that of her students.[29] After two years of using Twitter in my journalism classes, I'm noticing clearer and more engaging writing in their news stories. Their sentences seem clearer and crisper after tweeting an event. Twitter has helped them to say what they need to say without adding extra material to reach an editor's word count. After all, every character matters.

*About the author: Leigh Wright is an assistant professor of journalism and mass communications at Murray State University. Wright worked for nearly two decades as a reporter, section editor and columnist for a regional Kentucky newspaper. Follow her on Twitter @leighlwright.*

## How to cite:

Leigh Wright, "Tweet Me A Story," in *Web Writing: Why and How for Liberal Arts Teaching and Learning*, ed. Jack Dougherty and Tennyson O'Donnell (University of Michigan Press/Trinity College ePress edition, 2014), http://epress.trincoll.edu/webwriting/chapter/wright.

*See an earlier version of this essay with open peer review comments.*[30]

# Notes

1. Mark Briggs, *Journalism Next, Second Edition* (Los Angeles: Sage, 2013), 91.

2. Briggs, *Journalism Next*, 92.

3. Ryan Cordell, "How to Start Tweeting and Why You Might Want To," *ProfHacker*, August 11, 2010, http://chronicle.com/blogs/profhacker/how-to-start-tweeting-and-why-you-might-want-to/26065.

4. Author's tweet, April 17, 2014, https://twitter.com/leighlwright/status/456792663950630912.

5. "59% of Journalists Worldwide use Twitter, up from 47% in 2012," All Twitter, *Media Bistro*, June 28, 2013, http://www.mediabistro.com/alltwitter/journalists-twitter_b45416.

6. Carole Rich, *Writing and Reporting the News* (Boston: Wadsworth, 2010), 130.

7. Rich, *Writing and Reporting the News*, 131.

8. Leigh Wright, supplemental class materials for *Web Writing* book, *Wright on Writing*, 2014, http://leighlwright.wordpress.com/web-writing-why-and-how-for-liberal-arts-teaching-and-learning/.

9. John R. Bender, Lucinda D. Davenport, Michael W. Drager and Fred Fedler, *Reporting for the Media, Tenth Edition* (New York: Oxford, 2012), 225.

10. Amanda Sakuma, "Fifth Circuit stays Texas execution at eleventh hour," MSNBC.com, May 13, 2014, http://www.msnbc.com/msnbc/texas-execution-first-since-oklahoma-botched-lethal-injection.

11. See example of a television station's succinct news tweet, where the hashtag #BREAKING signifies the news is happening now and the @ symbol refers readers to the station's account. KRLD tweet, May 13, 2014, https://twitter.com/KRLD/status/466325516732338176.

12. Wright, supplemental class materials.

13. Wright, supplemental class materials.

14. Author's photo, Murray State University journalism students participating in a social media scavenger hunt in front of the Shoe Tree on campus, uploaded to http://epress.trincoll.edu/webwriting/?attachment_id=718.

15. Wright, supplemental class materials.

16. Wright, supplemental class materials.

17. Wright, supplemental class materials.

18. http://storify.com.

19. Hamish McKenzie, "From Bloody War to Social Media's Soft Power: Storify's Burt Herman on the New News Media," PandoDaily, April 8, 2013, http://pandodaily.com/2013/04/08/from-bloody-war-to-social-medias-soft-power-storifys-burt-herman-on-the-new-news-media.

20. "Iowans React: Teens in Isolation Cells at the State-Run Group Home," *Des Moines Register*, 2013, http://storify.com/dmregister/iowans-react-teens-in-isolation-cells-at-state-run.

21. Jeffrey Wilkinson, August E. Grant, Douglas J. Fisher, *Principles of Convergent Journalism*, Second Edition (New York: Oxford University Press, 2013), 55.

22. Sylvia R. Hamlin, "Spike Lee Rocks Lovett Stage," Storify, 2013, http://storify.com/SylviaRHamlin/spike-lee-rocks-the-lovett-stage; Tay Crum, "Spike Lee Invades Murray State," Storify, 2013, http://storify.com/TayCrum/spike-lee-invades-murray-state; Lexy Gross, "Lecturer Spikes Thought at Murray State," Storify, 2013, http://storify.com/lexygross/lecturer-spikes-thought-at-murray-state.

23. Leigh L. Wright, "TCLobster Mini-Season Off and Running," Storify, 2013, http://storify.com/leighlwright2/tclobster-mini-season-off-and-running.

24. Twitter feed for hashtag #JMC336town, 2012, https://twitter.com/search?f=realtime&q=%23JMC336town.

25. Michael Lund, *America's Continuing Story: An Introduction to Serial Fiction, 1850-1900* (Wayne State University Press, 1993), 15.

26. Rachel Ihara, "Novels on the Installment Plan: American Authorship in the Age of Serial Publication, from Stowe to Hemingway," (Ph.D. thesis, City University of New York, 2007), 10, http://books.google.com/books?id=SnWEpp44hY4C.

27. Ihara, 12.

28. Mallory Jean Tenore, "Author Jennifer Weiner on writers using Twitter, 'Leave Them Wanting More,'" *Poynter*, November 10, 2011, http://www.poynter.org/latest-news/top-stories/152513/author-jennifer-weiner-on-twitter-leave-them-wanting-more.

29. Anne Trubek, "Why Tweet? (And How To Do It)," November 30, 2011, http://annetrubek.com/2011/11/why-tweet-and-how-to-do-it.

30. Wright, "Tweet Me a Story," in *Web Writing* (Open peer review edition, Fall 2013), http://webwriting2013.trincoll.edu/engagement/wright-2013/.

# Civic Engagement

*Political Web Writing with the Stephen Colbert Super PAC*

*Susan Grogan*

In the fall of 2012, as a professor of political science at an undergraduate liberal arts college, I plunged my students—and myself—into the world of web writing centered around a campus-based, self-protesting Super PAC (Political Action Committee). The public writing that resulted reflected my growing interest in changing technologies in both the political world and the political science classroom. Super PACs after *Citizens United v FEC* have changed election dynamics, and web media have become a key means of political action.[1]

Web writing should be part of any political science curriculum. Our graduates aspire to careers in politics, advocacy, and journalism—all fields where writing competency is valued. Writing encourages students to process ideas, transcending the limits of learning by rote and periodic examination. In particular, Christopher Lawrence and Michelle Dion note that regular blogging is an effective learning mechanism especially well suited for political commentary:

> The unique features of blogging have lent themselves particularly well to political commentary. Political blogs tend to combine links to, and excerpts from, mass-media accounts of daily political events with political commentary by their authors, links to other blogs with commentary on these events, and (often, but not always) a comment forum associated with each post for visitors to contribute their own commentary and debate with other visitors or the post's author. They foster dialogue between bloggers and their audience, provide for the summarization and dissemination of political news and events, and help readers to conceptualize the political world.[2]

I found blogging particularly interesting for its positive correlation with higher levels of offline civic engagement.[3] I had already planned to incorporate civic engagement activities in my classes, recognizing that students who participate in elections become more familiar with the electoral processes and tend to remain engaged throughout their lives.[4] I considered blogging an effective supplement, enhancing the value of civic assignments.

In comparison to a traditional website built with static pages, blogs have a fluid, conversational nature that helps demonstrate the iterative nature of writing. Blogs, however, also encourage "quicker and more haphazard thinking, simpler (and even simplistic) analyses, and more ill-advised dudgeon"[5] rendering them less efficacious for more polished research and essays. Consequently, I assigned my students, as a public service, to adapt conventional research assignments for our class site, We Just Want Stephen Colbert To Come To Our College SuperPAC. The major departure from my past teaching was that students were now required to involve themselves in the political laboratory of the community and were encouraged to write for a public audience rather than strictly for their professor. Students were assigned online writing for my fall 2012 classes—Political Science 100: Introduction to Politics; Political Science 348: Parties and Elections; and Political Science 303: Law, Courts and Judges—and also my spring 2014 Political Science 201: American Politics class.[6]

## Background: We Just Want Stephen Colbert To Come To Our College SuperPAC

In March of 2012, political satirist Stephen Colbert offered his viewers, especially college students, an opportunity to purchase his Super Fun Pack that included instructions on starting their own Super PACs. As an enticement, Colbert also offered owners of Fun Packs the opportunity to enter his Treasure Hunt where, if they found Colbert's silver turtle hidden somewhere in the USA, they would win a visit by Colbert to their campus. The more attractive idea was that they could join with Colbert's "Americans for a Better Tomorrow, Tomorrow Super PAC" in a spontaneous campus-based protest of Super PACs and the Supreme Court's *Citizens United* decision. At the time, I was planning my upcoming fall classes around the election and was thinking in terms of creating a classroom environment conducive to civic engagement and web writing as a new peda-

# We Just Want Stephen Colbert To Come To Our College SuperPac

*The most honest Super PAC ever? (Politico)*

## NONPARTISAN

Introduction to
Politics Websites

Law, Courts, and
Judges Websites

Parties and Elections
Websites

*EVENT CALENDAR*

Professor Grogan

An Ordinary Person's
Super PAC Blog

*The "We Just Want Stephen Colbert to Come to Our College SuperPAC" course site.*

gogical focus. So, I jumped at the chance to center my classes on the greater Colbert campus-based Super PAC happening. I hoped to encourage students to act and write in terms of the audience of their peers, the demographic that watches *The Colbert Report*. We were one of about twenty Colbert Super PACs in 2012 and may be the sole survivor.

Having filed the requisite papers with the Federal Election Commission (FEC), I was caught off guard by media keeping track of new PAC registrations. *Politico*, recognizing the ambiguity in our Super PAC's name—slighting Colbert's Treasure Hunt, wanting just the prize—opined we might be "the most honest Super Pac ever"[7] The *Huffington Post* and the *New York Observer* also made inquiries. I responded with a press release, desiring to maintain an ambiguous stance toward Colbert and resorting to occasional humor, although I am not a professional satirist. The press release made a second joke of Colbert's *Treasure Hunt,* noting I already had a turtle collection and teasing that my Super PAC's motto was "Treasure None but Your Vote." The ambiguity seemed to work, my college president recognizing it as "political satire on political satire."[8]

I wanted the class setting to encourage direct engagement with the political process and to be interesting as well as fun. I felt it important, however, to continue an approach to Colbert that was neither adulation nor condemnation in order to leave room for a variety of student viewpoints. For example, *The Colbert Report* occasionally features a "Better Know a District" segment where a Congressional guest becomes the "straight man" of Colbert's pointed humor. As a foil to Colbert's faux interviews, we instituted "A Better Way to Know a District" where students registered voters throughout Maryland's Fifth Congressional District, holding two dozen voter registration events at seventeen locations.

## Introducing Web Writing into My Course Design

I first considered having students build a website for the SuperPAC, but inquiries to colleagues, discussions with college IT staff, and my own summer experiments with various templates and text editors soon dissuaded me. I did not want mastering website development to substitute for learning political science in my classes. The web writing and civic engagement assignments were to be integral course components and not mere add-ons. To facilitate this, I themed each of my 2012 classes. "Intro to Politics" became "Democratic Participation," and "Parties & Elections" became "Money and Votes." The challenge was "Law, Courts, & Judges," a junior-level course on the judicial process. Highlighting a contentious race for a local judgeship and the impact of the Supreme Court's decision in the *Citizens United* case reinforced the theme given this course: *This is an election year; who cares about courts and judges?* The question came with one answer: *Al Gore certainly did in 2000,* making the point that courts do matter in electoral politics.

## Class Assignments

The syllabi for these themed classes included writing regular blog posts, generally three per week, and commenting on other students' posts. Students were expected to demonstrate knowledge of course material and their ability to communicate that knowledge effectively. Students in the Parties & Elections course were assigned additional group research papers adapted to the web as static pages of the Super PAC website. I adjusted my grade-weighting scheme to make blogging a meaningful part of students' grades, 15-20% for 2012. These changes also left room for civic engagement activities, accounting for another 15% of final grades. In 2014, I transformed assignments traditionally completed in paper form into blog spots and web content on the Super PAC site, and therefore increased the weight for web writing to 50% of the final course grade.

As part of their civic engagement responsibilities, students trained to become voter registrars and took part in off-campus voter registration and "Get Out the Vote" (GOTV) events. Students in the Parties and Elections course were expected to serve as election judges in local precincts. Those unable or ineligible to do so were allowed options to volunteer as precinct "greeters" for candidates or parties, drive a shuttle to transport student voters to the polls, staff the Super PAC-sponsored Election Command Center and Hotline on campus, or observe the official canvass of provisional and absentee ballots.

For research assignments, students choose from placeholders on the Super PAC's homepage related to the theme of their class and the Super PAC's overall election and voting concerns. Among other assignments, my students in 2012 formed groups and created website content for "SuperPACs," "Gerrymandering," and "Voter Suppression."[9] Course syllabi are available on my pedagogy blog.[10]

## How-to

There are numerous options for publishing student writing on the web, and interested readers may refer to platforms and hosting services I considered.[11] Because of FEC regulations concerned about the sources and uses of political campaign funds, I was compelled to secure external hosting for the Super PAC, which is a political committee unaffiliated with any college. (The Super PAC raises funds for its pro-voter agenda and uses some funds to provide resources to college students.) I chose Hostgator as my hosting provider. With a low-level reseller account, I can host as many as 1,000 students as if each was a client purchasing hosting services from the Super PAC—only the Super PAC provides student accounts at no cost.[12]

Each student is provided her own WordPress web-blog. There is a trade-off between letting students have total control over the design of their sites or compelling them to use a standard design and format. To provide group thematic cohesiveness, to emphasize writing over design, and to minimize technical distractions, I generally restrict students to using the same free default theme and header image. The *2014* WordPress default theme is my current choice. Students are otherwise granted substantial leeway to customize their sites.[13]

Overall, setting up WordPress sites for students in advance has worked well because students can focus on content from day one rather than learning how to set up a blog account. Within the first two weeks, students easily become accustomed to WordPress. During this period, some class time is dedicated to technical aspects of WordPress—some preferably in a computer lab. It helps to provide simple how-to guides for a few basic tasks, which I publish on my blog as how-to stickies.

## In the Classroom

Because I had not specified particular questions to be answered or issues to be addressed, blog content varied considerably during 2012. A few students confined themselves to reporting political news with little commentary. Most students went well beyond that minimal effort. Some students took advantage of blogging's creative strengths, as in Jonathan Holtzman's "Ben Cardin: Senator, Second Banana, Invisible-Man?" and Matt Carney's, "The American Political Media: Why Bipartisanship is Going Extinct."[14]

Using new tools and methods in my classes reminded me that students will rise to expectations when given motivation and encouragement. To improve students' abilities "to summarize the story, to get to the heart, to the point, to sum up quickly and concisely,"[15] I now teach the Inverted Pyramid Style of journalism adapted for the web. Successful blogs often display the inverted structure in response to people quickly scanning web-content while looking for something interesting to read. Such posts often begin with compact and enticing "headlines and blurbs" that conclude the post up front, branching out into detail from there.[16]

My American Politics students have always prepared "thought questions" and "news reports" for each class. Five years ago, to improve the quality of the exercise, I began requiring students to email their "thought questions" to me before class. Now these assignments have been adapted to blogging. For each class, students write headlines, blurbs, and short posts with cited references or external links for a news item.[17]

I also presently require a weekly web-essay of 500 words plus blurb that is to be more polished than the typical blog post. I expect essays to evidence class material and current events, indicating that students have researched the issue a bit. Many weeks have scheduled web-essay topics. Others are student choice.[18] Since 2014, I have required students to prepare well-researched content designed for a static page of the website. This individual assignment of 2000 – 3000 words is turned in well before the semester ends in order to leave time for editing.

A great deal of time is invested in writing effective posts and finding one's topical style. As a class project, web writing taxes both students and profes-sor. Overall, I do not assign students more work than before, but it is more visible and they take it more seriously as a result. I find it is good practice to give students regular feedback by grading their work every couple of weeks using rubrics available to them on my pedagogy blog.[19]

## Student Responses: The Results of the Experiment

As students in my 2012 Introduction to Politics course wrestled with issues such as the difference between a nation and a state and why socialism seems to be a dirty word, I saw that they were learning the language of politi-cal science and the kinds of questions the field addresses. In some blogs, I identified interests not evident in the classroom as students more willingly personalized the theories and abstract materials we covered in their read-ings into "soapbox" opinion pieces, as is typical of bloggers, which became a pedagogical advantage.[20] Students in the Parties and Elections course also experimented with the form.[21] Two enterprising members of the Parties & Elections course went so far as to live blog one of the 2012 presidential debates. Prior to the debate, they tested several live-blogging plugins and got one up and running on their sites.[22]

Many students used their blogs to reflect on their 2012 civic engagement activities: the demographics of people they registered, what kinds of ques-tions they were asked, how hard it was to muffle their political views during registration and GOTV events, and the adventures they had as election judges.[23] There was an interesting spill-over effect from the class activities. I had launched a Facebook page for the Super PAC, and in response to some students comments, I granted them "content manager" privileges to post as the Super PAC.[24]

## Reflections

I made some changes for 2014. I try to grade blogs more often—every two to three weeks, providing comments. I convey higher expectations and structure blogging requirements more. I have added additional instructions and readings on web writing and plan to make a habit of inviting experi-enced bloggers to speak to the class. Class lectures now leave more time for critiques—first of external political blogs and then of student work. The expected class-then-blog relationship is often flipped to blog-then-class. A thread picked up from blog posts and comments can serve as the entrée into a subsequent class discussion. This reversal underpins blogging's integral role in the course.

Throughout the 2012 election, the pattern of our Super PAC-related course activities replicated patterns found in election campaigns. Until the elec-tion, the students (and I) had to balance limited hours, course objectives, on-going projects, and blogging... all within the fixed constraint of election timing, including the mid-October close of voter registration, the deadline for requesting absentee ballots, and the election itself. Following the big buildup to Election Day in early November there was a sudden release of tension and the question arose, "Now what?" We then shifted our focus from one kind of community outreach to another kind of publicness via more emphasis on the blogs. The nature of the blog writing thus changed during the post-election season after most had gotten in a few good comments on the outcome. Posts became more reflective, as in Emma Kaufman's, "What is the Point of Political Activism?"[25]

In 2012 I had approached web writing as a supplement to civic engagement, as a set of tools. In that sense, the semester was highly successful. Students did write—most of them a lot—about politics. They were more involved and invested in their writing and engaged a broader range of topics and concerns than they would have in traditional, narrow-themed academic papers guided by the *Chicago Manual of Style*. In addition, blog commenting can circumvent the dyadic nature of classroom discussions between students and their instructor as demonstrated by Nico Moore's post, "The Respect of the President."[26]

Today, web writing has become less a supplement and more another civic engagement activity in its own right. But, I believe it takes a critical mass to make the transition. Sparse external comments can discourage students. It has helped to have a visible website and exemplar work of previous students available for current students' reviews and class discussions, things which were not available to me before. Googling "gerrymandering" in class now returns our page twice on the first page of results. Searching "college student election judges" returns posts written by our own students. By the end of March 2014, Matthew Riedel's two-month old blog topped 37,000 page views not counting bots (class average is 13,000).[27] While earning stats is not the goal, such realizations can help students visualize themselves as taking part in something larger than just doing homework, and most respond.

On the civic engagement side, I have witnessed some truly outstanding commitment by my students. Some awoke at 8 a.m. on a Saturday or Sunday to register voters. Others spent 15 hours at the polls serving as election judges. (This duty was not without its rewards, as Jonathan Holtzman's post revealed.) Another pair of students who were ineligible to serve as election judges spent Election Day out in the cold volunteering for local candidates and greeting voters on their way into polling locations.[28]

Our Election Day efforts were recognized locally. Three of the students who served as Election Judges were interviewed by the local newspaper, and the Chief Election Judge at our local precinct emailed the day after Election Day, noting a marked increase in voter turnout for her precinct and attributed that to our efforts.[29]

Political scientists so far have focused mainly on the benefits and drawbacks of blogging in regard to their own scholarship and writing. John Sides, an author of the award-winning blog *The Monkey-Cage*, described how blogging could better position the political scientist in seeking tenure and advancement, in large part by inculcating better writing and research habits.[30] Robert Farley, an author of the less-structured *Lawyers, Guns & Money*, countered Sides, charging him in complicity with a "tenure and promotion system …built around an obsolete social and technological foundation, with career success built around posting a few articles in a few journals subscribed to by a few libraries and read by few people." Farley called instead for new incentives to reward academics who write blogs that "concentrate less on the transmission of academic research into the policy sphere and more on the direct application of research knowledge and skills to political and policy questions."[31] I find both these views value too much the political scientist as political or policy wonk and steer the focus of web writing too far away from its potential in the classroom. I agree with Juan Cole, author of the blog *Informed Comment*, that the issue of web writing and academic careers is misplaced. Cole says the question is "shameful."[32] My own focus is on applying both Sides and Farley's better premises to web writing pedagogy, which means I spend my free time administering student accounts, preparing web writing class materials in response to student progress in writing political commentary and research for the web, advising them personally as needed, and mostly reading their work. This leaves no time for me to routinely blog or write in the dedicated fashion of Sides, Farley, and Cole. However, my students are very familiar with these and other prominent political bloggers and read them more widely and in more depth than before, including analyzing writing styles and communicative effectiveness—from the students' own web writing experience base.

I plan to continue the civic engagement/public writing model in my political science courses. Plans for fall 2014 include civic engagement and web writing for a second Parties and Elections class, and I will launch *The Maryland Poll* as a project distinct from but with a similar pedagogical deployment as the Super PACs.[33] I have been awarded two Mellon Grants for Service Learning to cover the expense of civic engagement assignments in both fall classes, which also have been approved as Experiencing Liberal Arts in the World (ELAW) courses, satisfying a general College requirement.

Finally, I should note that Stephen Colbert has not come to our college. After agreeing to sell our t-shirts (with no profit to me or the Super PAC), my campus bookstore encouraged me to print a brochure that addresses the question, "Will Stephen Colbert Come To Our College?"[34]. I stated that I would prefer if Colbert came for what we had accomplished, implying I wouldn't want him to come too soon, not just because we have a catchy name and have adopted an adorable clown for a mascot. Also, I thought it impractical for Colbert to visit us back then out of fairness to the winner of his Treasure Hunt and the many other Colbertesque campus-based Super PACs. After all, the idea of a visit may be more civically engaging than the event. But in considering what on earth else we might have to accomplish to earn a freebie visit from His Grace, I must say, it does appear Stephen Colbert has set high expectations.

*About the author: Susan Grogan teaches political science at St. Mary's College of Maryland, a public honors college.*

### How to cite:

Susan Grogan, "Civic Engagement: Political Web Writing with the Stephen Colbert Super PAC," in *Web Writing: Why and How for Liberal Arts Teaching and Learning*, ed. Jack Dougherty and Tennyson O'Donnell (University of Michigan Press/ Trinity College ePress edition, 2014), http://epress.trincoll.edu/webwriting/ chapter/grogan.

*See an earlier version of this essay with open peer review comments.*[35]

# Notes

1. Citizens United v. Federal Election Commission, 130 S. Ct 876 (Supreme Court 2010).

2. Christopher N. Lawrence and Michelle L. Dion, "Blogging in the Political Science Classroom," *PS: Political Science & Politics* 43:1 (2010): 152.

3. Kenneth W. Moffett and Laurie L. Rice, "College Students and Blogging Activity during the 2008 and 2012 Elections," presented at the Annual Meeting of the American Political Science Association (2013): 3.

4. Robin Smith, "Embedding Engagement in a Political Science Course: Community College and University Students and the Help America Vote College Poll Worker Program," *Journal for Civic Commitment* 19 (2012): 6-15.

5. John Sides, "The Political Scientist as Blogger," *PS: Political Science & Politics* 44:2 (2011): 268.

6. Susan Grogan, "We Just Want Stephen Colbert To Come to Our College SuperPAC" parent website for political science classes, St. Mary's College, Maryland, 2012-14, http://wejustwantstephencolberttocometoourcollegesuperpac.org/.

7. Anne Palmer and Dave Levinthal, "Chesapeake Playing Both Sides in Clean Air Debate," *Politico*, June 13, 2012, http://www.politico.com/politicoinfluence/0612/politicoinfluence282.html.

8. Tyler Kingkade, "St. Mary's College Professor Starts Super PAC, Inspired By Stephen Colbert," *The Huffington Post*, June 14, 2012, http://www.huffingtonpost.com/2012/06/14/college-super-pac-stephen-colbert-st-marys-college-of-maryland_n_1597624.html; Colin Campbell and Hunter Walker, "Meet The Turtle-Collecting Professor Who Formed The 'We Just Want Stephen Colbert To Come To Our College Super PAC'", *Politicker*, June 14, 2012, http://politicker.com/2012/06/meet-the-turtle-collecting-professor-who-formed-the-we-just-want-stephen-colbert-to-come-to-our-college-super-pac/.

9. Susan Grogan, course parent website pages on SuperPACs, http://wejustwantstephencolberttocometoourcollegesuperpac.org/super_pacs.html; Gerrymandering http://goo.gl/ZNxq2Y; and Voter Suppression http://goo.gl/67YloI.

10. Susan Grogan, "Syllabi of Courses with Web-Writing Components," *Web-Writing in the Political Science Classroom*, April 26, 2014, http://profgrogan.wejustwantstephencolberttocometoourcollegesuperpac.org/syllabi-of-courses-with-web-writing-components/.

11. Grogan, "Platform and Hosting Options I Considered for Student Web-Writing," *Web-Writing in the Political Science Classroom*, April 7, 2014, http://profgrogan.wejustwantstephencolberttocometoourcollegesuperpac.org/platform-and-hosting-options-i-considered-for-student-web-writing/.

12. Grogan, "How To Set Up and And Use A Hostgator Reseller Account for Student Web-Writing," *Web-Writing in the Political Science Classroom*, April 7, 2014, http://wp.me/p4bWdW-2b.

13. Grogan, "Notes on Using WordPress for Student Web-Writing," *Web-Writing in the Political Science Classroom*, April 10, 2014, http://wp.me/p4bWdW-2e.

14. These and subsequent student posts on the parent course blog are cited with short-links to save space: Holtzman, http://goo.gl/i1N1MT and Carney, http://goo.gl/TCTj88.

15. Chip Scanlan, "Writing from the Top Down: Pros and Cons of the Inverted Pyramid," *Poynter*, March 2, 2011, http://www.poynter.org/how-tos/newsgathering-storytelling/chip-on-your-shoulder/12754/writing-from-the-top-down-pros-and-cons-of-the-inverted-pyramid/.

16. Douglas K. Van Dunne, James A. Landay, and Jason L. Hong, *The Design of Sites: Patterns for Creating Winning Web Sites*, 2nd ed. (New York: Prentice Hall, 2007): 297-302. See also Grogan, "Titles, Blurbs, and 'Inverted Pyramid' Writing Attract and Keep Readers," *Web-Writing in the Political Science Classroom*, January 28, 2014, http://wp.me/p4bWdW-1t.

17. See Jackson Ranheim's "#TAKEBACKAMERICANPOLITICALMEDIA," http://goo.gl/rE0oOa, and Kate Brennan's "HobbyLobby Lobs A Law Bomb," http://goo.gl/XrKztE, and a thought question in Peter Vicenzi's "Blurring the Lines Between Campaign Work and Political Advocacy," http://goo.gl/RDFKyT and Gabby Caligiuri's "Republican Playing Offense," http://goo.gl/Q92jO2.

18. See Nevin Hall's "Political Influence of A SMDP System," http://goo.gl/ViQZzM, and Erin Chase's "The End to Student Debt & Loans in Maryland May Be Coming Soon," http://goo.gl/agxxUH.

19. Grogan, "Why Use Rubrics?" *Web-Writing in the Political Science Classroom*, February 15, 2014, http://wp.me/p4bWdW-1P.

20. Kevin Wallsten, "Political Blogs: Transmission Belts, Soapboxes, Mobilizers, or Conversation Starters," *Journal of Information Technology & Politics* 4:3 (2008): 19-40. For student examples, see Knakia Francis' and Michelle Horne's blogs http://goo.gl/iA0aJg and http://goo.gl/NtS2aI, respectively. Martin Armstrong's "Court Jesters of the Modern Era" added his habits to our readings on Colbert and the media, http://goo.gl/6PoAYV. Luke Land's "A semester's wrap up" assessed what he had learned from the course, http://goo.gl/LLW3Qg.

21. See Kevin Schwarz's blog, http://goo.gl/K4K6vJ, and Taylor Adatia's *What's Wrong with the Voters of the United States?*, http://goo.gl/cjcs0e.

22. Nicole Zimmerman, "Live Blogging the Final Debate," http://goo.gl/YH7ovX.

23. Ame Roberts, "Getting Out the Vote," http://goo.gl/Sak6jI; Kira Schwartz, "What Shocked Me Most as an Election Judge," http://goo.gl/m1u6OD; Katina Burley, "Played a huge role in the election process, doing my civic duties," http://goo.gl/ZxAa88.

24. https://www.facebook.com/WeJustWantStephenColbertToComeToOurCollegeSuperPac.

25. Kaufman, http://goo.gl/cmZIKv.

26. Moore, http://goo.gl/aF35SZ.

27. Riedel, http://goo.gl/pjdHvf.

28. Holtzman, http://goo.gl/qoaotA; Allison Griffin, "Volunteering for Hoyer," http://goo.gl/VnZjqV.

29. "St. Mary's College Students Team up to Help at County Polls," November 2, 2012, http://www.somdnews.com/article/20121102/NEWS/711029870/1044/st-mary-s-college-students-team-up-to-help-at-county-polls&template=southernMaryland; John Warton,

"Plenty to Note Before the Vote: Election Judges, Precinct Hosts Scramble Toward Nov. 6," October 19, 2012, both in Southern Maryland Newspapers Online, http://www.somdnews.com/article/20121019/NEWS/710199836/1051/plenty-to-note-before-the-vote&template=southernMaryland.

30. John Sides, "The Political Scientist as Blogger," *PS: Political Science & Politics* 44:2 (2011):267.

31. John Farley, "Complicating the Political Scientist as Blogger," *PS: Political Science & Politics* 46:2 (2012): 384.

32. "Can Blogging Derail Your Career? 7 Bloggers Discuss the Case of Juan Cole," *Chronicle of Higher Education: The Chronicle Review* 52:47 (2006): B6.

33. The Maryland Poll, http://www.mpoll.org/.

34. http://wejustwantstephencolberttocometoourcollegesuperpac.org/PDFs/Brochure.pdf

35. Susan Grogan, "Creating an Environment for Student Engagement. . .," in *Web Writing* (Open peer review edition, Fall 2013), http://webwriting2013.trincoll.edu/engagement/grogan-2013/.

# Public Writing and Student Privacy

*Jack Dougherty*

## A Dilemma of Competing Values

Well into the fall semester of 2011, when I first assigned my class to write on the open web, I discovered a dilemma. On one hand, I had praised the pedagogical virtues of requiring my students to share our writing with the public. The reasons were both principled and pragmatic. The object of a liberal arts education is to fully engage with ideas that differ from our own in order to "free the mind of parochialism and prejudice," I told my students, quoting from our college mission statement.[1] One of the best ways to improve critical thinking and writing skills is to post work in public, beyond the four walls of the classroom, and to invite others to respond. Our prose has greater potential to improve when we author for real audiences (not just the professor), and revise our work in consideration of thoughtful feedback and alternative points of view. On the other hand, all students deserve—and are legally entitled under U.S. law—some degree of privacy in our educational institutions and ownership over the words they have authored. I was aware of these general issues due to my graduate training in educational policy, and as a digital scholar I had recently drafted an intellectual property statement for essays voluntarily submitted by contributors for another open peer-reviewed book at that time. But as a college educator, I was searching for an ethical way to balance the competing values of public writing and student privacy in my classroom.

Making student writing more public is not a new issue, and several faculty and librarians have devised ways to achieve this goal within legal guidelines. Some solutions are very low-tech. Down the hall from my office, for instance, a philosophy professor occasionally tapes anonymized student papers, with his comments, on the wall for other students and passersby to read.[2] Elsewhere on my campus, faculty assign students to post essays and comment on other students' work on password-protected course sites, or even deliver poster presentations at campus-wide events. Some academic units require senior thesis students to upload their final works into the library digital repository, where they have the option to limit readership to the college network or open it to the public. Some students volunteer to write for the college newspaper or literary publications, and a few publish their own blogs. Furthermore, a small number of students are invited to co-author scholarly journal articles or book chapters that may appear in print or online. But my pedagogical goal differed from the campus norm because I wanted *all students* in my mid-level undergraduate course to publish their writing on the public web, *preferably* under their real names, yet to retain *control over their own words.*

Current U.S. student privacy law is grounded in FERPA, the Family Education Rights and Privacy Act of 1974, and its subsequent amendments.[3] Greater awareness of this federal law has sharply curtailed past practices of openly posting student grades on a department bulletin board, or leaving graded papers for students to pick up on a hallway table, where anyone can flip through them. But exactly how the pre-Internet FERPA law applies to student writing on the public web is not perfectly clear. One crisis that prompted my dilemma in November 2011 was Georgia Tech's decision to erase class wikis with student writing on grounds that it violated FERPA.[4] The Georgia Tech decision was controversial because FERPA does not directly address the issue of student writing on the public web. For example, most colleges and universities interpret FERPA to prohibit the public disclosure of class rosters, as this is more detailed academic information than allowed in the standard "directory information" exemption of the law. In this sense, a faculty member who requires students to write on the public web, *using their full names*, effectively opens up the class roster for all to see. But does the law permit faculty to require students to publish student writing to the public web if names are optional?[5]

Since I am not a lawyer and have no legal expertise in this subject, I looked for guidance on how other academics interpret FERPA. My general understanding at that time (supported by subsequent writings by Kevin Smith and others) suggested that I *may* require students to post their writing in public as a course assignment (especially if my syllabus clearly states this in advance), but I *may not* require students to attach their names. Similarly, other students and I may publicly comment on writing, but all grades must be delivered privately to the student.[6] Based on my layperson's understanding of FERPA, I wrote up the following statement for my online syllabi, which explains my motivating principle behind public writing, while affirming students' rights to control their own words, with instructions on how to do so. See the statement with visuals and links in context.[7]

Public writing and student privacy policy:

This course requires students to post their writing on the public web because our ideas become clearer and more valuable when we share them and receive feedback from others. Unless marked otherwise, all content on this site is freely shared by Jack Dougherty and students under a Creative Commons Attribution-NonCommercial-ShareAlike 3.0 license. This means that the author(s) listed in the byline holds the copyright, but content may be freely adapted and redistributed under the same terms, if the original source is cited.

Although all student posts are publicly viewable and searchable, all grades are private and accessible only by the individual student, in accordance with the federal Family Education Rights and Privacy Act (FERPA). If a student desires additional privacy on the public web, s/he may publish posts for this course using only a first name, or initials, or a pseudonym approved by the instructor. If a student needs additional privacy, please speak with the instructor to arrange accommodations.

After an assignment has received a grade, students also have the right to change its visibility (to password-only, or private) or delete it from the site entirely. Students who co-author a post must reach this decision jointly. In turn, the instructor promises to maintain student posts until the course is offered again (or longer, if feasible), so that students have the option to link to their work on their resumes or personal websites. Additionally, the instructor will moderate and remove any inappropriate comments on student work on the class site.

Nowadays, when introducing this policy to my class, it is accompanied by a brief "Google Yourself" demonstration, usually by a volunteer student who has enrolled in one of my previous courses with web writing assignments. The volunteer types her or his full name (sometimes with the college name, if the surname is a common one) into Google Search on the classroom computer projector unit to find out where her or his prior coursework appears in the search rankings. The student's results usually appear within the top five listings. Judging from the audible gasps, several students are surprised by the outcome—and it still surprises me that some so-called "digital native" millennials do not already know this—and I briefly explain how Google's PageRank algorithm favors human-created links, particularly those from educational institutions. We briefly discuss the pros and cons of listing their full name, first name, or a pseudonym in the byline, and I offer two real examples. In the first case, a former student published a web essay under her full name, which helped her to earn a prestigious internship with a non-profit organization. In the second case, another former student published a web essay on a controversial legal topic, and initially decided to identify herself only with initials in the byline to reduce the risk of detection by authorities, then deleted it after the course ended. To wrap up the lesson, I demonstrate how students have control over how to display their name in their user profile settings of our site, and ask them to make an informed decision when assigning their first post. While this public-private side lesson takes only five minutes during the first day of class, the power to name oneself—or not—on the web lasts far longer.

How have students responded to the public-private policy? After implementing this change in 2011, I tracked responses by a total of 71 students in two different classes over two years. Both classes enrolled mid-level undergraduates from my academic unit and affiliated departments. *Educ 308 Cities Suburbs and Schools* is an elective seminar, and *Educ 300 Education Reform, Past and Present* is a required survey course for Educational Studies majors, which also counts for major credit in American Studies and Public Policy & Law. For all classes, I reviewed the students' final web essays to examine how they exercised their right to display their names in the byline or remove their writing from the class site, months after the class concluded (as of September 2013). Overall, the vast majority of students (87 percent) elected to display their full names on their public essays, while far smaller percentages chose to limit their essay by password, list themselves by first name only or a pseudonym, or removed the essay from the class website after the class ended. While the privacy protections are occasionally utilized, most of my students opt to modify their profile on our college's WordPress system from the default setting (their network username such as jsmith3) to their full name. [8]

How Students Elected to Display Bylines or Protect/Remove Final Web Essays, by percent

| Course (year) | Enrolled | Full name (public) | Full name (password) | First name only | Alias | Deleted by student |
|---|---|---|---|---|---|---|
| Ed 308 (2011) | 17 | 71% | 18% | | | 12% |
| Ed 308 (2012) | 11 | 100% | | | | |
| Ed 300 (2012) | 23 | 91% | | 4% | | 4% |
| Ed 300 (2013) | 20 | 90% | | 5% | 5% | |
| Total | 71 | 87% | 4% | 3% | 1% | 4% |

## If You Build It, Will They Come. . . and Comment?

In addition, some students express pride in their web writing by voluntarily adding brief "about the author" biographical statements at the end of their web essays to make more personal connections with readers. Other students demonstrate ownership over their works by including links to their essays in e-portfolios, job letters, or requests to other professors to admit them into advanced courses. When students discover ways to engage with broader audiences with their words, particularly in ways that I never intended or foresaw, it reminds all of us of the importance of writing for people other than the professor.

What if no one actually reads what I wrote? That may be the greatest fear of public writing on the web today. An empty comment box heightens this phobia, by suggesting (mistakenly) that the absence of visible feedback means that a writer's words did not successfully generate a public response.[9] By comparison, print authors do not experience this fear to the same degree. If no one thumbs through your obscure journal article or checks out your weighty tome from its dusty shelf, there is little evidence that your work has gone unread, except perhaps for library databases and citation metrics. For better or worse, web authors tend to rely on readers' comments for validation that our words have been seen and have value.

While introducing students to academic web writing over the past two years, I have experimented with different strategies for cultivating external readers and commenters. Mark Sample and other thoughtful educators have designed better blogging assignments and commenting roles for students in their classes.[10] But my focus has been on public engagement with readers outside our classroom walls. How might we build richer connections between students and broader audiences?

One experiment was the laissez-faire approach. During the spring 2012 semester of my *Educ 300 Education Reform, Past & Present* class, I did absolutely nothing to attract readers to my students' web writing. I did not email, tweet, nor promote their existence. In total, the entire class received precisely one external comment, or technically a "pingback" notification that one student's essay had been listed as an "online article that may be of interest" to readers of an academic journal.[11] While the absence of comments may suggest that my students had few readers, the web statistics tell a very different story. To avoid counting active student use, I tabulated web hits during the six-month break in this spring course, from mid-May 2012 through December 2012. Nearly 25,000 unique users visited our non-advertised course site. While most of these hits quickly bounced away from the site, and may have been robot web crawlers, most web traffic was driven by Google search queries on specific topics, which suggested significant interest by real readers. For example, the most popular student web essay, "Was Hurricane Katrina Good for the Education of Students in New Orleans?" attracted over 6,000 unique page views during this period, peaking on the seventh anniversary of the storm in late August 2012. Other widely-viewed student web essays—on topics such as community service in higher education, classroom technology, and the history of disability education law—attracted fewer unique page views (800 to 2,000), but retained visitors on the page for longer periods of time (between 5 to 7 minutes, on average). Of course, the quantity of hits is not necessarily linked to the quality of the student essay, but the average length of time spent by visitors on our course site suggested that, despite the absence of visible comments, my students had successfully engaged the public through their writing.[12]

A second experiment in public engagement was to commission recent alumni to serve as guest commentators on student web essays. At the conclusion of the Educ 308 Cities Suburbs & Schools seminar in Fall 2011,

I invited two recent Trinity College graduates (Claudia Dresser '10 and Devlin Hughes '09) to split a set of ten student web essays, post public comments based on our seminar's evaluation criteria, and then afterwards, meet the students in person to discuss the feedback they had delivered. The guest evaluators also privately shared with me their numerical scores for each essay, and with college funding I paid each a modest stipend of $150 for their time. As expected, these carefully selected commentators wrote substantive remarks that focused on desired aspects of expository student writing, such as the insightfulness of arguments, persuasive use of evidence, and effective integration of digital elements. While the guest evaluators posted at least one substantive comment per web essay, this exercise did not spark additional comments nor noticeably increase web traffic (about 3,000 unique visitors, averaging over 1 minute per page during the off-season from mid-December 2011 thru August 2012), perhaps due to the narrow focus of this specialized seminar. Still, the quality of reader feedback always beats the quantity of readers.[13]

A third experiment expanded upon the guest evaluator model to include student peers at other liberal arts colleges as part of a planned academic exchange. In Fall 2012, the second year of my Educ 308 Cities Suburbs & Schools seminar web writing assignment, a group of students from nearby Wesleyan University and I made a deal. The co-organizers of a student-taught course, Sociology 419: Education Policy in the United States, (Sydney Lewis '14, Catherine Doren '13, and Andrew Ribner '14) invited me to deliver a guest lecture at their campus.[14] In return, they arranged for the fifteen Wesleyan students in their course to divide up the work of guest evaluating seven web essays published by my Trinity students, based on our evaluation criteria, during a five-day period near the end of the semester. Furthermore, two of the co-organizers agreed to review all of the essays and guest evaluator comments, and to privately send me their numerical scores, which I averaged together as the assignment grade, to emphasize the importance of writing for real audiences beyond the instructor. Given that our two campuses are so close geographically, yet our students seem to rarely interact outside of athletic competitions, I was intrigued but nervous about this experiment, as the two groups never met face-to-face or even via videoconference. Overall, a vast majority of the guest student commenters made substantive remarks on my students' writing, and while not as in-depth as the two recent alumni commentators the prior year, the level of public engagement by arranged, yet unpaid readers made the exercise worthwhile.[15]

In sum, my approach to resolving the pedagogical dilemma between public writing and student privacy leaves some questions unanswered. Where is the line that divides instructor comments on students' public posts versus the private act of evaluating them? Should student writing be evaluated by other students? What would happen if a student agreed to post an essay, but objected to sharing it under the Creative Commons site license? These issues and others are not fully resolved. Nevertheless, while I do not argue that web writing is appropriate for every class, these initial results should challenge liberal arts faculty to consider news ways of engaging our student writers with the public, while protecting their privacy.

*About the author: Jack Dougherty is an associate professor of educational studies at Trinity College in Hartford, Connecticut, who tweets about web writing at @DoughertyJack.*

**How to cite:**

Jack Dougherty, "Public Writing and Student Privacy," in *Web Writing: Why and How for Liberal Arts Teaching and Learning*, ed. Jack Dougherty and Tennyson O'Donnell (University of Michigan Press/Trinity College ePress edition, 2014), http://epress.trincoll.edu/webwriting/chapter/dougherty-public.

*See an earlier version of this essay with open peer review comments.[16]*

# Notes

1. "Mission," Trinity College, Hartford CT, http://www.trincoll.edu/AboutTrinity/mission/Pages/default.aspx.

2. Photo of hallway paper by author, uploaded to http://epress.trincoll.edu/webwriting/?attachment_id=925.

3. Family Education Rights and Privacy Act, U.S. Department of Education, http://www.ed.gov/policy/gen/guid/fpco/ferpa/index.html.

4. Audrey Watters, "Georgia Tech Invokes FERPA, Cripples School's Wikis," *Hack Education*, November 15, 2011, http://www.hackeducation.com/2011/11/15/georgia-tech-invokes-ferpa-cripples-schools-wikis; Amy Cavender, "Protecting Student Privacy Without Going FERPANUTS" The Chronicle of Higher Education, *ProfHacker*, November 30, 2011, http://chronicle.com/blogs/profhacker/protecting-student-privacy-without-going-ferpanuts/37437.

5. Interestingly, the US Supreme Court ruled in 2002 that "peer grading" of student work by classmates does not violate the law, and federal regulations now clarify that peer-graded work is not considered an official "educational record" under FERPA until it has been collected and recorded by the instructor. See Owasso Independent School Dist. No. I—011v. Falvo, 534 U.S. 426 (U.S. Supreme Court 2002), http://www.law.cornell.edu/supct/html/00-1073.ZO.html;U.S. Department of Education, "Family Education Rights & Privacy Act (FERPA) Regulations," January 2012, p. 6, http://www2.ed.gov/policy/gen/reg/ferpa/index.html.

6. Kevin Smith, "Guidelines for Public, Student Class Blogs: Ethics, Legalities, FERPA and More," *HASTAC*, November 30, 2012, http://www.hastac.org/blogs/superadmin/2012/11/30/guidelines-public-student-class-blogs-ethics-legalities-ferpa-and-more; Kim Mann, "Online Assignments and Student Privacy," *Academic Technology at the College of William and Mary*, June 20, 2013, http://at.blogs.wm.edu/online-assignments-and-student-privacy/; Andrew G. McGinney, "A Guide to FERPA Guides," *CUNY Graduate Center Digital Fellows*, March 8, 2013, http://digitalfellows.commons.gc.cuny.edu/2013/03/08/a-guide-to-ferpa-guides/.

7. "Public Writing and Student Privacy" policy statement, Educ 300: Education Reform: Past and Present, Spring 2014, Trinity College, http://commons.trincoll.edu/edreform/resources/student-privacy/. In some seminars, I also point students to additional resources such as "Copyright Overview," Copyright and Fair Use, Stanford University Libraries, http://fairuse.stanford.edu/; and "About the Licenses," Creative Commons, http://creativecommons.org.

8. Student final web essays in *Educ 308: Cities Suburbs and Schools*, http://commons.trincoll.edu/cssp/; *Educ 300: Education Reform, Past & Present*, http://commons.trincoll.edu/edreform, both at Trinity College, CT.

9. See a brief history of the mid-1990s rise of Web 2.0 commenting in Michael Erard, "No Comments," *The New York Times*, September 20, 2013, sec. Magazine, http://www.nytimes.com/2013/09/22/magazine/no-comments.html.

10. Mark Sample, "A Better Blogging Assignment," The Chronicle of Higher Education, *ProfHacker*, July 3, 2012, http://chronicle.com/blogs/profhacker/a-better-blogging-assignment/41127.

11. Shanese Caton, "The Quest to Racially Integrate: African Americans and Higher Education," *Educ 300: Education Reform, Past & Present*, May 3, 2012, http://commons.trincoll.edu/edreform/2012/05/the-quest-to-racially-integrate-african-americans-and-higher-education/, cited in "Online Articles That May Be of Interest to JBHE Readers," *The Journal of Blacks in Higher Education*, May 9, 2012, http://www.jbhe.com/2012/05/online-articles-that-may-be-of-interest-to-jbhe-readers-15/.

12. Google Analytics data was collected on the Ed 300 class WordPress site, http://commons.trincoll.edu/edreform, using the Google Analyticator plugin, http://wordpress.org/plugins/google-analyticator/.

13. Screenshot of typical guest evaluator comment, uploaded to http://epress.trincoll.edu/webwriting/?attachment_id=82,from Educ 308 Cities Suburbs & Schools seminar web essays, Fall 2011, http://commons.trincoll.edu/cssp/web-essays/.

14. Sociology 419: Education Policy in the United States, Wesleyan University, Fall 2012, http://soc419.wordpress.com/.

15. Screenshot of typical Wesleyan student guest evaluator comment, uploaded to http://epress.trincoll.edu/webwriting/?attachment_id=83, Ed 308 Cities Suburbs and Schools seminar web essays, Fall 2012, http://commons.trincoll.edu/cssp/web-essays/.

16. Dougherty, "Public Writing and Student Privacy," in *Web Writing* (Open peer review edition, Fall 2013), http://webwriting2013.trincoll.edu/engagement/dougherty-pub-priv-2013/.

# Consider the Audience

*Jen Rajchel*

> "Technology proposes itself as the architect of our intimacies."
> —Sherry Turkle[1]

At one level, web writing is about writing *on* the web: the flexibility as a multimodal piece, the ability to nimbly circulate, and the capacity to create a network of texts. At another level, the practice is about writing *for* the web and situating ourselves as readers and writers within its evolving architecture.

The advent of social media platforms necessitates that the web may in fact be many places such as a WordPress blog (an open-source content management site often used for website and blogs), Twitter (a social networking site that allows its users to correspond in 140 character snippets), or Snapchat (an app that sends photos which delete from the recipients' phones after designated time period).[2] One of the biggest challenges and opportunities in digital publication is reaching out across multiple audiences with varied interests and deciphering which platforms are best suited to one's content.

However, such complexities of context and audience are not new. I first thought about these issues as an undergraduate English major through reading and classes, especially through poetry. Whether a poem be lowered through a window accompanied by gingerbread or delivered to a flickering screen on a subway, the spirit of its invitation often remains the same: to begin a conversation.

My thoughts about web writing and its connection with the liberal arts are shaped by my experience as a recent undergraduate English major at Bryn Mawr College, during which time I created a digital, poetry thesis. After graduating in 2011, my conversations about digital publication and its various manifestations continued with faculty, staff, and students at Bryn

Mawr, Haverford, and Swarthmore Colleges through my work with the Tri-College Digital Humanities Initiative (Tri-Co DH). I hope that my experiences might continue these conversations as part of the exciting and critical pieces in this volume.[3]

Web writing is about more than writing for the web—including the flexibility of multimodal pieces, the ability to nimbly circulate, and the capacity to create a network of texts. Web writing is also inherently about seeding the development of more opportunities to circulate student work while still foregrounding the difficult navigation of the public/private that accompany them.

## A Multimodal Approach to Poetry

What originally attracted me to the English major — or rather who — was Emily Dickinson. I was intrigued by her emphasis on reading "The Way I Read a Letter's This," complete with instructions on how I too might partake in her ritual of how to ready a space for reading.[4] Her role as author was just as carefully crafted; she even designed "envelope-poems."[5] It was through investigating Dickinson's blurred boundaries of agency between the reader and author and her bold approach to form that I began to explore the possibilities of new media publication and its role in the evolving, hybrid relationships between authors and readers.[6]

My thesis capitalized on my interests in poetic form and representations of readers across media by exploring the early poems of Marianne Moore (another poet who performed an intricate balance of public and private through her poetry) from Bryn Mawr's Special Collections via a website publication. I used hyperlinks to approach new ways of reading Moore's poems: the use of web design to visualize the ways in which poems opened out beyond a linear structure.

For example, Moore's poem "To My Cup-bearer" packs in allusions to Classical myths, literary works, and even a Bryn Mawr student secret ceremony. In visualizing these allusions together the weight of the role of the cup-bearer could be felt. By physically overwhelming the screen with hyperlinked windows to each allusion, the reader is both enlightened by the knowledge described in the poem and also engulfed by the ambition of its scope.[7]

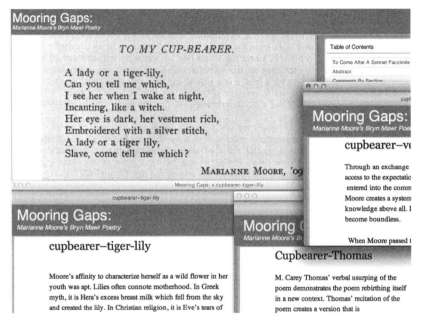

Rajchel, *"Mooring Gaps: Marianne Moore's Bryn Mawr Poetry."*

Before I was able to hack the hyperlink as a vehicle to various multimodal qualities, I had to learn more about the larger information ecosystem. But at the early stages of my web thesis, I didn't know what a server was or how it functioned, I wasn't clear on copyright, and I didn't know how to code.

Too often, the digital fluencies of incoming students are confused with mastery of platforms and software skills. Sophistication with media platforms should not be defined only by the ability to successfully complete a task on an interface (e.g. send a "private" message to another user, upload a video into a public channel, or complete forms on a profile page). Instead, we should define digital acumen by an overall awareness of the digital infrastructure. As an incoming freshman, considered a "millennial," my knowledge of digital tools was fragmented. I could hack Microsoft Word to work like a (very limited) version Photoshop, but I didn't read the terms of service or think about what happened to my data.

Constructing a digital senior thesis provided an opportunity for me to explore questions related to how information functions on the web, how to negotiate issues related to public versus private audiences, and a myriad of other questions related to media translation across platforms. When I began my work on a web-based thesis, the most beneficial experience was not jumping into the backend of WordPress (a skill I still use on a daily basis) but learning what kinds of questions I should ask when considering web writing of any sort.

I surveyed the platforms supported by Bryn Mawr College and talked with Information Technology staff about what it meant to be open-source. I narrowed the scope of the primary materials that I was using in Special Collections both as a way to ground my own work and to limit my materials to those in the public domain. Some of the letters that I originally intended to use were bound up in copyright, and while I learned the process for requesting permission, I knew being granted permission was unlikely to fit within my timetable.

This experience provided me with a set of guidelines that I use with every new media project. These guidelines allow me to critically approach platforms and assess the complexities of audience in ways that begin to build the kinds of interactions I hope for, and thus, position me to become an architect of my new media environment.

> 1. Is this medium adding a critical lens to the design of my
> argument?
> 2. Is this the audience I hope to be part of?
> 3. What are the terms of service and do I feel comfortable with
> the kind and amount of information I am sharing? (e.g. metadata
> and location services)

## Negotiating Publicness

In addition to having a better understanding of the infrastructure, the cycle of publication from an author's perspective also helped me to rethink my own writing practices. In my previous papers, I viewed citations and foot-notes as ways of tracing my thoughts or simply referencing evidence. How-ever, when writing for the web, I began to think of citations as a way of creating a path to discussion. Citations became central to my writing process because they contributed towards a broader dialogue among schol-ars and texts.

As Kathleen Fitzpatrick describes, web writing is a way of entering the are-na. Speaking at the Modern Language Association presidential forum in 2012, Fitzpatrick extended the boundaries of the blog so that it is defined not only as a "kind" of writing but as a location where both dynamic read-ing and writing occur:

> . . . the blog instead provides an arena in which scholars can work through ideas in an ongoing process of engagement with their peers. That spatial metaphor – the arena – is much to the point here: really grasping how something like a blog might serve scholarly communica-tion requires understanding that a blog is not a form, but a platform – not a shape through which are extruded certain fixed kinds of mater-ial, but a stage on which material of many different varieties – differ-ent lengths, different time signatures, different modes of mediation – might be performed.[8]

Fitzpatrick reminds us that through our writing we engage in performance and that when we choose a platform, we are also setting up a stage with multimodal capacities. When students write for the web, they should be prompted to become critical users who delineate the context, content, and circulation for each platform. Instead of merely advocating for one format or type of work, web writing assignments can provide room in a classroom setting to decide whether to converse on Twitter or Facebook, whether to write using Medium or WordPress, and how students might develop a rubric for platform adoption.

As an example of how the web can be used as a scholarly platform, I recently talked with a professor who was concerned about her privacy, copyrights, and intellectual property. She wanted a web presence but was thinking about deleting her Facebook account. However, when she considered her audience and the benefits of participating in conversations via Facebook, she recognized that some of the most exciting debates in her field are happening spontaneously on Facebook. While still critical of the trade-offs, she decided kept her Facebook account but committed to being thoughtful about which ideas she posted.

Transparency around scenarios like these are especially crucial for students who might not have begun to think about copyright or the long trail of their digital archive. Natalia Cecire, in her piece, "How Public Like a Blog: On Academic Blogging," illustrates the tensions of blogging. Cecile says academic blogging is filled with possibility and with potential risk for less established writers:

> Thinking in public is a difficult habit to get into, though, because public is the place where we're supposed to not screw up, and thinking on the fly inevitably involves screwing up. Blogging with any regularity in essence means committing oneself to making one's intellectual fallibility visible to the world and to the unforgiving memory of the Google cache.[9]

When students publish online, they assume the responsibilities of authorship. As Cecire notes, online authorship includes an online archival record that exists long after its publication. The consideration of such implications for visibility is crucial for students, especially those who might not have picked a career path.

One way we hope to raise awareness of such issues as part of the Tri-Co DH initiative is to ask our summer interns and researchers to report their work through blogging. Before publishing each blog, we ask to meet with students for a pre-publication discussion during which we draw out the possible stakeholders and readers: *Think about how someone from your internship might read this? How might that differ from your professor? Will you be sending this to family and friends? A potential employer? A scholar whose work you cite?* The goal of such questions is to reflect upon layered interests and stakeholders and to give students the opportunity to respond to such possibilities if they have not already.

Hema Surendranathan, a recent Tri-Co DII intern, points to the challenges of such performance in her blog, "How to be Cool or Thinking about Audience." Her post narrates her internship experience of being charged with sending emails to publicize the site's newly-published fiction. Knowing that there would be a deluge of emails that came before and after hers, she realized that she had to develop her pitch in the email subject line—and that to prompt a reader to read that it had to be "cool." Surendranathan further reflects in her blog post, "who could be interested?" and "how can I get them to listen?"[10]

Audience is perhaps the most difficult negotiation of web writing, especially as we manage the circulation through various social platforms and code-switch for several interested parties. Audience is also the most exciting.

When students were surveyed about why they chose to work in the digital humanities at Re:Humanities, a Tri-College undergraduate symposium on digital media, they unanimously responded that they want their work to circulate beyond the classroom. Stephanie Cawley, a recent Re:Humanities presenter, highlights the heightened sense of scholarly responsibility when writing online. As she explained in this short video about the symposium, "When you're producing something that's going to be online. . . you have a greater responsibility to engage more deeply, to understand everything you need to understand, because you have a greater responsibility to educate and reach out to a larger audience."[11] When students feel an increased level of investment in their projects and a heightened sense of responsibility to an actual audience, the work becomes less about grades and more about shaping their scholarship.

One way to increase opportunities for students to engage in public scholarship is to invite serious discussions in the classroom about social media platforms. Engineering opportunities for low-stakes media adoption that allows students to reflect thoughtfully and openly about their impact can invite a fruitful mingling between vernaculars of the scholarly and the social.

Take for example, Robinson Meyer, who Alex Madrigal profiles in his article, "How to Actually Get a Job on Twitter."[12] Madrigal emphasizes that it was not Meyer's "Klout score" which earned him the position of associate editor at *The Atlantic* as a freshly graduated Northwestern college student. Rather, it was his ability to synthesize information, read quickly and deeply, and also to engage in discussions with candor and humility.

These are the same skills that students learn in seminar style courses offered by liberal arts colleges: reading across disciplines, developing expertise, and delving into discussions. Students learn to challenge each other, and more importantly, themselves. But first, students have to be able to recognize that they are on stage and then they have to allow themselves to write for it.

I experienced this opportunity to write for a more public stage as a member of Katherine Rowe's "Global Shakespeares" course. We began the course by explicitly laying out a social media policy and our expectations for each other as a class.[13] We discussed the benefits of adding Twitter to the classroom, but also its limitations. After a robust discussion of what Twitter is and why we might use it, we decided to revisit the possibility of incorporating Twitter later in the semester.

Midway through the course, during two students' presentation on audience interaction, they asked their classmates to "paper-tweet" during a 20-second movie clip. After a quick introduction to the "rules of Twitter," notecards for tweets were passed out and the clip was played. Paper tweets were written and read aloud. What ensued was a variety of tweets: some the epitome of Shakespearean wit, others condensed, elegant meta-commentaries, and still others inside jokes that referenced class conversations.

Two main considerations arose from this experiment. The first concerned the length of audience participation. For the first time, everyone in class talked, and for the same length of time. We began to consider the economy of a medium that allowed for a variety of voices and how such a constraint could helpfully influence engagement. The flow of replying and attributing became conscious, and the act of thinking aloud stimulated the collaborative shaping of an idea. The second consideration emerged from the creative tenor of the tweets: why do we sometimes feel uncomfortable talking in the classroom in ways that engage wit and humor?

In the following class, the next pair of student presenters decided to run the paper-tweet experiment again. This time participants were asked to switch cards with a partner so that no one read their original post. The additional layer created authorial distance that mimicked the sometimes-removed self of online interaction. Our post paper-tweet reflections grappled with the questions of authorship and persona, topics that drew on theoretical texts we had read in class.

Following these paper tweets, we revised the class policy to allow tweeting in class for those who were interested. We confirmed the spaces and moments in which recorded interactions hindered rather than advanced our conversation and created cues for tweeting so that is was still possible to think through ideas that were unrecorded. The original concern of students who wanted to maintain the classroom as a place of thought experiment was upheld but others began to forge out into the Twitterstream with developed twitter voices. Ultimately, we were able to recognize the costs and benefits of Twitter as a platform in a low-stakes environment as well as within a thoughtful scholarly community.

## Looking Forward

There will never be a perfect schema for writing for the web. Interfaces are reconfigured regularly. Platforms wax and wane. From one day to the next, the conventions of how we interact online from reading and writing to connecting with friends, family, and employers rapidly shifts. Fortunately, liberal arts students who graduate with an understanding of historicized technological shifts and who are encouraged to recognize their experiences as part of a larger and longer framework of media change, are well-positioned to push the boundaries of their own scholarship and to become sophisticated readers and writers of the web.

*About the author: Jen Rajchel (@peasandpoetry) is a 2011 graduate of Bryn Mawr College. She now serves a dual role as the Assistant Director of Tri-Co DH and Digital Scholarship Curator at Haverford College.*

### How to cite:

Jen Rajchel, "Consider the Audience," in *Web Writing: Why and How for Liberal Arts Teaching and Learning*, ed. Jack Dougherty and Tennyson O'Donnell (University of Michigan Press/Trinity College ePress edition, 2014), http://epress.trincoll.edu/webwriting/chapter/rajchel.

*See an earlier version of this essay with open peer review comments.*[14]

# Notes

1. Sherry Turkle, *Alone Together: Why We Expect More from Technology and Less from Each Other* (New York: Basic Books, 2011), 1.

2. Danah Boyd wonderfully explains the draw to the ephemeral nature of Snapchat and how it differs from other social media like Twitter in her post "Why Snapchat is Valuable: It's All About Attention," *apophenia* (blog), March 21, 2014, http://www.zephoria.org/thoughts/archives/2014/03/21/snapchat-attention.html.

3. Tri-College Digital Humanities Initiative, http://tdh.brynmawr.edu.

4. Emily Dickinson and R. W. Franklin, *The Poems of Emily Dickinson* (Cambridge, Mass.: Belknap Press, 1999).

5. Emily Dickinson and Marta L. Werner, *Emily Dickinson: The Gorgeous Nothings* (New York: A Christine Burgin/ New Directions, 2013).

6. Many of my thoughts on this topic were influenced by Martha Nell Smith's *Rowing in Eden: Rereading Emily Dickinson* (Austin: University of Texas Press, 1992), accessible in Martha Nell Smith, Ellen Louise Hart, and Marta Werner, *Dickinson Electronic Archives*, 1995,http://archive.emilydickinson.org/archive_description_1997.html

7. Jen Rajchel, "Mooring Gaps: Marianne Moore's Bryn Mawr Poetry," (Senior Thesis, Department of English, Bryn Mawr College, 2010), http://mooreandpoetry.blogs.brynmawr.edu/2010/04/02/cupbearer/

8. Kathleen Fitzpatrick, "Networking the Field," MLA Presidential Forum address, *Planned Obsolescence (blog)*, January 10, 2012, http://www.plannedobsolescence.net/blog/networking-the-field.

9. Natalia Cecire, "How Public Like a Frog: On Academic Blogging," *Arcade (blog)*, April 20, 2011, http://arcade.stanford.edu/editors/how-public-frog.

10. Hema Surendranathan, "How to be Cool or Thinking about Audience," *Tri-Co Digital Humanities (blog)*, July 12, 2012, http://tdh.brynmawr.edu/2012/07/12/how-to-be-cool-or-thinking-about-audience.

11. Stephanie Cawley, "Re:Humanities '12," YouTube video, http://www.youtube.com/watch?v=59D2AAQHyYg. The Re:Humanities undergraduate digital media symposium began in 2010 and is sponsored by Bryn Mawr, Haverford, and Swarthmore Colleges, http://blogs.haverford.edu/rehumanities.

12. Alex Madrigal, "How to Actually Get a Job on Twitter," *The Atlantic*, July 31, 2013, http://www.theatlantic.com/technology/archive/2013/07/how-to-actually-get-a-job-on-twitter/278246.

13. Katherine Rowe, "Global Shakespeares" class, Bryn Mawr College, Bryn Mawr, PA, Fall 2012.

14. Rajchel, "Consider the Audience," in *Web Writing* (Open peer review edition, Fall 2013), http://webwriting2013.trincoll.edu/engagement/rajchel-2013/.

# Creating the Reader-Viewer

*Engaging Students with Scholarly Web Texts*

*Anita M. DeRouen*

It is late April, 2012. I am sitting in a small seminar room in our college library, eager to see the results of my Rhetoric of New Media class's engagements with their final project: a digital rendering of their final scholarly essays in the course. I am pleased with their results, chalking any misgivings I may have about their choices up to my own inadequacies as a teacher and the challenges of designing a new technology-focused course on a campus that often feels it would be more at home with the mimeograph and a fleet of IBM Selectrics.

The projects are varied: one student, interested in issues related to privacy and intimacy, renders her paper in the form of a Facebook wall. A business student turns his essay into the static Constant Contact newsletter; another student creates a dynamic video presentation of her data. Every project plays with existing forms, shaving and transforming the content to take advantage of the affordances of the new medium, but each proceeding in the same linear fashion as the original essay.

The project that excited—and challenged—me the most belonged to Mo Wilson. Mo, then a sophomore, used Tumblr to render his analysis of Kreyshawn's then-ascendance up the ladder of musical success through the lens of Richard Lanham's *Economics of Attention*.[1] The page was difficult to follow—like all Tumblr pages, it is a loose collection of curated images, words, and sounds. While there is something akin to linearity present, the reader who comes upon the page will have to cobble together an idea of the central arguments of Mo's project, the expected linkages and linguistic turns signaling the significance of one idea or the shift to another unseen in the gutter between the various posts that make up the rendering.[2]

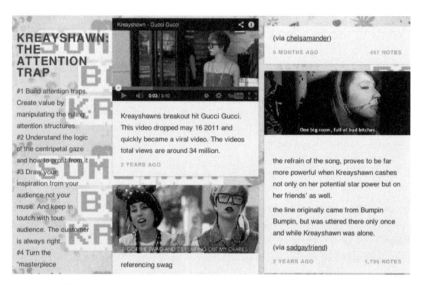

*Mo Wilson, "Kreayshawn: The Attention Trap."*

What I found most exciting about Mo's project was the difficulty it presented to the reader. Where does one begin? At the top? At the bottom? How does one "read" the videos and the GIFs and to what should the reader attach significance? As I turned over the challenges posed by the text, I realized that it could be read "as is." Perhaps the savvy reader could use a framework like Lanham's rules for creating an attention trap to muse on why a cluster of words and moving images helps us to understand Kreayshawn's success. Not all readers are savvy, though, and it's easy to imagine another reader—a fan, perhaps—coming across the site and not quite knowing what to make of it.

Mo's project intrigued me because it challenged my classroom practice. By selecting the Tumblr platform, Mo had chosen a site designed to "trap" attention; Tumblr pages provide endless opportunities to scroll deeper and deeper into a blogger's patterns of curation, and accessing site-wide content through the tag search features is a surefire way to kill many an idle hour. He also chose a site that relies upon reader association for making ideas—if any are intended by the site author—cohere. As I reflected on the term, I realized that as a teacher—teaching, of all things, a course focused on the rhetorical challenges and opportunities presented by this new set of media tools and platforms—I had focused on writing in a way that failed to give equal weight to the demands placed upon the reader. Planning the webtext—like any text—requires that the author do so with an eye toward communicating effectively, even when experimenting with new forms. Because I hadn't taught my students how to read the texts they were encountering, I hadn't made them as aware as I could have of how to read, let alone craft, a scholarly webtext that would best share the quality of their thinking. Here I share what we know about the challenges of reading webtexts to better understand the shifting literacy environment we currently occupy. By so doing, I hope to encourage faculty to pay closer attention to the connection between effective reading and effective writing and to help students become adept readers and creators of useful attention traps.

*** 

We tend to think of the reading portion of the literacy enterprise as the "already gotten," while writing is the "always to be gained." For example, Donald Leu et al note that, as written, the Common Core Standards (CCS) for writing are more progressive and aware of the need for sustained and explicit attention to developing student literacy in the areas of technology.[3] They go on to state that this is not the case for the standards pertaining to reading, a continuation of the under-recognized deficiency in our cultural model for literacy education. In my writing program administration (WPA) work, I have found myself constantly addressing the issue of student reading struggles with writing teachers who come to understand the relationship between the two components while trying to teach that even more elusive third element—critical thinking.

Add to that complexity the new challenges posed by multimodal platforms and approaches to writing—challenges we in the academy have largely been able to dodge so far—and the need for more explicit attention to the reading side of literacy development seems more urgent. We have been talking about hypertext and multimodal composition for quite some time; we should pause for a moment to consider the effects of hypertext and multimodality on reading.

In 1990, John Slatin wrote of hypertext's potential value and weakness:

> Perhaps the greatest value of hypertext is its ability to link enormous
> quantities of material that, in a conventional text environment, would
> be kept separate, perhaps even in different buildings, so that things
> which someone perceives as being related do in fact become related. [4]

The relationships between ideas—the connectives, transitions, qualifica-
tions, and other frameworks we use to "glue" ideas together—can easily go
missing (or be multitudinous) in a hypertext, and so, as readers, we must be
more and more aware of the various ways in which we are being led to put
them together.

As readers, we always make our own roadmaps. Some are just harder to
draw than others. We need to help students become what Frank Serafini
calls a "reader-viewer," a term that "expands the concept of reading to
include multimodal texts, graphic design elements, and visual images".[5] We
also need to be more aware of the challenges placed upon our comprehension skills—adopting the role of reader-viewer means, as Mary McNabb
notes, "continually [facing] decisions about which hyperlink to click on next
and why" and "[being] forced to make associations among lexias and create
[your] own narratives as [you] go".[6] These statements about reading and the
web may seem obvious, but the lack of attention to the changing realities of
what Donald Leu and Elena Forzani term the New Literacy in the Common
Core Standards for reading should alert us to an imbalance in the way that
we culturally consider and teach the enterprise of literacy.[7] It is not enough
to draw student attention to these new modes of communication as spaces
for creation of content; we need to attend to their development as reader-
viewers of the content as well.

An area of particular concern is the academic or scholarly webtext. I draw
attention to this genre because it is a place where I believe we can do more
work to advance the study of literacy in the multimodal environment. The
bulk of the work being done in multimodal literacy is conducted in the
K-12 setting and is conducted with texts that are fairly informative. Scholarly texts provide a particular set of challenges for undergraduate readers. Karen Manarin details her experiences teaching and researching the
strategies that undergraduate students use in reading texts.[8] She notes a
disconnect between student perceptions of themselves as readers and faculty perceptions of the students' ability to read in the manner that they

are expected to. Manarin asked students in two first year critical writing and reading courses to maintain a log of the strategies they used in the non-fiction reading they were doing for the course.[9] What she found was that students seemed to lean overwhelmingly to personal connection and imagery as the primary comprehension strategies, even when the material in the course was specifically selected for the difficulty of utilizing these approaches. When faced with challenges requiring new strategies, students tend to go with what they know even when they have been equipped with new things to try. We need to challenge our students' views of reading.

Reading comprehension is complicated and, like writing, should be considered in terms of both process and product. In a review essay, Paul van den Broek and Christine Espin present an Integrated Model of Reading Comprehension (IMREC) in an attempt to bring together what is known about comprehension to better instruct and assess students of reading.[10] The desired *product* of comprehension is a coherent mental representation of the text, "that is, the text elements (events, facts, and so on) are interconnected through semantic relations and form an integrated whole".[11] Readers build these representations through a variety of activities including inference and connection to background knowledge; this is what Walter Kintsch (1998) terms the "reader's situation model of the text" as opposed to the textbase itself and the surface model or "visual-perceptual representation of the text."[12] Like the paper submitted for external review, the product of reading comprehension is a more clearly definable goal. The comprehension *process* is more complicated. Van den Broek and Espin offer three overall observations about the process of "coherence-building": that readers constantly seek equilibrium between their understanding of the complete text and their "limited attentional or working memory resources"; that readers employ automatic and strategic processes; and that readers will use multiple strategies in a variety of combinations to understand any one text.[13]

The second of these observations—that "strategic processes must be learned," is of most value to this discussion; as van den Broek and Espin note in their discussion of automatic processes, the act of repeatedly engaging in explicitly taught strategies results in the creation of new automatic processes. The more practice we have reading a particular genre of text, the more adept we become at building coherent situation models of them.

Attention to process—and drawing our students' attention to the processes of developing their reading skills—should result in readers who better understand the demands of a world where literacy is now a deictic skill and who are well equipped to grow and shift with it.

Returning to Serafini, we get another insight into the changes demanded of readers in this new environment. Reading is a social activity, with readers adopting particular roles in relation to the author and the text. As texts shift from singular to multimodal forms they increase in processing complexity, shifting readers from four traditionally understood social practices (or "resources") in the first column of the table below to a new set of roles conceived by Serafini.[14]

### Traditional and Multimodal Reading Roles or Resources

| Reader as: | Reader-viewer as: |
| --- | --- |
| code breaker | navigator |
| text-participant | interpreter |
| text user | designer |
| text analyst | interrogator |

These reconceived roles require a great deal more from readers of webtexts, readers for whom the entire enterprise of reading—particularly in a new knowledge area—is already fraught with obstacles to their coherence-building activity.

Literacy studies focused on the acquisition of content knowledge in print and hypertext reading have repeatedly shown that the largest factor affecting a reader's understanding and coherence-building is the amount of prior knowledge of the subject matter readers bring to bear.[15] In particular, novice readers (those with the least amount of prior knowledge in a particular content area) need more in the way of explicit, coherent scaffolding to help offset the cognitive load of coherence-building in a new area. To put it another way: the more explicit the roadmap for the reader, the easier it is for the reader to make it to the writer's destination.

Our traditional mode of presenting scholarly work—in the case of this essay, the peer-reviewed journal article—has provided a challenging, but stable, means for students to engage with scholarly work as they explore disciplinary content. The IMRAD structure, for example, governs many texts in the sciences (Introduction, Methodology, Results, Analysis, Discussion), providing an excellent scaffold for novice and more advanced readers alike. For the novice reader, the sections signal rhetorical shifts in the writing, freeing readers to focus on the content of each section without having to ascertain the relationship of the section to the coherence of the piece. For the advanced reader, sections act as shortcuts to the information they seek.[16]

Moving the academic text from the static space of the journal or the print book to the dynamic web changes the game. As I shared my thinking and work on this project with colleagues, I often got blank stares when I stated that we needed to be more explicit in our teaching so as to prepare students to deal with scholarly webtexts. No doubt, my colleagues were visualizing the electronic version of a traditional print journal article, and wondering why on earth I thought students needed special training to read those (I do, a point I'll return to later). When I showed them what I meant, taking them to see something like Johndan Johnson Eilola's "Polymorphous Perversity and Texts" essay on the KAIROS website, they got the picture. These are not your advisor's journal articles, but they are indexed in the database right alongside them. When we as teachers and scholars embrace the possibilities inherent in what Johndan Johnson-Eilola calls the "polymorphous perversity" of text in this new environment, what does that mean for our students?[17] It means they've arrived in a new space that is, in essence, the old space with shifting architecture, the scholarly equivalent, perhaps, of the shifting staircases in Hogwarts.

We have to teach them attentiveness not only to text as object to be looked "through" but also as object to be looked "at." And so we return to Mo, my student with the webtext, and Richard Lanham's *Economics of Attention*, wherein we learn the difference between looking "at" and looking "through" and are challenged to "be able to relate judgments of [style] to judgments of [substance], to put style and substance into relationships that are as complex as human reality".[18] When reading a scholarly webtext, the style of the thing—the visual landscape, or, to bring our conversation back to Kintsch's model, the surface model of the textbase—can be of as much importance in developing the reader's situational model of the text as the textbase itself. Whereas we can more readily see the textbase and the surface model of the text as nearly indistinguishable in the traditional model of scholarly publishing, the webtext presents a less-stable and less readily discerned textbase.

Take Johnson-Eilola's "Polymorphous Perversity and Texts" for example. While the opening image is followed by several paragraphs of linearly-presented introductory text, the textbase is really found in the (reader's) sum of its parts—the path that the reader takes through the thirty lexias linked through the boxes in the graphic at the top of the page. Clicking the hyperlinks in the introductory text will take the reader to certain of the thirty lexias—or not, with several of the links actually pulling the reader off-site, away from Johnson-Eilola's text entirely, perhaps never to return. This is, perhaps, an intentional pushing of the reader into the sort of perversity that Johnson-Eilola explores in the webtext, but for the novice reader guided to this text via their university library's electronic search (indexed in ERIC under subject headings like "Computer Uses in Education," "Written Language," and "Writing (Composition)") the potential value of the text to their research and education may be utterly lost in the very perversity the author seeks to explore.

I don't mean to criticize Johnson-Eilola—or any of KAIROS's contributors or, for that matter, any scholar seeking to explore all that the web has to offer for communicative expression. What I hope, instead, is that I've enkindled in you, dear reader, a bit of a sense of the urgency and magnitude of the literacy problem our students are facing and will continue to face as our tools for communication allow for the building of more sophisticated and multi-faceted representations of our scholarly understandings of the world. Even if I never teach a student to craft their own multimodal webtext, I feel obligated to equip them with a more explicit understanding of themselves as always-developing readers and a more thorough grounding in strategies for reading across modalities of textual presentation.

The good news is that we already have the tools to do this. Jacqueline Urakami and Josef F. Krems, for example, found that providing novice readers with advanced organizers for texts where causal relationships may be missing (texts like Mo's Kreayshawn Tumblr, for example) created enough scaffolding to help them build more coherent representations of hypertexts.[19] Webtext authors frequently build such scaffolding into their texts, as Mo did, but readers may not always know to be on the lookout for them.[20]

Another possible tool is the reading log, which Manarin found useful for monitoring the strategies her students were using as they worked through the increasingly complex reading assignments in her first year course; it's easy to imagine the reading log maintained through any number of electronic spaces where students would be able to include their marked-up screenshots of particularly challenging lexias.[21]

Perhaps some of the strongest tools in the toolbox, though, are ones not necessarily meant for undergraduate eyes. Allison Warner's webtext, "Constructing a Tool for Assessing Scholarly Webtexts," presents a set of assessment criteria for web scholarship. The criteria incorporate expectations for print scholarship with regard to issues connected to coherence (like "content," "arrangement," and "documentation") while extending those criteria to document design concerns (like "form/content relationship," "link strategy," and "multimedia incorporation").[22] Cheryl Ball explores the pedagogical challenges of teaching and assessing the scholarly webtext and offers, if not a reusable scaffold for such assessment, a compelling discussion of what's at stake when we bring student writers into contact with these modes of production.[23] By sharing criteria of this type, we can draw student attention to the correspondences and differences between various modes of presenting scholarly work, thereby helping them to see both print and multimodal offerings as part of the larger enterprise of scholarly texts.

I've only scratched the surface of what we can do as instructors to encourage our students to develop their reading skills to better engage all types of scholarly materials they may encounter. We do not know what tomorrow will bring or what tomorrow's writers will create. What we can do to equip our students to meet the challenge, though, is to "talk about reading as a series of choices students can control."[24]

*About the author: Anita M. DeRouen is Assistant Professor of English and Director of Writing and Teaching at Millsaps College in Jackson, MS. She extends special thanks to Mo Wilson for the use of his project in this essay (and for just being an all-around delight to teach!). Anita tweets intermittently, occasionally curates, and sometimes even blogs.*

## How to cite:

Anita M. DeRouen, "Creating the Reader-Viewer: Engaging Students with Scholarly Web Texts," in *Web Writing: Why and How for Liberal Arts Teaching and Learning*, ed. Jack Dougherty and Tennyson O'Donnell (University of Michigan Press/Trinity College ePress edition, 2014), http://epress.trincoll.edu/webwriting/chapter/derouen.

*See an earlier version of this essay with open peer review comments.*[25]

# Notes

1. Richard Lanham, *The Economics of Attention: Style and Substance in the Age of Information.* (Chicago: University of Chicago Press, 2007).

2. Mo Wilson, "Kreayshawn: The Attention Trap," April 2012, http://kreayshawntheattentiontrap.tumblr.com. Note: The list of Andy Warhol's rules for creating an attention trap in the left sidebar of the image/page are taken from Richard Lanham's essay, "Economists of Attention," in *The Economics of Attention* on pages 53-54.

3. Donald J. Leu, J. Gregory McVerry, W. Ian O'Bryne, Carita Kilii, Lisa Zawilinski, Heidi Everett-Cacopardo, Clint Kennedy and Elana Forzani, "The New Literacies of Online Reading Comprehension: Expanding the Literacy and Learning Curriculum," *Journal of Adolescent and Adult Literacy* 55, no. 1 (2011): 9.

4. John M. Slatin, "Reading Hypertext: Order and Coherence in a New Medium," *College English* 52, no. 8 (1990): 881-82.

5. Frank Serafini, "Reading Multimodal Texts in the 21st Century," *Research in the Schools* 19 no. 1 (2012): 27.

6. Mary McNabb, "Navigating the Maze of Hypertext," *Educational Leadership* 63, no. 4 (2005): 76.

7. Donald J. Leu and Elena Forzani, "New Literacies in a Web 2.0, 3.0, 4.0, …∞ World," *Research in the Schools* 19, no. 1 (2012): 78.

8. Karen Manarin, "Reading Value: Student Choice in Reading Strategies," *Pedagogy: Critical Approaches to Teaching Literature, Language, Composition, and Culture* 12, no. 2 (2012): 281-97.

9. Reading strategies vary, but at the most basic level we might consider whether or not the student approaches all texts in the same manner--reading, for example, from start to finish as opposed to conducting a preview of the reading to determine where to place his or her focus or to understand what components comprise the text and how they relate.

10. Paul van den Broek and Christine A. Espin, "Connecting Cognitive Theory and Assessment: Measuring Individual Differences in Reading Comprehension," *School Psychology Review* 41, no. 3 (2012): 315-325.

11. Ibid., 316.

12. Walter Kintsch, *Comprehension: A Paradigm for Cognition* (New York: Cambridge University Press, 1998), quoted in van den Broek and Espin, 316.

13. van den Broek and Espin, 316-17.

14. Serafini, 27.

15. Franck Amadieu, Andre Tricot, and Claudette Marine, "Interaction Between Prior Knowledge and Concept-Map Structure on Hypertext Comprehension, Coherence of Reading Orders and Disorientation," *Interacting with Computers* 22, no. 2 (2010): 88-97; Dennis S. Davis and Carin Neitzel, "Collaborative Sense-Making in Print and Digital Text Environments," *Reading and Writing* 25 (2012): 831-856.; Mary McNabb, "Navigating the Maze of Hypertext," *Educational Leadership* 63, no. 4 (2005): 76.; Danielle S. McNamara and Amy M. Shapiro, "Multimedia and Hypermedia Solutions for Promoting Metacognitive Engagement, Coherence, and Learning," *Journal of Educational Computing Research* 33, no. 1 (2005): 1-29.; Thiemo Muller-Kalthoff and Jens Moller, "Browsing While Reading: Effects of Instructional Design and Learners' Prior Knowledge," *ALT-J, Research in Learning Technology* 14, no. 4 (2006): 183-98.; Andrew B. Pactman, "Developing Critical Thinking for the Internet," *Research & Teaching in Developmental Education* 29, no. 1 (2012): 39-47.; Ladislao Salmeron and Victoria Garcia, "Children's Reading of Printed Text and Hypertext with Navigation Overviews: The Role of Comprehension, Sustained Attention, and Visuo-Spatial Abilities," *Journal of Educational Computing Research* 47, no. 1 (2012): 33-50.; Pradyumn Srivastava, Shelley Gray, Marilyn Nippold and Phyllis Schneider, "Computer-Based and Paper-Based Reading Comprehension in Adolescents with Typical Language Development and Langauge-Learning Disabilities," *Language, Speech & Hearing Services in Schools* 43, no. 4 (2012): 424-437.; Min-chen Tseng, "Comparing EFL Learners' Reading Comprehension Between Hypertext and Printed Text," *CALL-EJ Online* 9, no. 2 (2008), http://callej.org/journal/9-2/tseng.html.; Jacqueline Waniek, "How Information Organisation Affects Users' Representation of Hypertext Structure and Context," *Behaviour & Information Technology* 31, no. 2 (2012): 143-54. (2012); and Jacqueline Waniek, Angela Brunstein, Anja Naumann, and Josef F. Krems, "Interaction Between Text Structure Representation and Situation Model in Hypertext Reading," *Swiss Journal of Psychology* 62, no. 2 (2003): 103-111.

16. While we should strive to make students aware of their role as rhetorical designers, it can be difficult to reinforce and extend that idea when their academic engagements across the curriculum tend to privilege these long-standing forms. Webtexts of the sort referenced in this

article have great potential to disrupt our notions of scholarly writing, but we must manage student experience of that disruption alongside the mainstream expectation.

17. Image of traditional print journal article, 1978, uploaded by author to http://epress.trincoll.edu/webwriting/?attachment_id=32; Johndan Johnson-Eilola, "Polymorphous Perversity and Texts," *Kairos: A Journal of Rhetoric, Technology, and Pedagogy* 16, no. 3 (2012), http://kairos.technorhetoric.net/16.3/topoi/johnson-eilola/index.html.

18. Richard Lanham, *The Economics of Attention: Style and Substance in the Age of Information* (Chicago: University of Chicago Press, 2006), 180.

19. Jacqueline Urakami and Josef F. Krems, "How Hypertext Reading Sequences Affect Understanding of Causal and Temporal Relations in Story Comprehension," *Instructional Science* 40 (2012): 277-295.

20. Author's image of scaffolding in Mo Wilson's "Kreayshawn," uploaded to http://epress.trincoll.edu/webwriting/?attachment_id=999.

21. Author's sample of a marked-up screenshot of Johnson-Eilola's lexia, uploaded to http://epress.trincoll.edu/webwriting/?attachment_id=998.

22. Allison Warner, "Assessment Tool for Scholarly Webtexts." *Kairos: A Journal of Rhetoric, Technology, and Pedagogy* 12, no. 1 (2007), http://kairos.technorhetoric.net/12.1/topoi/warner/tool/webtext-assessment-tool.pdf.

23. Ball, Cheryl, "Assessing Scholarly Multimedia: A Rhetorical Genre Studies Approach." *Technical Communication Quarterly* 21(2012): 61-77.

24. Manarin, 293.

25. DeRouen, "Engaging Students with Scholarly Web Texts," in *Web Writing* (Open peer review edition, Fall 2013), http://webwriting2013.trincoll.edu/engagement/derouen-2013/.

# Pulling Back the Curtain

*Writing History Through Video Games*

*Shawn Graham*

Let us dispense with the idea that there are such things as "digital natives".[1] The phrase has outlived whatever usefulness it may have had due to magic.

Arthur C. Clarke said, "any sufficiently advanced technology is indistinguishable from magic".[2] Unless you can build and program an iPad from scratch, it is magic. Unless you can build the algorithms that populate your browser with content, the web and associated technologies are again: magic. The Wizard of Oz, on the other hand, said, "Pay no attention to that man behind the curtain!" Maybe it's like the magic that the Wizard of Oz practices. Let's pull back the curtain. In this essay, I recount a pedagogical experience with 60 undergraduate history majors at Carleton University where students learned to write for the web and learned how the web is written, including how algorithms (sets of rules) create the content and the experiences that we have online.

I am not talking about writing essays. I am talking about making video games. Or more accurately, about learning to write history-through-algorithms.

The students' tasks explicitly included writing one's own algorithms to generate particular kinds of emergent engagement with historical materials. Think about a small child who is playing with a Lego playset, and the stories the child tells as she plays: that's emergent engagement.[3]

This kind of writing is alien to how we normally teach our students to write for it explicitly demands that the "writer" think about how the "reader" will make the story in the process of "reading." In 2005, William Urrichio pointed out the ways that video games represented history. He was not overly concerned with the graphical representation of the past (period-correct clothing and architecture) but rather with the ways that the rule-sets of the games allowed for different understandings of history itself to be represented. He suggested that historians should engage with video games, and the point of intersection was historiography. The rule-sets of games directly correspond with the historiographic traditions, the rule-sets of historical practice, within which historians write.[4]

In 2007, Ian Bogost coined the phrase, "procedural rhetoric" to express much the same thought.[5] The idea that the processes of computation embodies a kind of rhetoric and representation of how the world works is also a kind of cosmology. One can learn a lot about how game designers view the world by closely reading their code.[6] In the spring of 2013 I set out to explore these ideas with a seminar called HIST 3812 Video Games and Simulations for Historians.[7]

Let us agree that the rules of games represent something of how the game-makers/players view the world's workings. I put it to the students that what we were engaged upon, in learning to write history-through-algorithms, was akin to a kind of oracle or riddle building, a way of describing the world that the player – the reader – needs to explore. In this way, the reader may construct or build their own understandings not by reading and intellectually understanding arguments, but through experience.[8] Because we are engaged with the human past, it is also a kind of necromancy in that we might summon the spirits of the past forward, recreated and re-substantiated in digital form. These spirits of the past represent our own best ideas about the past, not the past directly, which of course we can never know. We project onto historical actors our best understandings. So too with these digitally-substantiated simulacra: the meanings of the past emerge from our playing with these digital spectres. We are more familiar with these when we encounter them pinned to the pages of a book or essay; but in silico they write themselves through interaction with each other and with the player.[9]

There was a bit of attrition during these first few weeks of the class.

There are a couple of reasons for this. Angela Cox identifies one of these when she writes about her own experiences treating games as texts to be analyzed in a composition class. On Cox's reading of her experience, one point of resistance is our colonization of what students perceive as a non-academic space: academics don't play games. It may be a surprise that this first issue should emerge in a classroom where "video games" was in the title, but:

> Postcolonialism may in fact provide the best explanation for some of the most frustrating student behavior I have witnessed in these classes, because if we see students as the marginalized group and the established academics as the center then student resistance to classroom activity and homework becomes a colonial struggle at the margins [...]. [...] videogames are outside the center's power and must be defended from further colonization. That is, [students] are resisting cultural appropriation.[10]

Bill Caraher has reflected on similar themes of student resistance to what and how we teach. He situates one location of resistance in student perceptions of the "trivial," that the learning is not "serious" enough.[11] This accords well with my own experience in another class (where we wrote for Wikipedia), where resistance emerged amongst my most historically-minded of students: what we were doing neither looked nor felt like what History was supposed to be about.[12] Kapell and Elliot identify a similar theme in the academic study (by historians) of video games and other simulations of the past, within intersections of historiography with ludology and narratology. If the process of history is composed of both selection (of facts) and assembly (of a convincing and sound narrative), then the kind of assembly that a video game allows is both good history and good pedagogy because the player actively constructs (reads) "history as a process" rather than grand narrative. The objection then, such as it is, is that video games allow the "non-professional to do her or his own 'assembly' of the past."[13] Historians and students object, and resist, alike.

## Assignment

The students had one major project to complete over the duration of this course: to design what the ideal game would look/feel/behave like.[14] The assignment prompt was:

> In small groups (assigned by the instructor), you will produce a 40-50

page game design document for an ideal history game (or meta game; a game about games) that distills what you have learned about telling history through interactive media. This document will also demonstrate in passing what you have learned as a result of this course. You will need to reference the appropriate games, history learning, games and history, design, psychology, cognitive science or other literatures to explain and show how your game/simulation would achieve its desired ends. For the purposes of this course you do not need to produce the actual game. Although, you may wish to create a playable mock-up or 'beta' of what the game might look like. It should demonstrate key concepts or gameplay mechanics, and be about 10 minutes worth of play. If you create a mockup along those lines, your written document can be correspondingly shorter.

Such a big project holds much potential for running off the rails. Numerous checkpoints were established throughout the term to keep the project on track (our term ran for twelve weeks).[15] The idea was that the students could then re-use these checkpoint materials in their final project design document. The first checkpoint was "the pitch", where they would be constrained to a single short paragraph to describe the game and their intended historical outcome. The next checkpoint asked them, in a single page, to identify the "problem space" and the principle game mechanic for addressing this space.[16] The problem spaces of a game are the challenges that the player must overcome; hence, to think of "history" as replete with problem spaces forces the student to think of how actors in the past were "confined by resources and rules of interactions with others." [17] This is a crucial benefit of writing history with video games: it forces understanding that the past was contingent, and not pre-ordained. Moreover, video games foreground the act of (re-)creation of the past in the present, focusing on the contingent rather than the grand master narrative.[18]

These two checkpoints were due during the third and fifth weeks of the term. It was not until the seventh week (over halfway) that students produced a document that finally addressed the game structures and the relationship to the "skin" of the game (that is, the difference between what the game is ostensibly "about" and what it actually "does"). The final checkpoint (week nine) described in detail the player's experience at each stage of the game, what they experience, feel, learn and do. Two weeks later each group had to present their work in progress in lightening timed presentations;

each group had ten minutes and thirty slides (set to auto-timer) to cut to the heart of their process. Writing algorithmically is about writing spare, being lean, and using the most effective amount of code to get the job done. While these students did not write code per se, they wrote academic code in a way that mimicked computer code, in contrast to that normal tendency to fluff, to expand, to meet page requirements.

Again, in keeping with the desire to promote lean and effective coding, the students also had to blog weekly, reacting to not just the readings and the class discussion, but also to what was happening in their groups.[19] "Accuracy" is a recurring theme. In the earliest posts, "accuracy" is conceived in terms of visual fidelity to the props of history such as proper uniforms, correctly rendered architecture, period-appropriate speech (that is, with the "skin" of the game rather than its underlying rhetorics). Roughly halfway through the course there is a pivot. I had the students play "Depression Quest," an interactive fiction (text adventure). The website provides this description:

> Depression Quest is an interactive fiction game where you play as someone living with depression. You are given a series of everyday life events and have to attempt to manage your illness, relationships, job, and possible treatment. This game aims to show other sufferers of depression that they are not alone in their feelings, and to illustrate to people who may not understand the illness the depths of what it can do to people. [20]

Working through how interactive fiction can produce emotional impact wrought a change in the idea of "accuracy" held by the class. By removing the graphics, by confronting them with a story generated by their own choices that focused on the experience of an illness, the earlier lessons of the course began to click with the students. Subsequent discussions in class were richer and nuanced (and the video game fan-boy element receded somewhat). As one student put it during a class discussion, "the strength of video games like this is that they create empathy; they're more like what we're used to reading when we read history, but because our interests and choices make a difference, we care more about what's happening to the characters."

## Outcomes

At the end of the course, there were six group projects submitted. Did students learn to be magicians? Did they see how algorithmic writing could produce knowledge, understanding, and empathy for actors in the past? Did they make the connection between what they were doing and the way information on the web is presented to them? For the most part, yes. One project ultimately missed the point entirely, but another project, "The Medic's War", exceeded all my expectations. Its creators wrote,

> Our [world war I] game looks to broaden the emotional range of video games and the players. We strive to illuminate the tragedy of war by creating an empathy with a group that has not been explored yet – the field medic. Many games that show history are focused colonizing, on conquering, about playing at war [...] Our game doesn't rely on domination but rather attempting to show the true nature of war; no matter which side you're playing on, there will be casualties, soldiers who are following orders, that need aid.[21]

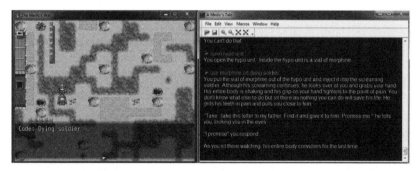

*A screenshot from the game prototype, "The Medic's War." It combined role-playing game elements (as in the left panel) with code words that unlocked interactive fiction texts (as in the right panel) to create empathy and an algorithmic experience of the pity of war.*

I had worried about these particular students. In one regard, they had bought in to what we were doing in this course *too much*. Every checkpoint document was vast and complicated. In their zeal to create *the* perfect game they had adopted a kind of kitchen-sink approach. The moment with *Depression Quest* was powerful for this particular group because it was also *alienating*. Angela Cox, in her class teaching games as texts, notes (when introducing older games and their conventions), "The notion that they had to type commands into the older games was utterly foreign to them; they struggled with it in much the same way that students struggle to read Middle English when we assign them Chaucer."[22] The zenith of interactive fiction occurred before these students were born; interacting with *Depression Quest* confronted the students with something that bewildered in its restraint. To drive home the idea of restraint, I had this particular group resubmit each of their checkpoint documents in the style of a tweet (140 characters only). In their resubmissions, they recognized that engaging with algorithmically generated (and read) texts could be used to create in the player the sense of confusion and despair that they identified in the diaries and letters of First World War soldiers and civilians. Thus, by writing not at the level of narrative but in the construction of possible outcomes, these students designed an emergent narrative to evoke the pity of war.

## Conclusion

Our last few sessions included a discussion about how the lessons that this course taught translated into other digital media, including Google Scholar, Wikipedia, and even the robots who are starting to write the sporting news.[23] Brittney, a self-described non-gamer, wrote on the course blog:

> If games [read, 'digital media'] allow the player to immerse themselves into the game in a natural manner, the choices and actions in the game become a sort of digital extension of the player's mind. This way, it is not just the never ending question of the accuracy of the facts and what is included or excluded [...] the player is left to their own devices and the more engaged they become, the more they take away from the game. THIS is what I consider good history. A person can engage with the storyline, the events of the past reconstructed in the game, and when they are able to immerse themselves into the game, they absorb the facts and repercussions of the past without having to be consciously aware of all of the minute details. Thus engaging them on a personal level with the past. Learning to play WHILE they are playing to learn.[24]

This is the value of encouraging students to use technology to learn how knowledge is produced, how history is constructed, and how values are passed on. In this digital era, we serve our students best by teaching them to pull back the curtain and look at what happens behind it.

*About the author: Shawn Graham is an assistant professor of digital humanities in the Department of History at Carleton University in Ottawa Canada. He blogs at electricarchaeology.ca, marshals some of his digital life at graeworks.net, and is all over twitter at @electricarchaeo. Currently, he's working on experiencing place-based history algorithmically via something he calls 'Historical Friction', with Stuart Eve.*

### How to cite:

Shawn Graham, "Pulling Back the Curtain: Writing History Through Video Games," in *Web Writing: Why and How for Liberal Arts Teaching and Learning*, ed. Jack Dougherty and Tennyson O'Donnell (University of Michigan Press/Trinity College ePress edition, 2014), http://epress.trincoll.edu/web-writing/chapter/graham.

*See an earlier version of this essay with open peer review comments.*[25]

# Notes

1. A phrase overused to excuse many ills. On the far more restricted original use of the term, see Marc Prensky, "Digital Natives, Digital Immigrants Part 1." On the Horizon 9, no. 5 (1 September 2001): 1–6, http://dx.doi.org/10.1108/10748120110424816.

2. Arthur C. Clarke, *Profiles of the Future.* (New York: Harper and Row, 1973), 21.

3. cf. Rob MacDougall, "The Action Figure Curriculum" robmacdougall.org http://www.robmacdougall.org/blog/2010/05/the-action-figure-curriculum/.

4. William Urrichio, "Simulation, History, and Computer Games" in *Handbook of Computer Game Studies* ed. Joost Raessens and Jeffrey Goldstein (Cambridge, MA: MIT Press, 2005), 336.

5. Ian Bogost, *Persuasive Games: The Expressive Power of Videogames* (Cambridge, MA: MIT Press, 2007).

6. As for instance, Mark Sample, "Rebooting Counterfactual History with JFK Reloaded," Play the Past May 19, 2011, http://www.playthepast.org/?p=1392.

7. Shawn Graham, "History3812 Winter 2013", Carleton University. Course blog at http://3812.graeworks.net.

8. Kevin Kee, Shawn Graham, Pat Dunae, John Lutz, Andrew Large, Michel Blondeau, and Mike Clare, "Towards a Theory of Good History through Gaming" *The Canadian Historical Review* 90.9 (2009): 303-326, http://muse.jhu.edu/journals/can/summary/v090/90.2.kee.html.

9. See for instance Shawn Graham "Practical Necromancy for Beginners," Play the Past http://www.playthepast.org/?p=559, January 20 2011.

10. Angela Cox, "Teaching Games as Text: The Problem." Part 3 of 4, *Play the Past* http://www.playthepast.org/?p=4605, April 9, 2014.

11. William Caraher. "Teaching, Learning and Resistance," *The Archaeology of the Mediterranean World.* March 31 2014, http://mediterraneanworld.wordpress.com/2014/03/31/teaching-learning-and-resistance/.

12. Shawn Graham, "The Wikiblitz," *Writing History in the Digital Age*, eds. Jack Dougherty & Kristen Nawrotzki (Ann Arbor: University of Michigan Press, 2013), http://dx.doi.org/10.3998/dh.12230987.0001.001.

13. Matthew Kapell and Andrew B. R Elliott, *Playing with the Past: Digital Games and the Simulation of History* (London: Bloomsbury Academic, 2013), 14.

14. I am grateful to Mark Sample for posting his teaching materials on video game criticism, which directly inspire this work. Mark Sample, "Videogames in Critical Contexts'" HNRS 353-002 (Spring 2012). George Mason University, http://samplereality.com/gmu/hnrs353/.

15. These checkpoints were developed and inspired from materials posted at the Learning Games Network; as of March 31st 2014 the site is under redevelopment at http://www.learninggamesnetwork.org/.

16. Jeremiah McCall, "Navigating the Problem Space: The Medium of Simulation Games in the Teaching of History." *History Teacher* 46(1) (2012): 9-28.

17. McCall, "Navigating the Problem Space," p 12

18. Kapell and Elliott, *Playing with the Past*, 14.

19. Shawn Graham, #hist3812 Digital History: Games & Simulations for Historians, Winter 2013, course blog, http://3812.graeworks.net.

20. Zoe Quinn, Depression Quest 2013, http://www.depressionquest.com/.

21. Mingarelli, Tucciarone, Bhandal and Lemieux, "The Medic's War: Final Assignment for HIST3812" April 4, 2013: 20.

22. Angela Cox, 'Teaching Games as Text: The Problem. Part 3 of 4' *Play the Past* http://www.playthepast.org/?p=4605, April 9, 2014.

23. On news writing robots see S. Levy, "Can an Algorithm Write A Better News Story than A Human Reporter?" *Wired: Gadget Lab* April 4, 2012, http://www.wired.com/gadgetlab/2012/04/can-an-algorithm-write-a-better-news-story-than-a-human-reporter/

24. Brittney, 'Wait...It's Not an Actual Sandbox? Or is It?' *#hist3812* March 20, 2013, http://www.3812.graeworks.net/2013/03/20/group-g7-r-brittney-wait-its-not-an-actual-sandbox-or-is-it/

25. Graham, "Learning to Write at a Distance," in *Web Writing* (Open peer review edition, Fall 2013), http://webwriting2013.trincoll.edu/rethinking/graham-2013/.

*Crossing Boundaries*

# Getting Uncomfortable

*Identity Exploration in a Multi-Class Blog*

*Rochelle Rodrigo and Jennifer Kidd*

In the United States, the K-12 student population is increasingly children of color while teachers remain largely Caucasian. In 2010, only 52% of American students were white,[1] while 84% of teachers were white.[2] Research suggests white, middle class teachers are often poorly prepared to effectively teach students from minority and lower income backgrounds,[3] meanwhile, a significant achievement gap persists between students from these backgrounds and their white, Asian, and middle-class peers.[4]

To become effective and culturally responsive, preservice teachers need to explore power, privilege, and prejudice, and to contemplate institutional and societal structures impeding the success of affected populations. However, teacher educators frequently report student resistance to discussing race.[5] Students deny race as a salient factor in their lives and see racism as a problem of the past.[6] They claim not to notice race[7] and to adopt what is known as a colorblind perspective.[8] Colorblindness suggests that because race should not matter, it does not matter. From a colorblind perspective, acknowledging a person's race is offensive and suggestive of underlying prejudice.[9] Accordingly, race is treated as an invisible characteristic that polite people neither see nor discuss. Such beliefs make frank discussions of power, privilege and prejudice challenging for educators and students.

## The Assignment

We designed a pilot project for pre-service teachers to write and share identity narratives in a multi-course blog in Spring 2013 with five sections of an educational foundations course at Old Dominion University. Shelley, the writing instructor/digital humanities scholar, and Jennifer, along with two other participating instructors, designed The Identity Exploration Assignment. This scaffolded web writing project asked students to engage with texts about identity development, reflect on their memberships in various social and demographic groups, produce "This I Believe" style essays exploring their most self-defining group membership, and submit their writing to a course blog.[10] Participants tagged their posts to help classmates identify and respond to peers both similar to and different from themselves and then concluded with a piece of reflective writing.

We hypothesized that students who reflected on their childhood identity development while reading narratives from diverse peers would discover how group memberships shape K-12 students' identities. We hoped witnessing diverse experiences via writing would increase participant receptivity to discussions of race and ethnicity in students' educational experiences and provide opportunities to improve writing skills. When students discuss racial/ethnic issues in interracial groups there is often a positive effect on student attitudes and learning.[11] Web 2.0 applications, such as blogs, enable such interactions.

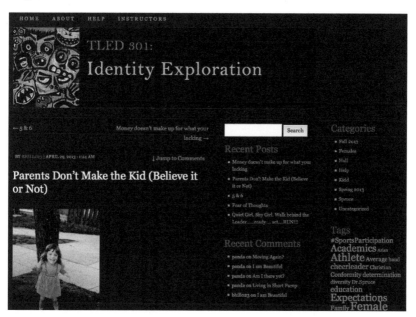

*The Identity Exploration course site.*

Identity development was a natural fit for this assignment for several reasons. First, attitudes associated with colorblindness are typical of white students in the first stage of racial identity development, what Helms[12] calls the contact developmental status.[13] We hoped studying identity would help students be cognizant of their own development and understand that developmental growth can be accompanied by feelings of anger, guilt, and discomfort. Second, as future teachers, these students will profoundly impact the identities of young people. Reading stories of young people's identity development — especially ones recounting the influences of teachers and peers — illuminates the powerful role and responsibility teachers have in shaping students' identities. Finally, engaging in reflective writing and thinking, exploring personal histories, acknowledging membership in different groups, and learning about the lives and experiences of other groups are specific activities suggested for education students to become culturally responsive teachers.[14]

We wanted participants to do most of their intellectual work, as well as demonstrate their learning, through writing for three reasons. First, writing-to-learn is a well-documented pedagogical strategy that provides students with writing assignments that allow them to think through what they are learning.[15] Students needed to slow down and critically think about the importance of group memberships and connect them to their own identity. Second, students would improve their writing while writing to learn.[16] Part of learning any discipline is understanding its theoretical and philosophical underpinnings which are present in the type, style, and genres of writing privileged in that discipline. Writing to learn would help the students process their own learning; learning to write would help them mature as future educators.

We layered the project so that students could write their way through their learning and continue to build upon their thinking in a scaffolded manner. Faculty who teach writing typically argue for scaffolding larger assignments,[17] especially research projects,[18] as a way to help students break up the tough intellectual labor of finding, analyzing, and synthesizing information from the similarly difficult work of arranging and presenting their thinking through writing.[19] Through the scaffolded process, students used write-to-learn activities to process what they were learning about diversity and their own identity development and then worked to present what they learned in a more polished manner.

We used a blog for two reasons: functionality and audience. Many scholars suggest benefits of various Web 2.0 applications[20] including the ability to share work more widely, and with a more diverse audience.[21] Of the students who participated, approximately 80% were female; 75% were white, 15% were Black, and 10% were other racial/ethnic backgrounds. These demographics are not so dissimilar to the current teaching population. With the tagging capabilities of the blog, however, students were able to select posts based on group memberships and purposefully seek out experiences both similar to and different from their own. All students were able to share their stories and then read others from students in different sections (and, eventually, prior semesters). User accounts in WordPress, outside of any institutionally affiliated software, gave students the option of using pseudonyms to discuss sensitive issues freely.

## Results

This Identity Exploration assignment was implemented in five course sections with a total of 153 students. Many students who completed the assignment appeared to meet both the primary objective of improving understanding of diversity as well as the secondary objective of improving writing skills. Prior to an instructional unit on diversity, students completed three diversity related surveys: the Professional Beliefs Scale,[22] measuring students' beliefs related to teaching; the Color-Blind Racial Attitudes Scale,[23] assessing students' racial attitudes; and fifteen items from the Multicultural Sensitivity Scale,[24] assessing interracial personal and teaching interactions. At the end of the course, students completed the same scales and responded to a researcher-designed survey evaluating students' attitudes toward the project. Ninety-one students participated in the study.

### Identity Development and Diversity

The three diversity-related instruments revealed a surprising combination of results. A significant difference in Professional Beliefs indicated participants had attitudes more accepting of diversity and more knowledgeable of institutional inequities at the end of the course. In contrast, there was no significant change in Colorblind Racial Attitudes suggesting beliefs about the salience of race did not alter much over the semester. Most interestingly, a significant difference in Multicultural Sensitivity scores suggested participants were more insensitive to multicultural interactions at the end of the semester. Specifically, students reported greater discomfort interacting with people from racial/ethnic groups other than their own at the posttest.

Although the students' experiences during the diversity unit seemed to make them uncomfortable, students evaluated the Identity Exploration Assignment very highly. The great majority of students found it a beneficial learning activity (84%) and enjoyed participating (84%). Participants reported learning about themselves (83%) and the effects of group memberships on identity (91%), often in ways they hadn't previously considered (86%). And, almost all the students found benefit in reading (90%) and reflecting on (91%) other students' stories, emphasizing the importance of the interaction facilitated by the blog.

Approximately twenty percent of students wrote about race or ethnicity; two thirds of these students were black, Asian or Hispanic. Interestingly, several black students did not mark their post with a race-specific tag (e.g. black), even if they named their race in their title (e.g."You're not like most black girls…"), instead opting for broader themed tags such as "Stereotypes" or "Expectations". This may indicate resistance to labeling, but it is likely the students did not realize the importance of the tags in helping readers find stories written by people from different demographic groups. Many students may not have posted in a blog previously nor used tags to label their writing. This is a technical detail the instructors need to address more thoughtfully in future iterations.

A few students appeared defensive about associating themselves with perceived privilege:

> Poor me, poor little white boy, that grew up in a white community, that was an only child, that had parents that loved him and supported him while encouraging him to be everything he wanted to be. So what defines someone like me you might ask?

This highlights the instructors' need to be sensitive to and supportive of members in dominant groups, to help them understand that privilege does not discredit their accomplishments nor make them a "bad person" and to broaden the definition of diversity so all students can celebrate their uniqueness.

The students who wrote about their race and ethnicity produced powerful narratives with lessons their peers could (and in some cases, did) learn from. Several African American females in the course challenged the notion of "acting white":

> They said to me that I am 'acting white'. I guess that acting white meant that I talked like them, I was smart like them, and I was listening to the same music, and dressing like them. But I didn't see it as me being more like them-but me just being me. I thought to myself, why is it that I have to be acting like them and not them acting like me?

About half of the responses to stories of "acting white" were made by black women sympathizing with similar accounts. Occasionally, comments from students outside the demographic group documented new personal insights:

> Your story was really inspiring to me. As a white male its often hard to think in terms of how other races might be dealing with having friends of different races and/or back grounds.

Another student wrote:

> It's so mind blowing to me that just because you are a certain race or ethnicity you are expected to 'act' a certain way or associate yourself with those specific people.

One student described how even her teachers adopted the stereotype that good students are white:

> In high school, my teachers always expected me to do very well. I have had 3 teachers that I can remember tell me that I wasn't black, 'because I show up for class,' or 'because I make good grades and behave well.' They really must have thought I was white. They were bashing my race right in front of me like it wasn't a big deal. I was born an African Amer-

ican, and no matter what I do, how I pronounce my words, nor how I act can change that.

This powerful and expressive post unfortunately received only one response. None of the posts about acting white received more than five comments, further evidence of the need for the instructors to do more to centralize stories of individuals from traditionally marginalized demographic groups.

Students frequently offered statements of support to their peers and the theme of overcoming hardships, especially when participants wrote about low expectations or criticism. For example, this comment was posted to the story of a Hispanic student whose aspirations to be a police officer were scoffed at by family and friends:

> What a great story. I am impressed by your motivation and the fact that you stuck to what you wanted in life. Sometimes children just except the answers their parents give them. When your parents told you that it was just a dream and assumed it would not come true you still went for what you wanted. This is a very inspirational story. I love the stories that show what individuals can do if they keep their focus set in the right direction.

Instead of critiquing expectations—their origin or influence, students focused on their peers' ability to resist prejudice and defy stereotypes. This fits well with colorblind ideology, suggesting people should be able to succeed regardless of circumstance, and a commitment to individual accountability rather than collective responsibility for equitable opportunities.

The most popular category of group memberships was extracurricular activities. Many students reported developing a strong sense of identity from participating on a team (e.g. sports, cheerleading, and band). The post that received the most comments (19), focused on the pervasive stereotypes of cheerleaders as unintelligent and promiscuous and provided a compelling account of hurtful comments and unfounded prejudices conveyed not only by the author's peers, but also her teachers.

> I got called all the names you could think of. I was told by my peers I wouldn't get good grades, I'd be called a slut, the whole nine yards.

> Teachers would pick on me and make fun of me because I was the stereotypical 'dumb blonde cheerleader.' Funny thing was though, I was a brunette and had all A's and B's throughout high school.

Students appreciated one another's narratives and most reached similar conclusions in their reflections. They acknowledged that everyone faced hardships; everyone "has a story". They preferred to frame experiences of discrimination as opportunities for personal growth rather than indictments of an unjust society. They focused on similarities and strengths, rather than on differences, injustice, or ignorance. There were critical reflections, however and calls to action:

> I really liked reading your story, because it gave me a whole new perspective. Unfortunately, I was always one of those to stereotype cheerleaders into the same categories you described... I never really thought about what you guys go through. It shocked me that so many people would be so cruel directly to you, or even behind your back.

As a teacher it is beyond important to understand the stereotypes for all the different students in class. Certain stereotypes can discourage students from not wanting to do their best in class, not wanting to really be themselves. As a teacher, if you don't try and understand *why* students are acting out or not doing their best, we can only make it worse on them.

## Writing

The primary goal of the Identity Exploration Assignment was to increase student understanding of diversity-related issues within the American education system, and in particular how students' identities are shaped by their group memberships and interactions with others. However, in using writing as a primary tool to help facilitate this learning, a secondary goal was to help students improve their writing. Many (78%) of the students somewhat or strongly agreed that the assignment "was a good opportunity to practice my writing skills." About one-third (35%) of the students made general comments about the benefit of reading and learning from one another's texts; they may have become more aware of themselves as potential audience members. Six made comments that demonstrated their awareness of the others reading their work; some of these comments included:

> When people commented on my story they gave praise and I knew that they were engaged into what I was saying. . .
>
> I was a little disappointed because I really put myself out there and only received feedback from one person. . .
>
> At first I was apprehensive about others being able to read my story. . .
>
> I did not feel comfortable sharing my story at all, and did not feel comfortable reading others as well.

Conversely, one student who claimed "It should be simply turned in on Blackboard" missed the assignment objective of learning from reading other students' work as well as learning from comments left by other students. Four more students emphasized that the assignment was "hard work" and took a lot of time. Three more participants mentioned the scaffolding, one praised the assignment being broken up into smaller pieces and two other students suggested that the assignment should have been smaller/shorter and had fewer sections.

We did not explicitly assess the writing of students during this implementation of the assignment; however, we plan to do so in the future. The general positive feedback on the assignment, especially the benefit of reading their peers' work, suggests students both learned, and were metacognitively aware they learned, through writing, reading, and comparing. To build on what we've started, we are revising the assignment so that students understand and practice the scaffolding process to both improve their thinking and learning as well as their writing (for example, we have explicitly built in a peer- and self-review process).

## Conclusions

The multi-course blog allowed students to explore the influence of group memberships on identity development with a more diverse cohort of peers than possible within their individual cohorts. Findings suggest students better understood the effects of group membership on interpersonal interactions and educational experiences as a result. Students' awareness of educational inequities increased. The most interesting finding was the increase in students' Multicultural Sensitivity Scale scores showing that students perceived greater discomfort interacting with others outside their racial/ethnic group at the posttest. It is, however, unclear exactly what caused these results. The class discussions on diversity-related topics, the Identity Exploration blog assignment, and 30-hour classroom observation placements may all have been contributing factors. Caution must be also used interpreting this finding as it is not clear whether students actually became less comfortable interacting interracially, if they became more aware of their discomfort, or if they are more willing to admit discomfort.

From a colorblind perspective, acknowledgement of race/ethnicity suggests underlying prejudice.[25] That participants in this study were more willing at posttest to admit they notice race/ethnicity and concede that interracial interactions are less comfortable for them to negotiate can be seen as a positive development. This discomfort may be indicative of the second stage of racial identity development, disintegration[26] where individuals become conflicted over unresolvable racial moral dilemmas, like believing one is nonracist yet not wanting to work with students of a different racial group. By sharing stories of identity, students may have progressed in their own identity development.

Although we believe that this version of the assignment was successful in making students more "uncomfortable" and therefore more aware of issues of diversity, we also believe we can more explicitly take advantage of the affordances of the blogging technology to help students emerge from their "filter bubble."[27] More thought needs to go into the tagging protocol to centralize narratives from authors of traditionally marginalized groups without making these individuals feel defined by their demographics and simultaneously allowing members of dominant groups to find and celebrate their own diversities. Students need more guidance identifying and critiquing power and prejudice in interactions in schools and discussing methods for teachers to dismantle dominant power structures in their schools and classrooms.

It is important to acknowledge that these changes are occurring in the first course in a teacher preparation program and that more instruction and intercultural interactions are needed before students graduate if these preservice teachers are to feel comfortable and competent interacting with students from diverse backgrounds in their future classrooms. While discomfort is a hopeful first step in the right direction, it necessitates subsequent steps. If the initial step is left unsupported, it could result in pre-service students stepping away from opportunities to work with diverse populations. The use of writing-to-learn activities supported by Web 2.0 technologies, like blogs, can be essential tools to facilitate greater intercultural interaction that enables this process.

*About the Authors: Rochelle (Shelley) Rodrigo is an assistant professor of English at Old Dominion University. She was a full time faculty member for nine years at Mesa Community College in Arizona. Shelley researches how "newer" technologies better facilitate communicative interactions, more specifically teaching and learning. In addition to co-authoring the two editions of* The Wadsworth Guide to Research, *Shelley was also co-editor of* Rhetorically Rethinking Usability.

*Jennifer Kidd is a senior lecturer in the department of Teaching and Learning at Old Dominion University. Previously she taught elementary school in Chicago, Virginia and Budapest, Hungary. Her research focuses on web 2.0 technologies to support teaching and learning. She received grants from HASTAC/The MacArthur Foundation and the National Science Foundation to support the production of a student-authored wiki textbook in her classes.*

### How to cite:

Rochelle Rodrigo and Jennifer Kidd, "Getting Uncomfortable: Identity Exploration in a Multi-Class Blog," in *Web Writing: Why and How for Liberal Arts Teaching and Learning*, ed. Jack Dougherty and Tennyson O'Donnell (University of Michigan Press/Trinity College ePress edition, 2014), http://epress.trincoll.edu/webwriting/chapter/rodrigo-kidd.

*See an earlier version of this essay with open peer review comments.*[28]

# Notes

1. Susan Aud, Sidney Wilkinson-Flicker, Paul Kristapovich, Amy Rathbun, and Jijun Zhang, *The Condition of Education 2013* (U.S. Department of Education, National Center for Education Statistics, 2013), http://nces.ed.gov/pubs2013/2013037.pdf

2. Emily C. Feistritzer, *Profile of Teachers in the U.S. 2011* (National Center for Educational Information, 2011) 11, http://www.edweek.org/media/pot2011final-blog.pdf.

3. Cathy Kea, Gloria D. Campbell-Whatley, and Heraldo V. Richards, *Becoming Culturally Responsive Educator: Rethinking Teacher Education Pedagogy* (NCCREST: National Center for Culturally Responsive Educational Systems, 2006),http://www.nccrest.org/Briefs/Teacher_Ed_Brief.pdf.

4. F. Cadelle Hemphill and Alan Vanneman, *Achievement Gaps: How Hispanic and White Students in Public Schools Perform in Mathematics and Reading on the National Assessment of Educational Progress (NCES 2011-459)* (Washington, DC: National Center for Education Statistics, Institute of Education Sciences, U.S. Department of Education, 2011),http://nces.ed.gov/nationsreportcard/pdf/studies/2011459.pdf; National Center for Education Statistics, *National Indian Education Study 2011 (NCES 2012– 466)* (Washington, D.C: Institute of Education Sciences, U.S. Department of Education, National Center for Education Statistics, 2012), http://nces.ed.gov/nationsreportcard/pdf/studies/2012466.pdf; Alan Vanneman, Linda Hamilton, Janet Baldwin Anderson, and Taslima Rahman, *Achievement Gaps: How Black and White Students in Public Schools Perform in Mathematics and Reading on the National Assessment of Educational Progress, (NCES 2009-455)* (Washington, DC: National Center for Education Statistics, Institute of Education Sciences, U.S. Department of Education, 2009),http://nces.ed.gov/nationsreportcard/pdf/studies/2009455.pdf.

5. Grace Cho and Debra DeCastro-Ambrosetti, "Is Ignorance Bliss? Pre-service Teachers' Attitudes Toward Multi-cultural Education," *The High School Journal 89* no. 2 (2005): 24-28,http://dx.doi.org/10.1353/hsj.2005.0020.

6. Ian F. Haney Lopez, "Colorblind to the Reality of Race in America," *Chronicle of Higher Education* November 3, 2006, http://chronicle.com/article/Colorblind-to-the-Reality-of/12577/; Sleeter, "Preparing Teachers for Culturally Diverse Schools," *Journal of Teacher Education* 52 (March 2001): 94-106.

7. Gay and Kirkland, "Developing Critical Consciousness," *Theory into Practice* 42 (2003): 181-187; Sandra M. Lawrence, "Beyond Race Awareness: White Racial Identity and Multicultural Teaching," *Journal of Teacher Education* 48 (1997): 108-117, http://dx.doi.org/10.1177/0022487197048002004.

8. Eduardo Bonilla-Silva and David Dietrich, "The Sweet Enchantment of Colorblind Racism in Obamerica," *The ANNALS of the American Academy of Political and Social Science* 634, no. 1 (2011): 190-206, http://dx.doi.org/10.1177/0002716210389702.

9. Janet W. Schofield, "Causes and Consequences of the Colorblind Perspective," in Prejudice, Discrimination and Racism, eds. John F. Dovidio and Samuel L. Haertner (New York: Academic, 1986), 91-126.

10. "TLED 301 Identity Exploration" course blog, Old Dominion University, 2013, http://tled301.courses.digitalodu.com/; "TLED 301: Identity Exploration Assignment, Old Dominion University, Google Document, 2013 https://docs.google.com/document/d/1tVWsfbj50IRLSPpT9NwyTtjO8PZp0L5EgbCCLrE9QwQ/pub; This I Believe, 2005-2013, http://thisibelieve.org/.

11. Mitchell J. Chang, "Does Racial Diversity Matter? The Educational Impact of a Racially Diverse Undergraduate Population," *The Journal of College Student Development* 40, no. 4 (1999): 377-395.

12. Janet Helms, *Black and White Racial Identity: Theory, Research and Practice* (Westport, CT: Greenwood Press, 1990).

13. Lawrence, "Beyond Race Awareness;" Beverly Daniel Tatum, "Teaching White Students about Racism: The Search for White Allies and the Restoration of Hope," *Teachers College Record* 95, no. 4 (1994): 462-476,http://www.tcrecord.org/Content.asp?ContentID=107.

14. Heraldo V. Richards, Ayanna F. Brown, and Timothy B. Forde, *Addressing Diversity in Schools: Culturally Responsive Pedagogy* (Tempe, AZ: National Center for Culturally Responsive Educational System, 2006), http://www.nccrest.org/Briefs/Diversity_Brief.pdf.

15. Robert L. Bangert-Drowns, Marlene M. Hurley, and Barbara Wilkinson, "The Effects of School-Based Writing-to-Learn Interventions on Academic Achievement: A Meta-Analysis," Review of Educational Research 74, no. 1 (2004): 29–58, http://dx.doi.org/10.3102/00346543074001029.

16. Ann Raimes, "Writing and Learning Across the Curriculum: The Experience of a Faculty Seminar," *College English* 41, no. 7 (1980): 799, http://www.jstor.org/stable/376219.

17. Kathleen Dudden Rowlands, "Check It Out! Using Checklists to Support Student Learning," *English Journal* 96, no. 6 (2007): 61–66, http://www.jstor.org/stable/30046754.

18. Helen Foster, "Growing Researchers Using an Information-Retrieval Scaffold," *TETYC* 31, no. 2 (2003): 170–178. http://www.ncte.org/library/NCTEFiles/Resources/Journals/TETYC/0312-dec03/TE0312Growing.pdf.

19. Barak Rosenshine and Carla Meister, "The Use of Scaffolds for Teaching Higher-Level Cognitive Strategies," *Educational Leadership* 49, no. 7 (1992): 26–33,http://www.ascd.org/ASCD/pdf/journals/ed_lead/el_199204_rosenshine.pdf.

20. Mark J. W. Lee, and Catherine McLoughlin, "Teaching and Learning in the Web 2.0 era: Empowering Students Through Learner-generated Content," *International Journal of Instructional Technology and Distance Learning* 4, no. 10 (2007), http://itdl.org/Journal/Oct_07/article02.htm.

21. Jason Tougaw, "Dream Bloggers Invent the University," *Computers and Composition* 26, no. 4 (December 2009): 251–268, http://dx.doi.org/10.1016/j.compcom.2009.08.002.

22. Cathy A. Pohan and Teresita E. Aguilar, "Measuring Educators' Beliefs About Diversity in Personal and Professional Contexts," *American Educational Research Journal* 38, no. 1 (2001): 159–182, http://www.jstor.org/stable/10.2307/3202517.

23. Helen A. Neville, Roderick L. Lilly, Georgia Duran, Richard M. Lee, and LaVonne Browne, "Construction and Initial Validation of the Color-Blind Racial Attitudes Scale (COBRAS)," *Journal of Counseling Psychology* 47, no. 1 (2000): 59-70, http://dx.doi.org/10.1037//0022-0167.47.1.59.

24. Maria Jibaja-Rusth, Paul M. Kingery, David J. Holcomb, W.P. Buckner Jr. and B. E. Pruitt, "Development of a Multicultural Sensitivity Scale," *Journal of Health Education* 25, no. 6 (1994): 350-357, http://dx.doi.org/10.1080/10556699.1994.10603060.

25. Schofield, "Causes and Consequences of the Colorblind Perspective."

26. Helms, *Black and White Racial Identity*.

27. Eli Pariser, *The Filter Bubble: What the Internet is Hiding from You* (New York: Penguin, 2011).

28. Rodrigo and Kidd, "Getting Uncomfortable," in *Web Writing* (Open peer review edition, Fall 2013), http://webwriting2013.trincoll.edu/crossing-boundaries/rodrigo-kidd-2013/.

# Writing as Curation

*Using a 'Building' and 'Breaking' Pedagogy to Teach Culture in the Digital Age*

*Pete Coco and M. Gabriela Torres*

As Wheaton College explores blended learning in the liberal arts, we have found that the technologies our students use for learning are fruitful objects of critical engagement in their own right. Re-orienting student writing onto the web potentially leverages liberal arts learning by engaging a critical process we call "building and breaking." This process asks students to think of their writing as a peculiarly digital form of curation in which they use digital platforms to "build" (curate new collections of alike digital objects), and "break" (critically engage with the curatorial decisions behind existing collections of alike digital objects).

This essay applies the frame of "building" and "breaking" to other classrooms where students engage critically with digital objects and collections. Drawing on case studies of students writing blogs at Wheaton College, this chapter uses excerpts of student writing from two blogging assignments in a course in anthropology to explore curation as a mode of online writing that simultaneously "builds" and "breaks." We suggest that as students learn to build web content they do so by engaging in two related processes: gathering a collection of relevant digital content and composing a written framework that reflects on the selected content's relevance. We propose that writing as curation, guided by assignments that direct student reflection, has the potential to encourage students to "break" the cognitive framework—both disciplinary and technological—when such writing takes place.

## Blog Writing as Curation

Blogs can "build" or curate knowledge about culture through reflection on key issues in the social sciences: the politics and ethics of representation, power imbalance and the circulation of knowledge, and social responsibility. In one online writing assignment, students were asked to draw on existing anthropological research and blog in response to the following question: "What can you do with anthropology?" Madison Spigel highlights research by anthropologist Morgan Ames on the negative effects that short-term visitors have on non-governmental organization technology projects and makes her own conclusion: the assessment of development projects requires ethnographic research because of the power imbalances inherent in development itself.[1] This kind of "building" assignment asks students to curate existing digital content in order to define and gather a new collection of digital items that has a signature logic and coherence.

The blogging assignment becomes a "breaking" activity that prompts critical reflection about the application of disciplinary knowledge when students begin to make conscious choices about what to include, why to include it in their collection, and how to organize and provide access to it. Writing on the politics and ethics of representation, student Lual Charles tackles his own reservations about engaging with the study of culture by drawing on the work of black anthropologist James Alves. Charles' reflection challenges or "breaks" the discipline's key methodology suggesting for himself a satisfactory way to engage with the study of culture.[2]

Assignment design, like blog writing, that pushes the real world application of knowledge borrows its ethic from current conversations in the digital humanities around "making" and its learning benefits, succinctly described by English professor Stephen Ramsay's "On Building" post.[3]

## 'Building' and 'Breaking' in Liberal Arts Teaching

Curating collections of similar digital objects can be assigned across the curriculum. For example, consider the following sample "building" assignments at Wheaton College:

- In a course on American folk music, students choose from a list of songs that each have a rich and varied recording tradition. Students create playlists in Spotify that show this change for one song and embed these playlists into blog posts that explain their choices and process.

- In a literary theory course, students use the MLA International Bibliography to find citations that together demonstrate how the critical response to a canonical novel has changed over time. Using TimelineJS, they create a timeline that includes particularly illustrative examples of that change. On the course message boards, students write about the citations they were closest to selecting but ultimately decided against.
- In a course on the history of Boston, students use Google Forms to nominate and choose a neighborhood of the city to visually annotate in Google Earth. They then use the Boston Public Library's collection of archival photographs to find images that they can plot to Google Earth.

Defining and collecting digital items through "building" activities like these encourage liberal arts students to understand the logic and coherence of information. On the other hand, assignments that use "breaking" make students critical users of existing digital objects and collections. For example, consider the following sample "breaking" assignments:

- Students examine a Wikipedia page with a high number of edits and consider the changes that were made to the page over time—and why.
- Students look at Google Poetics and use it to consider questions about authorship (who is the author of a "Google poem"?) and the definition of literature (Is a Google Poem literature?) while also exploring Google's design choices in its autocomplete search function.
- Students use a large image collection using a tagging folksonomy (Flickr) and compare its treatment of a particularly thorny or contested terminology to its treatment in a collection that uses controlled vocabulary (a library catalog).

Through critical and inferential engagement with the object(s), these assignments tease out the decisions made by designers. Students develop a critique of the designer's purpose and execution of that purpose. The focus of that critique can hinge on the discipline being taught, the tool itself, and/or student initiative. This method of assignment design stems from the scholarly conversation around critical information literacy, of which interested readers can find an elegant and comprehensive treatment in *Critical Library Instruction* as well as the work of James Elmborg.[4]

In both sorts of assignments (and particularly in their combination), writing output, as process-oriented reflection but also a product itself, is great for driving home the information fluency and content outcomes in a convergent way. By building knowledge in digital tools that visualize, organize, contextualize or otherwise curate our course content, our students engage with potential audiences in new ways. When we critically analyze, test, and attempt to "break" digital writing platforms and disciplinary principles that curate course-related content and then reflect on that act together and as individual writers, we become more critical users of digital technology. In fact, there are specific learning outcomes associated with each type of assignment:

### Learning Outcomes for Assignments that Build

Make and reflect on choices to:

- Find digital content
- Group digital content
- Present digital content
- Put together digital content with traditional print sources or data collected offline

### Learning Outcomes for Assignments that Break

Identify and critique choices implicit in an existing digital object:

- Where the objects came from
- How the content is grouped
- How the design is presented

## Beyond Blogging: Designing Assignments that 'Build'

Beyond blogging, digital objects can be collected on pretty much any website you and your students could build via three basic features of html: (1) hyperlinks, allow designers to connect pages within sites and to webpages outside of them, (2) embed codes, which allow you to borrow or "embed" content from other sites (like YouTube) directly onto your own pages, and (3) hosted image files, which are stored on your own sites and displayed there.

Other platforms make certain kinds of visualization and arrangements of collection objects easier to construct or can serve specialized needs. Prezi and other tools like Popplet allow you and your students to visually arrange collection items in a way that demonstrates their interconnections at multiple scales. Google Earth plots collection items to geographic location and TimelineJS plots them chronologically.[5]

Certain logistics are worth planning for in an assignment that builds. Critical questions to ask yourself upfront:

- Will students curate collaboratively or individually? What would be the trade-offs in each case?
- Will students need training to use the tools they need to complete the assignment? If so, will that be provided by you or by a guest presenter?
- Will students somehow use the final product of the assignment in-class, accompanying a presentation?
- What platforms will the class use to gather and display the final product(s)?
- Will the final products have a life beyond the classroom or the present semester? How will you plan for that?
- How much content will students be curating? How will students be prompted to reflect on curation? Will their reflections be apart of the content presentation or be pushed to another platform (a blog, a paper, a presentation, etc)?

- How much scaffolding can the assignment provide as students move through a potentially complex workflow?
- How will the student work be assessed? Will all projects be assessed along a single set of criteria or are there any circumstantial/topic-related factors that would make that unfair? Is the grading criteria focused on process and due diligence or the end product?
- To what extent will you give your students a role in making the above decisions–or access to your thinking as you make these decisions on their behalf?

It might be counter-intuitive, but using the assignment prompt to limit where students look for content can teach them more than leaving them to figure it out on their own. Restricting their search parameters allows the instructor to develop, in advance, a good sense of what sorts of content students will find and whether that truly fits with your goals.

## Designing Assignments that 'Break'

Assignments that "break" tend to begin with certain questions: How can students learn about a digital object's purpose and function by investigating its output? What choices and values went into the construction of this digital object? What learning outcomes related to course content can be deepened or complicated by a critical understanding of the given digital object?

Assignments that "break" can be logistically simpler than those that "build," but not all digital objects "break" equally well. Some will get to rich questions like the above more directly than others. Assignment design is crucial. Your students may not use most digital objects in the way you do.

"Breaking" assignments should be messy. Students will not all have the same experience "breaking" a digital object and that's okay. Sharing their experiences with each other via face-to-face or online discussion–as well as having you or a visiting expert on-hand to explain the variations of experience–is key and gives the fullest sense of the object being explored.

Consider an example of an assignment that we have used and revised over the years. To prompt students to consider the fundamental differences between using Google as opposed to a scholarly database, we designed an activity that asked them to search "Batman" in both systems and then compare and discuss the results. This worked well because Batman is considered in a lot of different and interesting ways in both scholarly and popular contexts. If the research activity were to allow students their own choice of superhero, more of them would have had, at least in the moment, a more bemusing experience. "I didn't really find anything on the Power-Puff Girls in the college library database," a student might complain. We are not surprised when this happens, but the students are. So together, we ask: why? There are several answers, and going through them with students—particularly as a group—can help them later with seemingly unrelated tasks, like choosing a manageable topic for their big research paper.

One way to think about "breaking" is to think of it as reverse engineering: given this output, what can we deduce about the design of this system? As a pedagogy, it puts students in a critical frame from the start. This is particularly important for assignments that leverage technologies that students already use for uncritical and goal-oriented purposes (like Google Search).

Depending on the focus, "breaking" can achieve learning outcomes about the cultural role that information systems play in the human experience. More pragmatically, however, "breaking"  teaches information literacy.

## Curating Culture Online: Cross-Cultural Blogging Project

It is clear that writing blogs have the potential to guide students into "building" and "breaking" the online space as an extension of classroom practices that deconstruct culture. Between 2007-2013 more than four hundred students blogged at Wheaton College in an Introduction to Anthropology course.

The assignment required each student to document the process of learning about culture in a public blog that curated the individual's encounter with unfamiliar cultural practice. Students learned to assume that culture is everywhere and that understanding this requires engaging with communities, and, crucially, a challenge to their own and each other's misunderstandings.

To learn cultural relativism, a basic concept of social anthropology, students are charged to "build" and "break" cultural knowledge online and in public either using their own names or pseudonyms. Curating self-reflection, together with web-based information and data collected in interviews or participant observation, the Cross-Cultural Blog Assignment challenged students to reframe both their conceptions of culture and writing:

> A cross-cultural encounter puts us in a situation where our understanding or our belief in how things 'are' or how things 'should be' is severely challenged. Cross-cultural encounters provide an excellent opportunity for understanding the discipline and practice of anthropology because they force us rethink ourselves and the worlds in which we live.

> Your professor and your peers will read your writing and it will be available to the public at large. Anyone may comment on your writing (your colleagues will) and part of your job will be to rethink your encounter with other's commentaries in mind.[6]

In our experience, student-authored blogs became a reflexive curatorial exercise that both creates and questions knowledge in public. In practice, students actively engaged with web communities and with each other to begin their journey into understanding how culture works and how knowledge about culture is created. In a liberal arts curriculum that focuses on developing writing skills as well as multidisciplinary and global learning, writing in collaborative online spaces opens a unique space to "build" and "break" culture. Through blogging, our students began to understand the politics of representation and the complexity of public scholarship and culture; key learning goals of more advanced anthropological research.

The inherently interactive and public format of blogging pushed students beyond their comfort zone by design. Writing and rewriting with an audience in mind, students regularly reported how their online interactions proved transformative to their ideas and perspectives. The opportunity and space to rethink, rewrite and "break" the very idea of authorship. This was often a frustrating experience for students used to handing in research papers for a single audience. They carefully crafted their narratives as they engaged with the questions: "Why does this thing go with this other thing and not that one?" and "How will my audience react?" In their narratives and responses to commentary, student-bloggers typically were compelled to make their taxonomies, hierarchies and breadth of cross-cultural experience explicit.

Curating the knowledge of informants with their own, student-authored blogs challenged the usual approach to undergraduate paper writing. Kyla Baxter's *An Unfamiliar Culture* blog used insight from her informants via online messaging or direct conversation to reflect upon. What emerged is a complex process of thinking and writing that enables students to curate already circulating information in sophisticated ways:

> I was reading through my comments and someone posted a very insightful and interesting comment on the blog I wrote about the man who was an ex-Baha'i turned Christian. They said how it was true about the Baha'i faith as seeking individual exploration but it wasn't only about that. I think this is true, there is a social aspect to the Baha'i community, but I think the important thing about the individual exploration of faith is that you are able to explore those parts of faith that you most connect with and you can explore other faiths and in that way link the faiths up together.[7]

Kyla's example is one of many that show that students can develop, strengthen, and sustain a voice and space of one's own as it relates to the work and practice of other writers or knowledge producers.

Blogs that elicited engaged audience commentary demonstrate the potential of web writing to develop the curatorial skills of public scholarship. Students acted as audiences for their peers but their writing was also offered up to an infinite public community. One example of this is found through the exchange that occurred after a comment was posted on Laura Starr's *Culture of War* blog on Ugandan child soldiers. In a thorough and charged comment, one of her readers concluded the following reaction to her blog. He wrote:

> I just stumbled across your blog, so first things first, welcome to Uganda (when you get here …) Secondly, I don't know who the source of

your information on Uganda is, but most of it is outrageously incorrect.[8]

After reading this comment, Laura reached out to the reader and began an offline conversation that became key to her cross-cultural encounter. The learning experience is eloquently represented in the concluding entry to her blog. She writes:

> This experience was the closest I have had to an actual cultural encounter and this encounter, while only communicating online, was what helped me most in writing my blog. I had my first flash of recognition after receiving the comment from Tumwijuke in Uganda. I realized the power that words have, especially when you are writing or talking about something that you are unfamiliar with. I now understand how important it is to dismiss my own beliefs and thoughts before engaging in something I am unfamiliar with and become open to learning about something new. People are not all so different when it comes to war and trauma. Writing this blog has been one of the most eye opening experiences because it allowed me to learn about another culture through my own mistakes, which I believe are inevitable, and expanded by encounters with others outside of my life circle.[9]

Comments to blog posts allow student authors to curate their own voice with a collective sense of shared knowledge that resides in a public sphere. Blogging about culture required an understanding of the author's culture, and it required the search for a collaboratively-inclined ethnographic voice through which we can speak respectfully about others and ourselves. The collaboration in this practice of web writing extends beyond the students own experience and forces students to simultaneously "build" and "break" their own cultural knowledge.

Caroline Letourneau, writing in her *Understanding the United States Military Academy* blog, curates information from the course on language with information on West Point Military Academy in print and information from informants to "build" and "break" knowledge about the workings of language and culture:

> Within the first dozen pages of *Absolutely American*, David Lipsky brings up 'The Theory and Practice of Huah' (11). Huah? Right. In addition to basing everyday speech on acronyms, apparently the military

has its own vocabulary. Lipsky writes 'There's a word you hear a lot at West Point: huah. . . Huah is an all-purpose word' (11). It seems that huah is something that you can say to anyone at any time. It can be attached to the end of a question signifying 'right?', it can be used as an adjective to describe someone who is ready for action, or it can be used as a response to most questions ('How are you doing today?' 'HUAH!'). I guess that huah is the military's version of 'Supercalifragilisticexpialidocious,' something to say when there's nothing else to say.

I decided to bring up the idea of 'huah' with my ever-patient acquaintances at West Point. I received an instant response when I uttered the word, but it was not quite the response I had anticipated. I was immediately told that I was spelling it wrong. Apparently the spelling has changed since the publishing of *Absolutely American* in 2003. Nowadays it seems that this magic word is spelled H-O-O-A-H. Once we moved away from the technicalities of the word, I asked the cadets what hooah meant. I received an absolutely brilliant response: 'hooah is everything and anything, but "no" ' (Anonymous). The cadets then went on to describe how hooah is the Army version of 'good,' except if you're good then you're alright, but if you're hooah then you're motivated, physically and mentally prepared, and ready to perform. It seems that hooah carries more baggage than one would originally think.

Tying this word into the anthropological study of culture, I think that it serves to create identity. According to the dictionary, hooah/huah is not a word, yet it is quite obvious that at the United States Military Academy it is a word, and a very important one at that.[10]

## Conclusion: Everyone's a Curator

Both "building" and "breaking" work from the same assumption: everyone using and sharing digital content is a curator, whether they mean to be one or not. Curation is best done deliberately. It also involves skills we can cultivate in our students.

Because the scale of digital content and data now accessible is sublimely massive, none of us can engage with it without first making choices about which discrete segments are relevant. Curation of cultural knowledge discussed in our case study of blog writing demonstrates that online curation is an art that requires students to foreground audience and to sequence and stage the presentation of information. Most importantly, however, curatorial writing that "builds" and "breaks" culture online requires a self-conscious understanding of the student author as culture-maker.

"Building" and "breaking" work especially well in tandem. Putting students on both sides of the decisions that content curators make for their users makes easy answers less satisfying. The point, in our experience with blog writing and beyond, is never that designers and curators are "wrong" to make the decisions they make, but those decisions involve trade-offs and are too easily obscured to users. As a practice of reflexive writing, curation is not simply an administrative task in information sorting but a form of critical reflection in its own right.

Moreover, as curation becomes a greater factor in commerce and culture we increasingly find ourselves at the mercy of curators. The stakes can be high. Some will curate irresponsibly or for reasons that might be obscure, intentionally or otherwise. Whether we are discussing how Reddit users up-voted conspiracy theories that accused innocents of the Boston Marathon bombings to the "front page of the Internet,"[11] or the provenance of an ad in a given user's Facebook newsfeed, curation is an act with human, ethical, and technical dimensions that can be explored in any classroom that engages with digital objects.

In fact, we would argue that curation is a matter of such broad consequence that it can be considered meaningfully across disciplines and as a key skill for liberal arts graduates to bring into the workforce. A humanities classroom might ask whether a collection fairly or fully represents the human record and relevant experiences of a topic; social science courses can consider how and why people curate as they do; natural science courses can explore the vagaries of algorithmic function or as an example, at scale, of emergence. In an important sense, these are all different approaches to the same question.

Whatever the questions we ask about curation, they can be framed by an approach of "building" and "breaking." But the fundamental question is universal: "Why does this thing go with this other thing and not that one?" The space for subjectivity and judgment in any curator's answer to that question makes it a solid foundation for writing in the digital age.

*About the authors: Pete Coco (@pfcoco) is the digital learning strategist at Wheaton College in Norton, MA. M. Gabriela Torres (@MGabrielaTorres) is an associate professor of anthropology at Wheaton College, MA. She is a teacher/scholar whose innovative work with technology in the teaching of anthropology has been featured through the National Institute for Technology and Liberal Education, the American Association of Colleges and Universities, and Bryn Mawr's Blended Learning in the Liberal Arts Conference.*

## How to cite:

Pete Coco and M. Gabriella Torres, "Writing as Curation: Using a 'Building' and 'Breaking' Pedagogy to Teach Culture in the Digital Age," in *Web Writing: Why and How for Liberal Arts Teaching and Learning*, ed. Jack Dougherty and Tennyson O'Donnell (University of Michigan Press/Trinity College ePress edition, 2014), http://epress.trincoll.edu/webwriting/chapter/coco-torres.

*See an earlier version of this essay with open peer review comments.*[12]

# Notes

1. Madison Spigel, "Visiting Your Development Project Does No Good," *What Can You Do With Anthropology?* blog, April 21, 2014, http://whatcanyoudowithanthropology.wordpress.com/2014/04/21/visiting-your-development-project-does-no-good/.

2. Lual Charles, "My Conflict with Anthropology," *What Can You Do With Anthropology?* blog, May 3, 2014, http://whatcanyoudowithanthropology.wordpress.com/2014/05/03/my-conflict-with-anthropology/.

3. Stephen Ramsay, "On Building," personal blog, January 11, 2011, http://stephenramsay.us/text/2011/01/11/on-building/.

4. Maria T. Accardi, Emily Drabinski, and Alana Kumbier, eds., *Critical Library Instruction: Theories and Methods* (Library Juice Press, LLC, 2010), http://books.google.com/books?id=kw4AmX8uh8EC; James Elmborg, "Critical Information Literacy: Implications for Instructional Practice," *The Journal of Academic Librarianship* 32, no. 2 (March 2006): 192–99, http://dx.doi.org/10.1016/j.acalib.2005.12.004.

5. Prezi, http://prezi.com/; Popplet, http://popplet.com; Google Earth, http://www.google.com/earth; TimeLineJS, http://timeline.knightlab.com.

6. M. Gabriela Torres, "Cross-Cultural Blog Assignment Description," Anthropology 102 syllabus, Wheaton College, MA.

7. Kyla Baxter, "The Final Glimpse," *An Unfamiliar Culture: A Glimpse into the Baha'i World* blog, May 1, 2008, http://kybblogger.blogspot.com/2008/05/final-glimpse.html.

8. Tumwijuke, comment on Laura Starr, "The Civil War in Uganda," *Culture of War and Child Soldiers* blog, October 17, 2007, http://cultureofwar.blogspot.com/2007/10/civil-war-in-uganda.html.

9. Laura Starr, "Reflection," *Culture of War and Child Soldiers* blog, December 6, 2007, http://cultureofwar.blogspot.com/2007/12/reflection.html.

10. Carrie Letourneau, *Understanding the United States Military Academy* blog, April 22, 2008, http://whywestpoint.blogspot.com/2008/04/supercalifragilisticexpialidocious.html.

11. Leslie Kaufman, "Bombings Trip Up Reddit in Its Turn in Spotlight," *The New York Times*, April 28, 2013, http://www.nytimes.com/2013/04/29/business/media/bombings-trip-up-reddit-in-its-turn-in-spotlight.html

12. Coco and Torres, "Curation in Writing," in *Web Writing* (Open peer review edition, Fall 2013), http://webwriting2013.trincoll.edu/crossing-boundaries/coco-torres-2013/.

# Student Digital Research and Writing on Slavery

*Alisea Williams McLeod*

In Holly Springs, Mississippi, where Rust College (where I teach) is located, there are intact former slave dwellings still situated behind their respective "big houses."[1] For the last three years, I have invited students taking my Composition II (research and writing) course to go on a walking tour of the town. We have walked through both antebellum mansions and slave dwellings. Were it not for the tour, the students might not even know of the existence of these remnants of slavery. The students seldom find reason to venture into the town's old neighborhoods. The experiential study of history is part of an introduction I provide to the study of American slavery and African American Civil War experience, an ongoing research focus for the course. Students can choose to study this history as their course project or propose other topics. In the two years that I have offered the historical research option, about twenty percent of my students have elected it. When they do choose to participate, they become involved as student-researchers in the Eaton-Bailey-Williams Freedpeople's Transcription Project (hereafter referred to as the Freedpeople's Transcription Project or FTP). The project is named for John Eaton, Jr., General Superintendent of Freedmen. Two former slaves, Africa Bailey and Daniel Williams, were enlisted in Eaton's army unit. The families of Bailey and Williams lived at a "contraband" or refugee camp during the war; the names of their family members are included in the Register of Freedmen (ROF), the Civil War camp log upon which FTP is based.

FTP is my own research project, centered upon transcription and analysis of the ROF. This 1864 record includes names of more than 2,100 formerly enslaved persons living at Camp Shiloh in Memphis and the names of several hundred former masters. Since 2010, the transcribed ROF has been available online.[2] In the first year of student involvement, 2012, these emerging researchers were assigned to study slaveholders from Marshall County, where the college is located, as well as planters from two nearby

Tennessee counties: Shelby and Fayette. The objective of this second phase of FTP, following transcription, was to abstract, from eight to ten-page research papers, short (100 to 250-word) biographies to be freely published on a project wiki.[3] A collection of student-authored biographies, published at (but not written at) the project wiki, Digisense, would complement the transcribed and published ROF.[4] The biographies are transferred to the site rather than composed there. Most of the writing instruction students received was for the purposes of the longer, traditional paper; however, students were also given instruction and directives on authoring and publishing on the project site.[5] Because many of our students come from areas represented in the ROF, I considered the possibility that some might discover personal connections. This was a pedagogical goal that seemed in keeping with the main goals of FTP: giving history new dimension and reconnecting descendants, including student-researchers, to the past. Connections have occurred in both expected and unexpected ways. In theory, WikiSpaces are powerful platforms for disseminating knowledge of lost or obscure histories, but recovery and commitment to its lengthy process require buy-in from would-be student authors who may not be prepared to engage a cosmology and an epistemology of the past.[6]

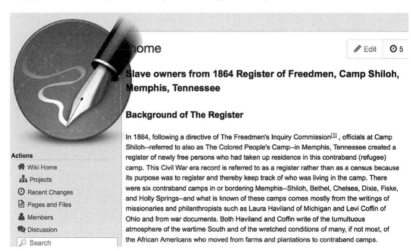

*The Digisense Wikispace.*

From the outset of this initiative I have been hyper-conscious of the ethics of merging teaching and learning within a college setting with what could be fairly viewed as social, digital activism. I find some justification for the merger in the pedagogy of service learning (SL). Still, I realize that unlike with perhaps other SL projects, even if a majority of my students do not discover a personal connection to the ROF, I am nudging them into a past they might—for conscious or unconscious reasons—rather not enter. Students electing not to do slavery research undoubtedly make such a choice for all kinds of reasons including simply having greater interests in other topics. However, it is plausible to suggest that they also, through such choice, exercise control over their own temporal constructions. Their choices and acts of temporal construction have a relationship to society, so it may be reasonable to expect that the level of interest students have in the topic of slavery may be influenced by the degree to which the larger society engages history. Other influences may include students' families and the professor's valuations of history communicated to students both knowingly and unknowingly.[7] My students' historical scholarship assists reconstruction of American and African American history while potentially reconstructing their own senses of time. I have no better proof of possible effects of the work of FTP on some students than from post-research survey comments and in conversations after the course had ended. The comments ranged from changed, more positive, attitudes about history, slavery, and the research process, to personal stories of mystical experiences. Of the twelve students involved the first year, half shared views and experiences that suggest they had become more deeply involved in the work than they had expected. However, disappointingly, of these six students, a majority chose to end involvement in the work after the course was over while two, who seemed from the beginning to have deep interest in and commitment to our subject, chose to continue working without course credit. While I feel confident in stating that these two students (as well as the others) exercised a right of choice in determining their focus for the course, I believe that an imminent infusion of history into American culture—through digitization and through social media as purveyor—may before long raise an issue of a students' right to his or her own temporality as we increase exposure to controversial, historical documents. Electing not to be an active purveyor of history through web writing/digitization may be a choice that appears quite rational in both modern and postmodern milieus, an allowance that Sara Ahmed gets at when she suggests that we are happily oriented toward certain objects and unhappily oriented toward others.[8] It is not difficult to believe that some students, if not all of them, are not happily oriented toward slavery, in which case moving them toward activism in this area may be a challenge from the outset.[9]

A significant factor preventing greater student involvement in FTP is their hesitance to buy into the idea of membership in the Digisense site, reluctance that has translated into most of them not uploading the biographies of the slaveholders assigned them. In fact, of the first group of student-researchers, only one uploaded his writing. With student permission obtained, I uploaded and published the work of some of the other students. The biographies were abstracted from the "Findings" section of the I-Search paper, which was due very near the end of the course. The longer paper was in fact the main work of the class, making up the bulk of the students' grades, and it included several steps (a bibliography and an annotated bibliography, for instance) and drafts. By comparison, the biography was worth only five percent of the grade, equal to a required PowerPoint presentation. Clearly, practical matters such as completing the various course assignments and consideration of incentives for performing well on one type of work versus another played a part in the low-level of participation by the students in the project wiki. When the course ended, I quickly realized that student buy-in could undoubtedly have been improved by weighting the wiki participation more heavily, placing it at the center of the course, and having it take the place of the PowerPoint. Issues of timing and student evaluation of requirements would be easy to fix. However, without department approval, I cannot substitute digital publication of the short biographies for the traditional paper (its structure, length, and purpose), radically moving the biographies from a placement, which may have felt to the students like an afterthought, to the center of our course activities. Changing student views of digital publication might be achieved through intense moral suasion—stronger statements by me concerning the potential value of our work to the public and also through conversation among colleagues about new formats for academic publication.

In a post-research survey, several students offered a somewhat surprising evaluation of the work of the course even without their own active participation in final digital publication.[10] One student, Larance, a social work major, wrote concerning a paucity of information currently available on American slave owners:

> Certain information should be available, and because slavery was such a big part of American history, the biography of a slave-owner should be one of those things. Such records should be kept accurate and able to be easily accessed by anyone, but in particular, African Americans.[11]

Larance's sense of "historical accountability" comes through in his statement, yet his expressed concern does not include a suggestion that persons like himself—students, African Americans, or private individuals—might become providers of the desired information.[12] Larance was one of several students who did not publish his research, and he was no longer involved in FTP after the course despite his having indicated on his survey that he would likely continue such research. I did not speak further with him about his decisions. While I would continue to see him around campus, he never again mentioned the topic of slavery. For most of his peers as well, involvement in the project and even conversation about it ended with the course.

However, two other students, Naomi and Joshua, both English majors, immediately expressed interest in continuing the work once the course ended. For Naomi, investigations into the life of Ebenezer Nelms Davis, one of the largest slave owners in Marshall County, had become political. She had been outraged to learn that Davis had owned a second plantation in Alabama. After finding that he had "refugeed" in Alabama during the war, she concluded that as war had approached, he had become even more committed to the institution. Before our course ended, she and another student, Terry—who was researching Mississippi Governor Joseph Matthews—engaged in several heated debates after class on the question of whether slave owners and slave holding were humane. A month after the end of the course, Naomi revised her initial paper for an upcoming undergraduate research conference; this time framing it around the central question of slavery and (in)humanity. Her biography of Davis would eventually be published at Digisense, but–like her other classmates–she expressed little interest in helping to develop the wiki. Rather, she seemed especially motivated by more traditional formats and publication. Joshua likewise prepared a paper for the conference. His strong interest in Internet research seemed to lead naturally to active involvement in the project wiki.

He was the only student to publish his work there without my nudging or assistance.

The level of student participation in our project wiki should not be the sole standard by which I judge the success either of Digisense or FTP. I had hoped to get this work underway at Rust because of the college's history and mission, its location, and the demographics of its student population. Despite not achieving the level of participation I had hoped for, I nevertheless revel in the fact that Naomi and Joshua have continued the research, even working on related papers in the summer of 2013 while studying as fellows at Emory. I see their conventional work as parallel with writings published at Digisense. This prompted me to consider whether more traditional forms of writing and publication better fit student purposes—a focus on course completion—and if more traditional writing assignments, because they have a clear beginning and ending and because they usually remain private, also are a buffer between the student and the public on the one hand and the student and uncertain elements (figurative or literal ghosts of the past) on the other hand. Simply put, I thought maybe students are reticent about allowing the public to read their writing even when it is offered anonymously. Entry into the public realm of the Internet may, in the minds of these students, decrease their sense of control over their work—who gets to view, comment, and evaluate it, as well as their active and serious participation in the universe of the Internet. Larance's comments, for instance, might be described as pre-activist in that he sees an injustice in need of redress, but he has not yet imagined himself as a public researcher or writer. His hesitance may involve several issues that include the difficulty of the topic of slavery. Additionally, there may be some concern not solely for protecting privacy but for protecting one's sense of self in history. While on the surface of things this possibility seems not to have been a concern for Joshua (who in fact has continually sought engagement with the public about our work), Naomi's view of public interest in her research is expressed in a description of her experience visiting one of the town's antebellum homes. In her conference paper, she wrote that she felt "swarmed" by Holly Springs' elite matrons and gentleman, who held her captive to their entreaties concerning the "better" sides of slavery and the benevolence of their ancestors.[13] Long after the visit, Naomi's experience as a researcher of slavery continued to be characterized by this same sense of being swarmed or overwhelmed if not by actual persons then by subconscious thoughts expressed mostly in her dreams. Joshua too indicated that the theme of slavery was surfacing in his dreams.

In the fall of 2012, Naomi and I were selected as William Winter Fellows. We later attended the 2013 Natchez Film and Literary Festival whose theme for the year was the Civil War in Film. At this point, Naomi continued experiencing a heightened sense of the past. As we traveled even deeper into the South, her feelings grew even more intense and she implored me to explain to future students who might become involved in FTP what she felt was a spiritual or mystical aspect of the work. I promised her that I would. I also explained that my neglect in doing so with her cohort was due to an assumed inappropriateness in bridging the spiritual and the academic, especially in a traditional research course involving mostly conventional methodology. It was not so much that I doubted students would disassociate themselves from anything "ghostly," but I doubted that the modern field of composition studies lacked a contemporary discourse for even broaching the topic of the spiritual in writing and research. Even while Naomi was attending and I was teaching at a private, religious-affiliated institution, I had found no easy way to suggest that taking, as Larance put it, "steps back into history," might in fact engage a cosmology and an epistemology more in keeping with my students' African ancestors than with the perspectives of their living elders or with the teaching practices of most of the professors at Rust. How might I reasonably suggest and defend a step back as a spiritual crossing of a delicate line between The Good Red Road of the living and the blue or black roads that are "the worlds of the grandfathers and grandmothers?"[14] Despite the fact that Rust is affiliated with the United Methodist Church, students at the college who profess a Christian faith do not appear to consider their own prayers to Spirit or their belief in Christ's transcendence of time and space as being related to academic work in which they might summon and engage ancestral spirits. The idea that writers and researchers might experience visitation or assistance from the spirit world might resonate with creative writers who insist on the reality of the muse, but how might one explain such experience as a part of "objective" research? Both in his paper and in subsequent conversations, Joshua suggested that we were indeed awakening sleeping dogs, an act about which his family had forewarned him. Although he expressed the deepest commitment to the work, he saw journeying into the past both as a movement back and as a reopening.[15]

One could certainly argue that engagement of the spiritual is a decentering of the subject or researcher. For many years, I have been intrigued by the research theory and practice of anthropologist Paul Stoller, who has suggested not that the ethnographer is merely decentered but that she is consumed.[16] Offering a sensual and embodied scholarship that challenges Cartesianism, Stoller goes beyond resurrection of the human body—as text—to an acceptance of the body as receiver of spirits. He writes, ". . . I argue that embodiment is not primarily textual; rather, the sentient body is culturally consumed by a world filled with forces, smells, textures, sights, sounds, and tastes, all of which trigger cultural memories."[17] Might it be appropriate to ask if the kind of information found in the ROF, as well as findings of my student-researchers concerning former slave owners, is experienced through the bodies of these students if not through their whole beings? And could this be the reason that a majority of them chose to limit their involvement in slavery research to the confines of our course? The challenger to Naomi's thesis concerning slavery and inhumanity, Terry, resurrecting Gov. Matthews, wrote of his own experience:

> It was almost as if I was living out his life through third person just by reading, and trying to imagine the things he had been through or seen. . . I couldn't put the book down or turn off my computer while doing research. However, I was still far from done with my journey traveling through this gentleman's life.[18]

As with Larance, Terry, a biology major, did not choose to continue his involvement in FTP despite or perhaps because of feeling, as Stoller suggests, consumed. In conversation with me, Terry expressed trouble with sleeping during his research experience. Focus and extra energy, their source or sources unclear, had kept him late into the night working on recovering the life of Gov. Matthews. During the course, Terry seemed to have given over control of his own habits of structuring time.

In the field of Rhetoric and Composition, scholars have renewed considerations of the once abstract concept of time and its potential role in the teaching of writing. Deborah Mutnick, arguing for a reconfiguration of a cultural polarity of academic writing and personal writing, suggests that Bakhtin's chronotope, or time and space, might be a way to invite young writers to engage "the personal" in the writing classroom.[19] Mutnick's appeal is part of ongoing debate of the place of the personal within composition, and in her approach to this question, a turn toward investigation of time and space in the lives of students, she perhaps unwittingly expands the universe of the classroom as she nudges students to go where they have perhaps not thought to or been encouraged to go before. On the one hand, this turn brings the political as well into the classroom in a new way since, as Mutnick explains, "worldviews and social realities are forged by the interaction of space and time, history and location, content and form."[20] Because students, like their instructors, are situated within certain temporalities, both constructed and acculturated, they cannot be said to be innocent of the implications of the worldviews and social realities that rely on the temporal and spatial constructions. Does this mean that neither I nor my student-researchers can claim innocence as some of them seek to keep history at bay and as I, at the same time, gently push them to engage it? Mutnick's sense of the value of the chronotope may be more worldly than spiritual; however, I think she would agree both that student writing about "the personal" might invite the spiritual and that teaching that suppresses the supernatural constructs time and space for students and perhaps teachers alike. It may be that most, if not all, of my students have accepted this order of things: an efficient world that leaves the pasts of those who were enslaved, as well as those who enslaved, unexplored. However, while Rust students taking my Composition II course may have had the option not to engage the topic of slavery, or to shy away from playing an active role in disseminating information on the subject within the digital sphere, ongoing digitization of historic records like the ROF make it all but inevitable that they, and the entire world, will soon have to confront problems and possibilities that come from widespread re-infusion of the historical. In his theorization of the work of archivists, James O'Toole writes that historians are just beginning to use records to understand the slave's point of view.[21] He is correct, and the digital universe promises that such use will multiply exponentially in the next few years and that the democratization of access to records is also likely to increase continually. Political, theological, and pedagogical implications of these two facts cannot be ignored if we intend our students to be digitally active.

*About the author: Alisea Williams McLeod is an assistant professor in the Humanities/English Division at Rust College in Holly Springs, Mississippi. She specializes in critical literacy and is especially interested in the ways that students and others construct time and space.*

How to cite:

Alisea Williams McLeod, "Student Digital Research and Writing on Slavery," in *Web Writing: Why and How for Liberal Arts Teaching and Learning*, ed. Jack Dougherty and Tennyson O'Donnell (University of Michigan Press/ Trinity College ePress edition, 2014), http://epress.trincoll.edu/webwriting/chapter/mcleod.

*See an earlier version of this essay with open peer review comments.*[22]

# Notes

1. Author's photos of Holly Springs, MS, Flickr, https://www.flickr.com/photos/peeling_paint/sets/72157629276541881.

2. "Register of Freedmen," Camp Shiloh, Memphis, Tennessee, circa 1864, *Last Road to Freedom* website, http://www.lastroadtofreedom.com/uploads/3/1/1/7/3117447/register_of_freedmen_ii.pdf.

3. McLeod, English 136 "Module Project: Researching and Remembering," Google Document, Rust College, Spring 2012, https://docs.google.com/document/d/1RP-I3SD7Gu319HQ-VRt8gBcxBRXJSrEmE3ksy2O9tAY/pub. This project also used Wikispaces, which are not edited by organizational editors or by the public without permission from the wiki owner (in this case, me).

4. "Marshall County, Mississippi, Slave Owners in the 1864 Register of Freedmen, Digisense wiki, http://digisense.wikispaces.com/Marshall%20County%20Mississippi%20Slave%20owners.

5. McLeod, "Authoring at WikiSpaces: Directions for Preparing Your Abstracted Biography," Google Document, https://docs.google.com/document/d/1ysOKwmS4RaLL9Xyq1F77OT_i32q0oHbdAD7DCNMrsYE/pub.

6. For more on this issue, read McLeod, "Structural Constraints," Google Document, https://docs.google.com/document/d/17Z-o0_TMQh7prTpRLLrkY0Y9GXo9HLnL2P5V6fkwI-c/pub.

7. McLeod, "Moving and Maybe Hoarding History," HASTAC blog, February 19, 2012, http://www.hastac.org/blogs/amcleod/2012/02/19/moving-and-maybe-hoarding-history.

8. Sara Ahmed, "Happy Objects," in *The Affect Theory Reader*, edited by Melissa Greg and Gregory J. Seigworth, 29-51 (Durham, NC: Duke University Press, 2010).

9. McLeod, "Barriers vs. Pathways to Student Digital Activism," HASTAC blog, May 15, 2014, http://www.hastac.org/blogs/amcleod/2014/05/15/barriers-vs-pathways-student-digital-activism.

10. Fifty-two percent of students enrolled in the course returned one of two separate surveys (based on research topic). Fifty percent of students conducting slavery research returned surveys, three choosing to respond anonymously.

11. This student and others gave permission for their names, survey responses, and papers to be used in this essay. Larance Carter, "The Life and Lineage of Matthew Lacy." Unpublished paper, Rust College, Holly Springs, Mississippi, April 18, 2012.

12. I borrow this term from James O'Toole, "Archives and Historical Accountability: Toward a Moral Theology," *Archavaria* 58 (Fall 2004): 4.

13. During the town's annual Pilgrimage, in which several antebellum mansions are opened to the public, Naomi and Joshua both visited Burton Place, owned by local attorney David Person, whose relatives held a slave by the name of Henry Totten. Naomi Rahn, "'To Treat the Slaves as Kindly as Their Conduct Will Allow': A Question of Humanity or Inhumanity." Unpublished paper presented at the Mid-South Undergraduate Research Conference, Southern Arkansas University, Magnolia, Arkansas, October 3-5, 2012. The title of Naomi's conference paper is taken from a contract between Ebenezer Davis and an overseer, which appears in the Audubon Mississippi/ Strawberry Plains Finley Collection, MUM01701, Series II, Department of Archives and Special Collections, University of Mississippi, http://www.flickr.com/photos/peeling_paint/ 14181934364.

14. Jamie Sams and David Carson, *Medicine Cards* (New York: St. Martin's Press, 1999), 13, 22.

15. Joshua Stampley Gardner, untitled, unpublished paper, Rust College, Holly Springs, Mississippi, April 18, 2012, 2.

16. Paul Stoller, *Sensuous Scholarship* (Philadelphia: University of Pennsylvania Press, 1997), 55.

17. Ibid, 55.

18. Terry Dent, "Is There a Good or Bad Slave Owner: A Questioning of Slave Owners." Unpublished paper, Rust College, Holly Springs, Mississippi, April 18, 2012, 5-6.

19. Deborah Mutnick, "Time and Space in Composition Studies: 'Through the Gates of the Chronotope,'" *Rhetoric Review* 25 (2006).

20. Ibid, 43.

21. O'Toole, 13.

22. McLeod, "Student Digital Research and Writing on Slavery," in *Web Writing* (Open peer review edition, Fall 2013), http://webwriting2013.trincoll.edu/crossing-boundaries/ mcleod-2013/.

# Web Writing as Intercultural Dialogue

*Holly Oberle*

My original motivation to begin experimenting with blogging in my classroom was twofold: first, a commitment to a feminist pedagogy and thereby a desire to explore alternative modes of the "classroom discussion," which has the tendency to alienate female students; and similarly, a desire to harness the cultural diversity of my students, especially those not inclined to speak, as a pedagogical resource in and of itself. The former stems from my academic interests in feminist linguistics and international relations; the latter from my personal experience of being an international student for seven years in four different countries. As an international student, I often found my personal blog to be one of few places where I was able to process culture shock. As an educator, my goal was to find a tool that had the potential to recalibrate the face-to-face discussion as well as foster more meaningful intercultural learning among diverse students. My experiment with web writing serves as a call for educators to treat their increasingly diverse classrooms as an instructional resource rather than a happy accident—a resource that can be (carefully) cultivated through the web. This essay explores the delicate relationship between diversity and the web and, by extension, the potential difficulties and risks of web writing in the liberal arts classroom.

## Defining Intercultural Dialogue

While the term "intercultural" is often used to refer to the interaction between people of different nationalities, I use it here to encompass not only the international, but also the exchange among those of different ethnicities, genders, sexual orientations, religions, and socioeconomic classes. Due to my own international orientation, however, the examples discussed herein focus on dialogue among different nationalities, but my strategies and recommendations can be applied to any form of diversity.

Diversity policies in higher education take on many forms including the recruitment of traditionally under-represented domestic populations as well as international students, institutional support structures targeting these students, and the development of curriculum designed to satisfy an intercultural learning requirement. These approaches aim not only to increase the number of students from different backgrounds, but also towards specific educational outcomes related to cultural awareness and identity exploration. However, there is little evidence to indicate that these desired outcomes are actually happening, an issue to which I will return shortly.

If diversity policies are designed to foster intercultural learning, the time has never been better than now. According to the Institute for International Education, the 2011-2012 academic year was witness to the largest ever enrollment of international students in the United States with nearly 765,000 students.[1] And a recent report from the Western Interstate Commission for Higher Education predicts that by 2020, 45 percent of high school graduates in the US will be "minorities," most of whom are destined for college admission.[2] These trends indicate both a challenge and a chance for educators to go beyond merely adding a "global perspective" to their curriculum and truly seize upon the increasingly diverse classroom as an avenue through which to achieve that perspective.

## Strange Bedfellows: The Web and Diversity Policies

The web and educational policies have a number of rather remarkable things in common. First, both have been credited with the power to foster a "global village:" a more inclusive global society and a space free of prejudice.[3] Perhaps it is because of this imagined outcome that both continue to aggressively shape the mission statements of institutions worldwide. And while the enthusiasm for the utopian vision of the web's potential has quelled somewhat, it is also finding new traction with the rise of Web 2.0 platforms and social media.[4]

Yet, as Selfe points out, the global village may be less about the dissolution of borders and more about the age-old American belief in technological progress as social progress.[5] Scholars are now fleeing the village for what

Van Alstyne and Brynjolfsson call "cyber-Balkans:" fiercely isolated and homogeneous groups identifying along more salient dimensions than mere geography.[6] Similarly, several have observed that students in otherwise diverse institutions tend to self-segregate along ethnic, religious, or even gendered lines, leaving the classroom as the most promising setting for cross-cultural exchange.[7]

I suspect that the failure of both the web and diversity programs to construct an open space for intercultural dialogue stems from the same root: the belief that simple contact with others will lead to significant cultural interactions.[8] This is a seductive theory to be sure. However, while contact is a productive first step, meaningful intercultural learning requires more. It demands thoughtful and deliberate approaches that are sensitive to a variety of learning styles as well as those that incentivize students to collaborate with those outside their normal circle. I have found that using strategically structured blogging assignments as a complement to, and at times, a substitute for, in-class discussion has the potential to prompt not only contact with others, but the *application* of these experiences towards a more sophisticated and culturally-informed understanding of the curriculum itself.

## Web Writing as Intercultural Dialogue: Exploring Women and Leadership

The following is a description of a web writing project that I have attempted to streamline over the teaching of several separate "Introduction to Gender and International Relations" classes taught in Berlin, Germany. These courses were always attended by students from multiple European countries, several North American exchange students, a significant number from the Middle East, and a few from elsewhere. This is a class that counts towards a diversity requirement for undergraduates and, for most, it is their very first exposure to gender studies. While the blogging assignment has certainly evolved since my first attempt, I still consider the specific structure of the assignment to be a work in progress.

I set up a restricted-access WordPress site to facilitate the course. The site is dedicated to two separate on-going web writing projects that progress throughout the semester, the first of which aims to create an "ethnography" of female leaders worldwide. First, I asked students to think about an influential woman in their own country or personal experience and to write a very short blog post about her. For example, an Indian student wrote about Sampat Pal Devi, the founder of a woman's activist organization in Northern India that trains women in self-defense and puts pressure on local police departments to more seriously address rape. Second, I asked students to review a handful of their peers' posts and to leave one to three questions in the comments section. Over the course of the next few weeks, the original posters were instructed to choose a few of the questions to respond to. I then assigned each student one of the women being discussed in the blog (apart from their own original contribution) and asked them to do a bit more digging and post content from the public web about her (if available), along with questions or comments on that article.

Following this exercise, we took a break from structured blogging (although students were encouraged to continue posting) and focused instead on in-depth class discussions and lectures on particularly theoretical or complex ideas. The examples and questions on the blog were continually brought into the face-to-face conversation or the lecture in an attempt to bridge the gap between the abstract ideas found in the required readings and the students' own lives. Educators often attempt to draw theory out of the clouds through the use of vivid examples, but this exercise utilized illustrations drawn directly from student's own work, narrowing that gap even further. We discussed why, for example, the majority of the Western students chose to blog about a female politician, while many of the non-Western students wrote about women in more varied capacities. this discussion was related to a reading on cultural and gendered definitions of leadership.[9]

I attempted to draw cultural comparisons between the ever-evolving research on the blog during class discussions. We compared the description of Sampat Pal Devi from the student-generated blog post with the media portrayals from the public web. The Indian student who wrote the original post pressed the Western students to explain why the American media portrays the Gulabi Gang, the organization Devi founded, as "vigilantes." In response, an American student pointed out that the American media was not always kind in its portrayal of Code Pink, a somewhat similar organization in the United States that challenges the priorities of authority figures. A conversation began about whether women are more peaceful than men. Various examples from nearly everyone's personal experiences were offered to either support this hypothesis or refute it. Although it was not on the original syllabus, I canceled the assignment for the following week and opted for a new reading that tackled the issue of women as peacekeepers and whether this is naturally or socially constructed.

Students were assigned yet another woman and this time they were asked to provide a lengthier piece of original research to be appended to the original post and the article from the public web, and the original posters were asked to review the research and make comments. This peer review system reinforces, once again, that students are not merely passive recipients of information but can also take on the role of the instructor and guide the research process. In my experience, students seem genuinely pleased to have a second opinion about their work from someone other than the professor.

Throughout this process, I attempted to allow the online discussions to unfold organically without much intervention unless necessary. If I felt that the blog, in general, or a certain line of discussion was getting off-track somehow, I endeavored to redirect it in class rather than through the blog. Admittedly, I did not even attempt to read every comment and every response. A particularly active group of students can easily produce hundreds of comments in a short period of time. I did not purposely read all the comments in order to facilitate a sense of ownership and accountability by the students for their peers and to contrast the authoritative style of in-class discussions and lectures, which are largely guided by the instructor.

## The Evidence of Intercultural Learning

No consensus has been reached as to what specifically constitutes "intercultural competence."[10] However, I find compelling evidence of intercultural competence in the students' final research papers. Before introducing the blog assignment, students would consistently write about either a person or event that the student had some sort of preexisting knowledge of, or they would ask me for a topic. After the blog assignment, students began writing their final papers on one of the women introduced by *other* students on the blog rather than their own original post. Because the women being researched were often local (and sometimes without even so much as a Wikipedia page), students had to rely on their peers as secondary sources, and these students directed their colleagues to local newspapers or websites to further their projects. I encouraged students to use their peer's comments from the blog as a resource to improve their papers and even cite them when appropriate.

Some of the international students later reported to me that they were completely taken aback by the fact that someone might find a local leader in their community worth researching. It seemed to improve their intellectual confidence, their sense of self-worth, and I also speculate that it might have helped them process culture shock. I believe this to be the case due to subtle changes in international students' behavior in class as well as the evolving nature of their writing, which can be easily traced using WordPress. Research suggests that international students, non-native English speakers, women and other traditionally under-represented groups can be hesitant about participating in face-to-face discussions due to individualist or combative argumentation styles, language ability, learning culture and general social adjustment factors.[11] Once their peers took a genuine interest in their lives and cultures, I noticed some of the previously hesitant students tentatively participating in face-to-face discussions on a more consistent basis. I also found that the more vocal students began to listen more in class, and I also noticed that as the blog took shape, the *quality* of everyone's written and oral contributions improved. Therefore, the blog was not just a way to accommodate students who are less inclined to speak in class; it seemed to elevate everyone's intellectual development.

Because this is a project that is almost entirely peer-facilitated, students are learning *from each other* and using their colleagues' experiences as the source of serious academic research. As Christopher Hager describes in this volume, students can begin to see themselves and their experiences as valuable sources of research and thereby *creators* of knowledge. Finally, some students developed an attachment throughout the semester with some of the women on the blog, and they were honestly interested in learning more about them. They requested that, with the author's permission, the final research papers be published on the blog so that the entire class could read them. When was the last time you had undergraduates *requesting* to read each other's final research projects?

## Public Versus Semi-Private Web Writing

While the web has blurred the boundaries between the public and the private, web writing need not be public in order to count as such. Due to concerns by German universities (and my own) about student privacy in regards to public blogging, links to or even screenshots of the project I discuss in this chapter are not available for public consumption. In fact, all of the blogs were permanently deleted two months following the conclusion of the course. Many of the contributors to this volume see the public aspect of web writing as one of the most compelling reasons for its adoption. With the exception of Jack Dougherty's chapter, few consider the potential legal and ethical consequences. Certain courses may benefit greatly from public engagement on the web. But as I have suggested, the web can be a rather hostile environment. Feminists have done a particularly good job at documenting the use of extreme sexist, racist, and abusive language on Twitter and elsewhere and how those attacks haunt victims in their real lives.[12] As someone who has been on the receiving end of such language on the web, I am not prepared to subject my students to the potential trauma that cyber-balkanization poses as they grapple with complex issues that are often directly relevant to their own lives and identities. In this sense, web writing is not always as reflective and accountable as we might hope. Furthermore, we should not underestimate the conceivable consequences of a blog post written by a young undergraduate that, without the benefit of context, might appear insensitive, ignorant, or even offensive. We know that companies are now Googling potential hires and even requesting access to their Facebook page. Therefore, we should assume that any public writing will be used to evaluate a student's credentials, a practice which could either help or severely hurt a student's future career prospects.

Keeping a course's web writing amongst the immediate participants allows students to "experiment" with public writing before throwing themselves into the multifarious and unpredictable world of the Internet. Writing within the safe space of the course also gives them the opportunity to properly reflect on the nature of public writing before actually doing it. When students see how their peers respond to their writing, they are given the opportunity to consider how to communicate clearly in order to avoid being misunderstood, and they learn how to keep web discussions on topic and to be respectful. Part of our mission in molding more culturally competent students should also be producing more thoughtful digital citizens, but this requires guidance. To this end, I plan to incorporate Storify into future classes to demonstrate how a seemingly innocuous tweet can quickly go viral and how sexism and racism can fuel the epidemic.[13]

However, while I plan to continue to keep class blogs closed, the contributions to this volume have inspired me to think of creative ways to broaden my student's audience in ways that do not risk their privacy or their integrity. I think the best way to accomplish this is to maintain a private course blog for safe reflection and peer review, and then filter that content into existing public infrastructures with clear guidelines. The result of my ethnography project is a loose but remarkably profound collection of under-researched women from all over the world. Considering that Wikipedia has a well-known "woman problem" among other biases,[14] I may follow Siobhan Senier, also in this volume, and encourage students to use their blogging assignment as a stepping stone towards contributing to the Wikipedia and improve upon the site's breadth and global scope. Finally, I would like to utilize Global Voices Online in future courses. This community of international bloggers brings together young, voluntary writers who contribute unique stories with a particular focus on those parts of the world the professional media tends to ignore. Not only does the site provide a wealth of creative stories to inspire further inquiry by my students, they may also suggest topics from their own countries and perhaps even make contributions. In my view, Global Voices provides a model for how intercultural web writing should be done.[15]

## Choosing the Right Platform

Issues of privacy and culture provoke the question, "What sort of web-based platform should we use to best accomplish our pedagogical goals?" If our goal is to employ intercultural exchange as an educational resource, the tool we use to achieve this end must be deliberately collaborative in nature, flexible in its architecture, and able to accommodate both horizontal and vertical content sharing.

It is for this reason that I use WordPress rather than an existing Learning Management System (LMS). While LMS platforms may be secure and private, they also tend to be rather rigid and primarily designed for administrative efficiency rather than student-generated activities.[16] In short, Learning Management Systems are a remnant of a Cartesian epistemology, while blogging sites such as WordPress represent the shift towards social learning. Many Learning Management Systems by now include interactive elements such as discussion boards, wikis, and even integration with social media, but I often feel as though these additions are after-thoughts rather than part of the system's philosophical underpinnings. WordPress has proved to be extremely adaptable for any number of purposes due to its openness, simplicity, and endless options for customization. Most importantly for my purposes, WordPress is easy enough to learn for those students with no previous experience, and does not operate with any sort of preexisting workflow except that which the user defines. The former is important because it needs to be accessible to all students of varying degrees of digital literacy; the latter is important so as to inspire critical thinking rather than forcing students into a strict and predefined pattern. I also like WordPress because, with only minimal effort, it can be made to look professional and unique, which I find encourages students to participate because it is easier for them to imagine it as *their* space, rather than an institutional one.

This is not to suggest that WordPress is a flawless platform or that there is no room for an LMS in the modern classroom. In fact, a platform that blends the best of both worlds might be the most productive. There are now WordPress/LMS plugins and some universities are beginning to utilize the metrics and automation features of an LMS and feed that information into course-specific and student-owned blogs.[17] But as a tool to harness cultural diversity in the classroom, most Learning Management Systems are too steeped in institutional culture rather than student culture to be suitable.

## Some Conclusions and Cautions

In summary, the best promise to inspire meaningful intercultural dialogue in the classroom is an expansive repertoire of teaching methods; one of which should include writing on the web. Fusing traditional pedagogy with web-based methods has the potential to accommodate different learning backgrounds, develop better dialogue among diverse students, and cultivate more responsible users of technology.

We should approach web writing with the full knowledge that the web is not a value-free or powerless environment. Even the most well designed online forums can be just as intimidating as face-to-face conversation, and the voices of traditionally under-represented groups can easily dissolve into consensus as defined by all the usual power structures from the real-world. As web writers, we must resist the naive and indeed Western perception of technology as the "great leveler." I see web writing as a medium that can prompt intercultural dialogue, but that dialogue must extend from the digital to the physical classroom in order to be effective. Thus, as students write more on the web and bring those insights into the "real" world, it is essential that we constantly interrogate our relationship to the digital and make our students not only culturally sensitive individuals, but sensitive and critical users of technology as well.

*About the author: Holly Oberle is the author of College Abroad, a guide for American students who wish to fully enroll in university outside the United States. She also is a Ph.D. candidate at the Free University in Berlin, a teaching fellow at the Asian University for Women in Bangladesh, and has lived and studied in Hungary, Israel, and Spain.*

### How to cite:

Holly Oberle, "Web Writing as Intercultural Dialogue," in *Web Writing: Why and How for Liberal Arts Teaching and Learning*, ed. Jack Dougherty and Tennyson O'Donnell (University of Michigan Press/Trinity College ePress edition, 2014), http://epress.trincoll.edu/webwriting/chapter/oberle.

*See an earlier version of this essay with open peer review comments.*[18]

# Notes

1. Institute of International Education, "International Student Enrollment Trends, 1949/50-2011/12," Open Doors Report on International Educational Exchange, http://www.iie.org/opendoors.

2. The increasing racial diversity will mostly come from students of Hispanic, Asian, and Pacific-Islander decent, while white and black enrollment is expected to decrease. Eric Hoover, "Wave of Diverse College Applicants Will Rise Rapidly," *Chronicle of Higher Education*, January 10, 2013, http://chronicle.com/article/Wave-of-Diverse-College/136603/.

3. On the Internet as a "global village," see Nicholas Negroponte, *Being Digital* (New York: Random House, 1996); as it relates to international education, see Richard Pearce, "Developing Cultural Identity in an International School Environment," in *International Education: Principles and Practices*, eds. Mary Hayden and Jeff Thompson (London: Kogan Page, 1998), 60-83. For an early assessment of how these two mediums can work together to foster tolerance, see Ringo Ma, "Computer-Mediated Conversations as a New Dimension of Intercultural Communication between East Asian and North American College Students," in *Computer-Mediated Communication: Linguistic, Social, and Cross-Cultural Perspectives*, ed. Susan C. Herring (Amsterdam: John Benjamins Publishing Co., 1996), 173-186.

4. John Seely Brown and Richard P. Adler, "Open Education, the Long Tail, and Learning 2.0," *Educause Review* 43, no. 1 (2008), 16-32, http://open.umich.edu/oertoolkit/references/mindsonfire.pdf.

5. Cynthia L. Selfe, "Lest we Think the Revolution is Revolution: Images of Technology and the Nature of Change." in *Passions, Pedagogies, and 21st Century Technologies*, eds. Gail E. Hawisher and Cynthia L. Selfe (Logan, UT: Utah State University Press, 1999), 292-322.

6. Marshall Van Alstyne and Erik Brynjolfsson, "Global Village Or Cyber-Balkans? Modeling and Measuring the Integration of Electronic Communities," *Management Science* 51, no. 6 (2005), 851-868, http://dx.doi.org/10.1287/mnsc.1050.0363.

7. Rona Tamiko Halualani et al., "Who's Interacting? And What are They Talking about?—Intercultural Contact and Interaction Among Multicultural University Students," *International Journal of Intercultural Relations* 28, no. 5 (2004), 353-372, http://dx.doi.org/10.1016/j.ijintrel.2004.08.004; CindyAnn R. Rose-Redwood and Reuben S. Rose-Redwood, "Self-Segregation Or Global Mixing?: Social Interactions and the International Student Experience," *Journal of College Student Development* 54, no. 4 (2013), 413-429, http://dx.doi.org/10.1353/csd.2013.0062.

8. This is known as the "contact hypothesis" and remains influential among sociologists and psychologists. Gordon W. Allport, *The Nature of Prejudice* (Cambridge: Addison-Wesley, 1958).

9. I realize that dividing the world into Western and non-Western borders on Orientalism. For the purpose of brevity, I ask the reader's forgiveness with this glib terminology.

10. Patricia M. King, Rosemary J. Perez and Woo-jeong Shim, "How College Students Experience Intercultural Learning: Key Features and Approaches." *Journal of Diversity in Higher Education* 6, no. 2 (2013), 69-83, http://dx.doi.org/10.1037/a0033243.

11. Maureen Snow Andrade, "International Students in English-Speaking Universities Adjustment Factors," *Journal of Research in International Education* 5, no. 2 (2006), 131-154, http://dx.doi.org/10.1177/1475240906065589.

12. See for example Jill Filipovic, "Blogging while Female: How Internet Misogyny Parallels Real-World Harassment," *Yale Journal of Law & Feminism* 19 (2007), 295-303.

13. For one example from Storify, https://storify.com, see Zen Vuong, "Suey Park's 'Hashtag Activism' Brings Racism Out of the Woodwork," *Storify*, April 5, 2014, http://www.pasadenastarnews.com/media/20140404/suey-parks-hashtag-activism-brings-racism-out-of-the-woodwork.

14. Stine Eckert and Linda Steiner, "(Re)Triggering Backlash: Responses to News about Wikipedia's Gender Gap," *Journal of Communication Inquiry* 37, no. 4 (October 01, 2013), 284-303, http://dx.doi.org/10.1177/0196859913505618.

15. Global Voices Online, http://globalvoicesonline.org.

16. I am not alone in this observation. See Lanny Arvan, "Dis-Integrating the LMS," *EDUCAUSE Quarterly* 32, no. 2 (2009); Lisa Lane, "Insidious Pedagogy," *First Monday* 14, no. 10 (2009), http://firstmonday.org/ojs/index.php/fm/article/view/2530/2303.

17. For specific examples, see John Mott, "Envisioning the Post-LMS Era: The Open Learning Network," *Educause Review* (2010), http://www.educause.edu/ero/article/envisioning-post-lms-era-open-learning-network.

18. Oberle, "Web Writing as Intercultural Dialogue," in *Web Writing* (Open peer review edition, Fall 2013), http://webwriting2013.trincoll.edu/crossing-boundaries/oberle-2013/.

*Citation and Annotation*

# The Secondary Source Sitting Next To You

*Christopher Hager*

Like a lot of people who teach in the humanities, I have spent years complaining about the ways my students use secondary sources in their research papers. Most often, a choice excerpt gets dropped into a paragraph with only quotation marks separating it from the surrounding prose. Slightly better, a student may call out the author of the source—"Smith writes, 'The Great Gatsby is a scathing critique of the American Dream'"—without showing any awareness of what Smith has to say beyond the single quoted sentence. Students come to my office hours and tell me, "I'm not too worried about this paper—I found some good sources and have a lot of quotes that support my point." When I explain why a writer shouldn't be citing only those sources which support his or her point, the student sitting my office generally looks at me as if I am extolling the virtues of driving on the wrong side of the road. Why cite a source, the student seems to think, if not to borrow its authority for my argument?[1]

Cobbling together isolated, disconnected "quotes" to produce a research paper is not just a bane of writing teachers. It is symptomatic of students' deficiencies in what many librarians now refer to as "information literacy." Researchers with The Citation Project studied a sample of student writing and found (unsurprisingly, any humanities professor will probably say) that students virtually never summarize entire sources but rather pluck individual sentences out of them for quotation or paraphrase—raising the question of whether student researchers actually *read* their sources or merely skim them for useful bits. Wendy Holliday and Jim Rogers have observed tendencies among students—and, to an extent, among writing instructors and librarians—to talk about "finding sources" rather than "learning about" a subject. The consequence, they argue, is that sources become "reified as objects"—of which, in many common assignments, students are required to track down and cite some minimum number. When students regard sources as acquisitions toward a quota, they do not see them as ideas, outcomes of a fellow researcher's analysis, or reflections of an author's scholarly agenda.[2]

## An Experiment

A few years ago, when I was preparing to teach one of my college's First-Year Seminars, I asked myself: what am I most dissatisfied with about students' preparedness for my courses, and how could I try to prepare them better at their point of entry into college? It was this shallow and utilitarian relationship to secondary sources that I wanted to change, and I decided that changing it would be the hidden curriculum of my seminar on a single year in American history and literature, "1862: America Undeceived." I had also been interested, for a variety of reasons, in moving more of my students' writing on to the public web, and I conceived an idea to marry the two goals.

If I could "publish" my students' writing—and I very easily could, using WordPress—could students see their peers' essays as secondary literature? If I asked them to cite sources written by the very people sitting next to them in the classroom—to see "sources" as the work of actual peers, rather than of invisible "authorities"—would they begin to regard those sources not just as reservoirs of ready-to-use quotations but as the products of particular thinkers' research processes, inflected by particular points of view?

In a two-part assignment that was the centerpiece of my seminar, I first asked the fifteen students to conduct primary-source research on the events of a single day in 1862. They used digitized newspapers and periodicals, among other sources, to locate artifacts of their chosen day. They practiced writing about these artifacts in blog posts (on Moodle, my college's course management system—visible only to other students in the class). After a series of in-class workshops focused on these blogs—designed to model and teach effective description and interpretation of primary sources—the students crafted essays reporting their research on single days. These essays were posted to a WordPress site near the middle of the semester, and they became required reading for the class.

In the second phase of the assignment, the students had to construct an argument about continuity or change over time in 1862. They needed to cite at least three essays written by their peers (about three different days), supplementing that with additional secondary research. These final essays were published online, too, to form a student-authored anthology on America in 1862.[3]

# 1862: America Undeceived

a student-authored anthology on Civil-War America

Home    Part I: Days at a Time    Appendix: the Assignment

*The student-authored anthology, "1862: American Undeceived."*

My most basic goal was that students would leave the course with a clear understanding of the difference between primary and secondary sources. Further, I hoped that, when students cited their peers in the final essays, they would be highly aware that their "secondary sources" were not the final word on how to interpret historical material. They would have seen the research process behind each source, beginning with the blog posts in which their fellow authors initially described their primary sources. Students reading a peer's essay might see that the peer had further developed or even changed his or her analysis since the blogging stage.

I also aimed for students to understand that research is the work of a scholarly community. Their anthology would be, necessarily, an interconnected web of cross-referenced research. I announced to the seminar at the outset that, at the end, I would measure each class member's "impact factor" —

how many times was each of the first-round essays cited during the second phase? — and award a prize to the most frequently cited author.[4]

## Its Results

What were this experiment's outcomes? In certain respects, they were disappointing. A majority of students (about 10 out of 15) persisted in engaging with secondary sources—the work of their peers—primarily by quoting isolated excerpts. At worst, a few students only re-used primary source material from peer essays ("quoted in. . .") or cited their fellow students' work as the source for such information as that 22,000 men died at the Battle of Antietam.

In other respects, the results were more satisfying. The students' final essays *did* evince a greater tendency (compared with my experience giving research assignments to other beginning college students) to assimilate research and adapt it to new ends. Even those students who primarily only quoted from their peers' work, as opposed to summarizing it, were not lining up those quotations to bolster a prefabricated thesis they had hatched. Most of them were drawing connections among multiple researchers' analytical assertions, if only at the level of isolated sentences. In some of the best essays, students apprehended both the information and the point of view in their peers' essays and—as good researchers do—applied that information in other contexts. One student, writing about the role of religion in Americans' endurance of the Civil War, cited a peer's essay about December 25, 1862. The student summarized part of that essay ("argues that Christmas gave soldiers a break from the harsh realities of war"), quoted a relevant portion of it, and adduced soldiers' Christmas celebrations as evidence of Americans' recourse to religious observances for coping with the duration of the conflict.

It pleased me to see my students taking each other seriously and treating their peers as authorities. The student writer I just mentioned engaged with her peer's work (the Christmas essay) no differently than she did (in back-to-back paragraphs) with the work of James McPherson, one of the most eminent living Civil War historians. In this sense, the class really did come to function as a small scholarly community. Although my students were universally unaware of the role "impact factor" plays as a metric in academic literature, and at first only dimly grasped the idea that citations register kinds of influence, my end-of-term review showed that they had been astute readers of their secondary sources. Although I feared they might tend to cite mainly the essays from which they found it easy to pull quotations—ones about high-profile topics, for instance — the essay with the highest impact factor turned out to be the one to which I had given the highest grade: a subtle analysis with little topical connection to other students' essays but with a thoughtful and illuminating perspective.

There were some ancillary benefits of this assignment, too. Although its effectiveness in addressing the problems I set out to tackle was mixed, it had an apparently positive impact on other aspects of students' writing. In evaluating the seminar, one student reported feeling "very motivated to do great work since I knew all my classmates were going to see my work." Another found that seeing—and reading carefully—other students' essays "allowed me to get a better grasp for what I was and was not doing right in my own writing." And several students appreciated the way in which online publication dignified their writing. As one student put it, turning student writing into assigned reading was a way of "giving our hard work the credit it deserves."[5]

As an intervention in students' information literacy, then, the experiment was at best partially successful. It was not powerful enough—at least as a one-time exercise—to dislodge all students' habits in writing research papers. Those who see "research" as plucking quotations from sources will not easily be transformed into deep readers of secondary literature. A First-Year Seminar may not have been the ideal setting in which to try this, and I hope to undertake something similar with more advanced students.

The assignment seems to have been more successful as a form of academic socialization. It did literalize the metaphor of scholarly "conversation." And it definitely succeeded in getting students to assimilate new knowledge and adapt it to new contexts. They really *read* and synthesized their secondary sources. This success may not have been an effect of the assignment's web-based dimension at all, or even of its peer-authorship feature. Probably more important is that I did not ask the students to begin their research by coming up with a topic. Unlike the classic research-paper sequence (choose a topic, go find sources, then write paper), in effect I gave the class a finite repository of sources — their own first-round essays — in which they had to find meaning. The assignment redirected students' energy from *finding sources* to understanding what the sources had to say. That restriction of scope is not exactly a feature of doing a web-based assignment—almost the contrary—but web-based publishing did ease the logistics of it.

*About the author: Christopher Hager is an associate professor of English and co-director of the Center for Teaching and Learning at Trinity College. He is the author of* Word by Word: Emancipation and the Act of Writing.

## How to cite:

Christopher Hager, "The Secondary Source Sitting Next To You," in *Web Writing: Why and How for Liberal Arts Teaching and Learning,* ed. Jack Dougherty and Tennyson O'Donnell (University of Michigan Press/Trinity College ePress edition, 2014), http://epress.trincoll.edu/webwriting/chapter/hager.

*See an earlier version of this essay with open peer review comments.*[6]

# Notes

1. An earlier version of this essay first appeared in Christopher Hager, "The Secondary Source Sitting Next to You," *MediaCommons*, May 20, 2013, http://mediacommons.futureofthebook.org/question/what-does-use-digital-teaching-tools-look-classroom/response/secondary-source-sitting-next.

2. Rebecca Moore Howard, Tricia Serviss, and Tanya K. Rodrigue, "Writing from Sources, Writing from Sentences," *Writing and Pedagogy* 2.2 (2010): 177-192. Holliday and Rogers, "Talking about Information Literacy: the Mediating Role of Discourse in a College Writing Classroom," *Libraries and the Academy* 13.3 (2013): 257-271; quotations on 257 and 262. Also see Barbara Fister, "From Conversations to Things," *Inside Higher Ed*, 2 December 2013, http://www.insidehighered.com/blogs/library-babel-fish/conversations-things-0.

3. "1862: America Undeceived: A student-authored anthology on Civil War America," First-Year Seminar with Christopher Hager, Trinity College, Fall 2012, http://commons.trincoll.edu/1862. I opted to publish the essays anonymously (they appear online as having been posted by me or by Sophie Goldsmith, the peer mentor for the seminar) and told students they could request to

have their byline added. None requested this. Although authorship is not publicly identified, students in the class *did* know the authorship of all the Part I essays, because they knew which of their peers were working on which dates. Therefore, most students' names do appear on the public web—in the Part II essays in which they are cited by their fellow students.

4. The prize? A complete DVD set of Ken Burns's PBS miniseries, *The Civil War*.

5. Student course evaluations and emails, FYSM 207: "1862: America Undeceived," Fall 2012, Trinity College.

6. Hager, "The Secondary Source Sitting Next to You," in *Web Writing* (Open peer review edition, Fall 2013), http://webwriting2013.trincoll.edu/citation-annotation/hager-2013/.

# Web Writing and Citation

*The Authority of Communities*

*Elizabeth Switaj*

The web is made of citations. Without citations, there would be a world-wide collection of unconnected digital spaces instead of a web. Hypertext markup language (HTML) would be text markup language. In the online world, citation is not an arbitrary requirement enforced by authority figures but, rather, a necessary, community-based value. The communities and cultures that come together online tend to value citation, even if they do not value copyright. Downloading a movie is fine; claiming to have made it is not.

Despite the importance of citation to its organization and architecture, the Internet has often been blamed for plagiarism.[1] Certainly students can copy and paste passages from websites and other digital documents more easily than from printed matter. Instead of looking at the influence of the web and digital cultures as a problem to be solved, however, instructors should take advantage of the importance of citation in online communities to help students understand the logic behind different ways of crediting sources and to help them see that, while academic citation formats may seem esoteric and arbitrary, they are akin to practices in which students who are active online engage on a daily basis. In other words, web writing presents an opportunity to teach citation as a community practice—and to make giving credit something students want to do, rather than something they have to do. In composition and writing-intensive courses, this goal can be reached by studying existing web writing, producing web writing embedded within existing communities, and by developing a unique set of citation standards based on the class's authority as a community.

Traditional ways of teaching citation are authoritarian and follow what Paulo Freire called the "banking model" of education.[2] Knowledge is treat-

223

ed as a set quantity; citation standards are depicted as unchanging ideals that must be deposited into students' minds. Teaching citation through observation of and participation in online communities, by contrast, acknowledges that expectations for giving credit depend upon culture and community. By allowing students to engage with the logic of citation in different communities instead of asking them to follow regulations, instructors prepare them to discuss and debate the role of citation. Students can contribute to our understanding of what citation should be if we give them the tools to understand current expectations and the reasons for them. This approach resembles the one taken by Gerald Graff and Cathy Birkenstein's *They Say / I Say* in that it focuses on teaching students how to join conversations in their writing.[3] Where it differs is in locating these conversations specifically within communities and in viewing these communities as authorities on the rules of these discussions. Such a focus could be achieved without the online element, but using web writing for this task makes explicit the connections between students' activities outside the classroom and the practice of citation in academic writing. Also, on the Internet, conversations happen faster and more visibly, making the communities in which they take place easier to observe and participate in, especially given the time limitations imposed by semesters or quarters.

Communities develop citation standards, and authorities codify them. A number of examples of these two aspects of the development of expectations for giving others credit online can be given to students. Ryan Cordell has described using examples from social media to explain citation practices to students: "You wouldn't steal somebody's post on Twitter, he explains to them. Instead you mark it with 'RT,' for retweet. Same with Facebook: 'If you get something cool from someone, you tag them.'" Academic citation, similarly, shows where ideas comes from.[4] Descriptions of the connections between the logic of academic and of social-media citation can be much more detailed, however.

The history of citation on Twitter provides examples of the importance of citation and of various kinds of citation practices. Users quote each other by retweeting. This feature only became automatic a few years ago. Originally, retweeting had to be done manually, by copying text and prefacing it with "RT @[username]"—a convention that became widespread on Twitter within a year of its launch. Some people on Twitter still use this method, especially when they want to add a comment before the quotation. (Sometimes the comment is placed afterwards, with a character such as "|" dividing the quoted material from the original.) "RT" is changed to "MT" ("modified tweet") when the wording is altered. Less commonly used, and originating with blogs, are "via" and "h/t" ("hat tip") to denote intermediary sources. The early development of "RT" by Twitter users illustrates how much online communities value giving credit. The distinctions between "RT," "MT," and "via" or "h/t" show the value placed on accuracy in giving credit; they can be compared to academic citation practices for quotations, paraphrased passages, and intermediary sources. Including "@[username]" also creates a conversation, since the cited user receives a notification of the tweet from Twitter. Scholarly citation, too, is a kind of conversation, though a less efficient one. On Twitter, linking to external articles is also a citational practice, especially when those links are prefaced with a quotation from or summary of the piece. This particular practice, however, is about more than credit: the whole article provides an additional, fuller context as well. One of the purposes of citation in both online and academic communities is to allow one's readers to access one's sources. Finally, Twitter provides an example of how academic citation standards are formed by communities, as the Modern Language Association (MLA) released a standard style for citing tweets due to demands from the community that uses the MLA style. Discussing this particular example also provides an opportunity to illustrate that academic disciplines form communities.

At the same time, not every borrowing of material on Twitter needs to be cited. Memes in which specific phrases or pictures are played with to respond to different situations are rarely credited to their creators. No one ever provides a citation when they do something "for great justice." Memes are an example of the kind of intertextuality that Susan Blum refers to when she describes students quoting media to each other without the kind of boundaries between the speaker's and others' ideas that academic writing requires.[5] In fact, web communities regard memes as a kind of common knowledge. Some pieces of common knowledge are, as Amy England argues, used to proclaim membership in a discourse community.[6] Only someone who is new to a community, and thus not fully cognizant of the community's standards and assumptions, would think that I invented Serious Cat if I tweeted a picture of him with the caption "Serious Cat. He's seriously common knowledge."[7] Teaching how the discourse community determines what is considered common knowledge presents a challenge for teaching, as students without direct experience within said community will struggle to judge precisely what knowledge is considered common. New members of online and academic communities should proceed cautiously, citing whenever in doubt and checking with more experienced community members along the way.

In addition to describing the history of citation within a particular digital community, instructors can also assign students to observe and describe the citation practices of specific communities. The description can take the form of an essay, a blog post, or an oral presentation and can be completed individually or in small groups. In any case, making this project public (through an unprotected blog post or a recorded presentation uploaded to YouTube, for example) will potentially allow members of the community discussed to comment on whether they believe the students have accurately described their expectations. Students might also contact community members directly and quote or paraphrase them in their reports. Having students explore and consider the role of citation on the web in this way allows them to understand more deeply the uses of citation (perhaps even discovering functions unknown to the instructor) and to develop their abilities to adapt to the expectations for citation of different communities.

Online communities also provide examples of what happens when expectations for giving credit are violated, and when members of a community hold different expectations. A widely debated case occurred when white feminist blogger Amanda Marcotte of Pandagon was accused of plagiarizing the work of a woman of color blogger who, at the time, went by the pseudonym Brownfemipower.[8] The ensuing discussions, which took place in posts and comments on numerous blogs, considered not only the precise definition of plagiarism but also how issues of power and privilege affect citation. For many in the communities drawn into this debate, citing commentators who represent less-heard perspectives is a matter of social justice. A blogger for major feminist blog *Feministe*, going under the name Holly (no surname), related the controversy to a broader context in which ideas espoused by people of color are not heard, let alone valued, until a white person restates them.[9]

During the Spring 2014 semester, I divided my ENG 102: Composition II course at the College of the Marshall Islands into small groups to write rhetorical analyses of blog posts about this controversy, using a Google Drive document to collaborate. This assignment could also be used in various cultural studies courses. After students read each other's analyses, they discussed the issue and generally agreed that it mattered less whether something can be labeled plagiarism and mattered more that failure to pay attention to what someone else has said on a subject, and to demonstrate that attention through citation, is disrespectful. Asked how such actions differ from their collaborative writing, since Google Drive does not record who wrote which sentence, students pointed out that they had agreed to work together—if they had so wished, they could have each written a paragraph and signed it—while in the case discussed no such agreement had been made.

Failing to cite someone else's work on a subject, whether through intentional plagiarism or a failure to fully explore what had already been written, can be disenfranchising. Good citation requires good research first, and while the precise definition of plagiarism does matter, it is more important that students understand how to cite well. Instead of teaching the avoidance of plagiarism, we must teach the practice of good research and citation so that when students, through their writing, participate in conversations they do so as conscientious members of the communities in which they are writing.

Having explored community-based citation practices online, classes can consider the distinction between these expectations and the legal standard of copyright. Sometimes, copyright overlaps these expectations. For example, in the Cooks Source case, a small magazine copied content from food bloggers without permission or sufficient credit; the initial discovery of a theft of material led to a crowdsourced search for examples of plagiarized content. Traci Gardner has described a lesson-plan on plagiarism, the Internet, and the public domain based around this controversy. Gardner suggests a number of pages on the incident that students can read before answering such questions as, "Where are public domain materials on the Internet?" and "When do you need permission [to reproduce others' work]?"[10] In contrast to that situation, sometimes copyright stifles discussions within communities—perhaps the most famous academic case being that of the James Joyce Estate. While many of us would prefer to live in a more ideal world where alternative sharing-based models such as Creative Commons or Copyleft reign, students should still be aware of the potential implications of copyright law for any public web-writing they might produce.

Once students have practiced observing and analyzing the citation practices of online communities, and understand the implications of copyright for citation practices, the next step is for them to produce work embedded in such communities. Doing so provides students with the experience of meeting standards and (potentially) being corrected by peers and authorities beyond the classroom. Moreover, as they become more involved in these communities, they also become more likely to continue participating and writing in them even after the course concludes. Online communities, even ones without specifically pedagogical aims, can support life-long learning.

Given that citation matters so much to Wikipedia that the community's designation for insufficiently sourced information ("[citation needed]") became the subject of a web comic that spurred a meme, Wikipedia may seem to be an ideal community for this kind of project. Indeed, plagiarism and insufficient citation are often caught quickly by Wikipedians. Recently, however, there has been some negativity among active, experienced Wikipedia editors towards such assignments. They believe student editors are more prone to making flawed edits that have to be reverted.[11] These stories can be used to frame assignments that involve editing Wikipedia pages in order to emphasize the need to understand and follow the community's standards. Siobhan Senier's "Indigenizing Wikipedia" essay (in this volume) describes one possible assignment that engages with community standards about what kinds of sources need to be cited to establish notability in particular. My own favorite Wikipedia assignment to give students is embedded in a longer research project. I require students to consult the site as part of their initial research. Then, after they complete the bulk of their secondary research, they must return to the articles they read and add any new information they have found. This process allows them to see not only that citation matters (as failure to cite sources will result in their edits being reverted) but also how to gauge the value of Wikipedia articles more accurately. Because the original articles vary in quality, I either use this assignment as an ungraded in-class activity or grade students based on a reflection paper.

Another way to allow students to produce web-writing embedded in communities is for students to begin their own blogs, or contribute to a group blog, designed to be part of a specific blogosphere (feminist, fandom, etc.). The disadvantage of this assignment is that, at least at first, the writing will be less immersed in the community; fewer readers from the community means fewer chances for the community to react to violations of its expectations for giving credit. The advantage is that, in order to make their blogs part of a community, students must cite blogs already established in the community, especially through links within blogposts that send trackback comments; they must, in other words, conduct online research and participate in ongoing conversations.

At the same time that students writing publicly can participate in outside communities, a class creating web writing forms its own community. The classroom community is entitled to create its own standards for citation, though the development of these standards has to be constrained somewhat by membership in broader institutional and academic communities. It would be a disservice to allow students to decide, for instance, that they should be allowed to copy and paste whatever they want without any credit (and if students did suggest such a standard, it would likely indicate that they had not taken the assignment to develop standards seriously).

Demanding that students use an existing citation style can cause developing writers anxiety and, especially given the proliferation of formats in different disciplines, has questionable value in undergraduate education.[12] When students are responsible for their own citation rules, instead of running a white-knuckle Google search for "MLA citation animated GIF linked Facebook hosted Tumblr" (for example), they can ask their classmates to decide on a standard, if time permits. Otherwise, they are more likely to be able to make a logical decision about how to cite a resource for which there is no specific citation format because they will have a thorough understanding of the reasons why their footnotes, endnotes, or in-text citations look the way they do.

As part of the process of inventing their own standardized citation style, students might also be asked to consider whether it would suit any of the purposes of citation to name things that have contributed to their papers that are not usually credited in academic work. How much of the research process should be documented? At the end of a brief article on the effects of Google, Chris DiBona suggests an alternative approach to citation in the age of Google by listing the searches he undertook while completing the piece.[13] A list of search terms might help readers discover the broader intellectual context of issues and ideas being discussed and to more thoroughly understand the writer's approach. That search results change over time and due to "personalized search" settings is an issue that might be raised during the discussion about whether to include search terms. Another example of work that could be credited, but usually is not, is software used by students. Do word processing programs, citation managers, and their developers not deserve credit?

Whatever students decide, their knowledge about the kinds of considerations that go into the development of citation styles will allow them to understand whatever systems they may be required to use in the future and to make similar judgments later in life. Because they will be required to think about the placement of commas, periods, and other punctuation marks, they will also have a greater awareness of the level of detail at which citation templates need to be read. Those students who go on to work in academia or in publishing may also be able to apply this experience to the revision of existing stylesheets and citation formats.

Citation is not condemned to cramped footnotes in arcane tomes and single-reader term papers. However, students will think that citation practices are simply rules to follow when citation guides are presented without any indication of where they came from or how they connect to practices many students already engage in on a daily basis. Perhaps even more troubling, many pedagogical approaches to citation do not focus on engaging in good practices but instead focus on avoiding bad ones. This negative focus creates distrust of the online world and a climate of fear in the classroom. Instead of wanting to give credit where it is due and to participate in community conversations, conscientious students panic over periods versus commas in bibliographic entries. Less well-intentioned students try to game the system—doing just enough work to avoid (provable) plagiarism. Teaching citation through web writing will not prevent all such cases, but it can help students develop intrinsic motivation to practice good citation as defined by whatever communities they participate in. When students are provided an understanding of the reasons for existing citation practices, they can also contribute to discussions of when citation should happen and how it should look. They can shape the future expectations of communities both within and outside of academia. Preparing students to participate fully and rationally in their present and future communities is, after all, one of the most important goals of higher education.

*About the author: Elizabeth Switaj is a Liberal Arts Instructor at the College of the Marshall Islands. She blogs at www.elizabethkateswitaj.net.*

## How to cite:

Elizabeth Switaj, "Web Writing and Citation: The Authority of Communities," in *Web Writing: Why and How for Liberal Arts Teaching and Learning*, ed. Jack Dougherty and Tennyson O'Donnell (University of Michigan Press/ Trinity College ePress edition, 2014), http://epress.trincoll.edu/webwriting/chapter/switaj.

*See an earlier version of this essay with open peer review comments.*[14]

# Notes

1. Dan Greenberg, "We've Got a Monster on the Loose: It's Called the Internet," *Brainstorm: The Chronicle of Higher Education*, February 27, 2008, http://chronicle.com/blogs/brainstorm/ weve-got-a-monster-on-the-loose-its-called-the-internet/5738; Jonathan Zittrain, *The Future of the Internet and How to Stop It* (New Haven: Yale University Press, 2008), 244, 317; Susan D. Blum, *My Word! Plagiarism and College Culture* (Ithaca, NY: Cornell UP, 2009), http://books.google.com/ books?id=J3uv5MQsdIkC&printsec=frontcover, 1; Thomas S. Dee and Brian A. Jacob, "Rational Ignorance in Education: A Field Experiment in Student Plagiarism," NBER Working Paper Series, National Bureau of Economic Research, January 2010, JEL No. I2,K4, http://www.swarthmore.edu/Documents/academics/economics/Dee/w15672.pdf, 3-4.

2. Paulo Freire, *Pedagogy of the Oppressed: 30th Anniversary Edition* (New York: Continuum, 2000).

3. Gerald Graff and Cathy Birkenstein, *They Say / I Say: The Moves That Matter in Academic Writing* (New York: W.W. Norton & Co., 2010).

4. Marc Parry, "Escalation in Digital Sleuthing Raises Quandary in Classrooms," *The Chronicle of Higher Education*, November 6, 2011, http://chronicle.com/article/Escalation-in-Digital/129652/

5. Blum, *My Word!*, 7-8.

6. Amy England, "The Dynamic Nature of Common Knowledge," in *Originality, Imitation, and Plagiarism: Teaching Writing in the Digital Age*, ed. Caroline Eisner and Martha Vicinus (Ann Arbor, MI: University of Michigan Press, 2008), 104–113, http://hdl.handle.net/2027/spo.5653382.0001.001, 100.

7. "Serious Cat" image, uploaded by author to http://epress.trincoll.edu/webwriting/wp-content/uploads/sites/12/2014/07/Switaj1-SeriousCat500px.jpg.

8. Problem Chylde, "Don't Hate; Reappropriate," Blog, *Problem Chylde*, April 8, 2008, http://problemchylde.wordpress.com/2008/04/08/dont-hate-appropriate/.

9. Holly, "This Has Not Been a Good Week for Woman of Color Blogging," Blog, *Feministe*, April 10, 2008, http://www.feministe.us/blog/archives/2008/04/10/this-has-not-been-a-good-week-for-woman-of-color-blogging/.

10. Traci Gardner, "An Easy-as-Apple-Pie Plagiarism Lesson," *Bedford Bits: Ideas for Teaching Composition*, November 23, 2010, http://blogs.bedfordstmartins.com/bits/plagiarism/an-easy-as-apple-pie-plagiarism-lesson/.

11. Michelle McQuigge, "Toronto Professor Learns Not All Editors Are Welcome on Wikipedia," *National Post*, July 4, 2013, http://news.nationalpost.com/2013/04/07/toronto-professor-learns-not-all-editors-are-welcome-on-wikipedia-when-class-assignment-backfires/; Nick DeSantis, "U. of Toronto Class Assignment Backfires in Clash on Wikipedia," *The Ticker: The Chronicle of Higher Education*, April 8, 2013, http://chronicle.com/blogs/ticker/u-of-toronto-professors-class-assignment-backfires-in-clash-on-wikipedia/58225; "Wikipedia: Education Noticeboard," *Wikipedia*, http://en.wikipedia.org/wiki/Wikipedia:Education_noticeboard.

12. Kurt Schick, "Citation Obsession? Get Over It!" *The Chronicle of Higher Education*, October 30, 2011, http://chronicle.com/article/Citation-Obsession-Get-Over/129575/; Isaac Sweeney, "Throwing the Citation Handbook Away," *On Hiring: The Chronicle of Higher Education*, July 23, 2012, http://chronicle.com/blogs/onhiring/throwing-the-citation-handbook-away/32581; Nels P. Highberg, "Plagiarism: An Administrator's Perspective," *ProfHacker: The Chronicle of Higher Education*, March 17, 2011, http://chronicle.com/blogs/profhacker/plagiarism-an-administrator's-perspective/31775.

13. Chris DiBona, "Ephemera and Back Again: Open Source and Public Sector, Google," in *Is the Internet Changing the Way You Think?: The Net's Impact on Our Minds and Future*, ed. John Brockman, (New York: Harper Perennial, 2011), 224–27.

14. Switaj, "Web Writing and Citation," in *Web Writing* (Open peer review edition, Fall 2013), http://webwriting2013.trincoll.edu/citation-annotation/switaj-2013/.

# Empowering Education with Social Annotation and Wikis

*Laura Lisabeth*

> Language is allowed to change and flow as needed by the world. —
> (Kristen, sophomore English major, in Group 1 Wiki)[1]

In *Empowering Education: Critical Teaching for Social Change*, Ira Shor cuts to the heart of one of our education culture's toughest issues when he says, "A good student answers questions but doesn't question answers. Knowledge and authority are fixed and unilateral." [2] This essay looks at a one-semester classroom research project that I undertook in an Introduction to English Studies class in which I tried to address that issue as it manifests in institutional assumptions about what constitutes acceptable academic writing and language. Students used a wiki as a format for socially "annotating" an iconic guidebook to good writing: *The Elements of Style* (hereafter *TEOS*) by William J. Strunk and E.B. White.[3] "The Elements of Styl(in)" project was a casual testing of the boundaries of the book, and *this* book in particular, as a cultural object—an examination of the way such a textbook authorizes standard academic discourse, an exploration of how our concept of text is changing with digital affordances, and a consideration of what could happen to text and to classroom power structures when "marginalia becomes demarginalized" in digital spaces.[4] Marginalia— "skirmishes against the author"[5] as poet Billy Collins once said—are what we in the Humanities cherish as the reader's act of individual empowerment in authorized spaces. In digital space these annotations can become a transformative public act as the text being annotated takes a backseat to the collective backchannel.

"The little book," as Professor Strunk called *TEOS*, originated as a short set of rules put together in a pamphlet for his composition students at Cornell University in the early part of the twentieth century. After being edited and embellished by White, a former student of Strunk, *TEOS* was published in 1959 and widely promoted in the college textbook market by The Macmillan Company. It has since come to represent, as a familiar and concise writing handbook wrapped in White's emblematic prose voice, a kind of standard knowledge assigned in a variety of courses by hopeful and well-intentioned professors as the go-to resource for error control. A quick internet search of syllabi nationwide finds *TEOS* a required text for a range of courses, from Composition and Writing classes to Environmental Policy and Rap Music and Hip-Hop Culture. Some of these course syllabi communicate an awareness of the ideological nature of Strunk & White's ideas of English language usage. A Michigan University's "Writing, Style and Technology" course includes an assigned "remake" of *TEOS*.[6] However, requiring that all student work "follow the rules for English Composition found in Strunk,"[7] is also a typical directive.

As a composition teacher, I thought it might be valuable to create a critical awareness around Strunk & White's book as a way of historicizing one of academic writing's more persistent texts, along with challenging the larger cultural norm of a universal and transparent academic discourse. Articles published recently in the inaugural issue of *Literacy In Composition Studies* resonated deeply with my experience of the split consciousness that attends the teaching of writing: the tension between a pluralized notion of literacies and persistent institutional and cultural expectations for a monolithic standard academic literacy. "Writing to pass," as Kate Vieira points out in "On The Social Consequences Of Literacy,"[8] is a common experience of freshman writers, and standard discourse of the sort prescribed by *TEOS* is a stubborn marker for success. Even when "other" literacies are valorized in classrooms, they maintain that categorization as *other*, or *out of school*, and what Brian Street has called "autonomous literacy" remains intact;[9] students often remain accountable to it, and its ideology stays "unchallenged and un(der)theorized," according to Carmen Kynard.[10] I wondered what kinds of questions would arise from having student writers engage rhetorically and ideologically with a writing text that has been widely regulatory, used as a quick reference, and mostly "unchallenged and un(der)theorized."

A relatively new venturer in digital pedagogy, I was curious to know how a public classroom engagement with annotating *TEOS* through a wiki might impact students' critical approach to this canonical work. How would engaging in discussion in a multimodal public forum impact student agency with regard to an authoritative text? Part of my purpose in conducting this experiment was to understand more about how digital writing practices might facilitate annotation as a form of "student protest," a component of Ira Shor's "empowered" classroom model in which students are explicitly given the freedom to challenge the substance of the course curriculum, and to critically examine Strunk and White's kind of "standard knowledge through which the status quo tries to promote and protect its position," [11] as Shor says:

> Because some groups in history have had the power to establish standard knowledge and standard usage, these canons need to be studied critically, not absorbed as a bogus common culture.[12]

Shor's notion of protest seemed to be an answer to Horner's call for a recognition of students' ongoing acts of "interpretation. . . reading the social environment and engaging and remaking that environment through communication."[13] Jesse Stommel, writing in the online journal *Hybrid Pedagogy*, warns of the danger of digital pedagogy replicating "vestigial structures of industrial era education" and sees digital pedagogy as one and the same with critical pedagogy: "Digital pedagogy demands that we rethink power relations between students and teachers — demands we create more collaborative and less hierarchical institutions for learning."[14] Bringing the guiding principal of transformation into student use of social forms of annotation in the classroom seemed like a goal worth pursuing, one that could challenge a canonized object like *TEOS* and broaden the concept of a student-produced academic text, while at the same time testing the collaborative learning potential of a digital composing tool.

In digital space, what is it like to leave a trace on an authorized text, to decenter it with jottings from margins that may only exist in the abstract? The internet is marked and in some ways defined by public comments features that can range wildly in their value as discourse. Some of the more successful text annotation sites like SocialBook and RapGenius offer simple platforms for students and classes to experience public engagement on the internet but generally the annotations on these sites replicate the close-reading practices of traditional literary studies. The computer interface allows what N. Katherine Hayles describes as a cognitive move from linearity to "large numbers of connections between. . . networks layered onto one another. . ."[15] The move to networked knowledge-making through combinations of visual, audio and alphabetic objects, allows for more critical engagement with social, cultural and historical networks. Unlike the historic model of marginalia as the act of an individual book owner, the wiki, as I imagined it, would be a collaborative space for purposeful bricolage, a less hierarchical model of authorship and critique, and a format in which the often unexpected links *between* digital objects would be at least as significant as the objects on their own: a use of digital pedagogy for critical engagement and "difficult thinking"[16] rather than for a re-creation of close-reading practices.

I asked students a question: What kinds of things do Strunk & White seem to be saying about writers, readers and the function and purpose of language?

Students worked in groups of three to four, collaborating on their final wiki pages, and leading a class discussion based on their work and on the comments their classmates made on their wiki presentations. (See sample excerpts from my students on this wiki page, which represents the type of thinking and writing they shared with me and their classmates.)[17] Groups worked together on choosing excerpts from *TEOS* that they wished to speak back to. I encouraged them to be creative and playful. A second form of annotation was created through the class comments on each group wiki presentation.

When the assignment was working best, Strunk and White's text acted like a philosopher's stone in the way its seeming neutrality concealed the power to release and reveal issues of class, race, gender and power embedded in student writers' understanding of academic discourse and "correct" usage of the English language.[18]

## 'This Is How We Do Things': Negotiating Identity

In *How We Think*, Hayles points out that human and machine intelligence interact in ways that demand a new framework for practices like reading and responding to text. Digital affordances reconfigure the objects of our fields as humanities teachers:

> . . . objects are seen not as static entities, that once created, remain the

same throughout time but rather are understood as constantly changing assemblages…[19]

This description is true as well for the English language, which is far from
a static object, though, as a dominant discourse, it is often treated as such.
English is a constantly evolving, "changing assemblage" of vernaculars, other languages and historical layers of standard usage. The wiki opened a
space for creative play (a definition of bricolage) with *TEOS* that material-
ized this concept of flux. Play itself is a form of critical inquiry, according to
Sean Michael Morris, Pete Rorabaugh and Jesse Stommel. Digital writing
enables practices that are "multimodal, collaborative, and playful — that
push the boundaries of disciplinary allegiances, and don't always wear their
brains on their sleeves, so to speak."[20]

In the following example, the associative leap one student made from
White's "Rule: 1" to a car commercial provided an opportunity to trace a
path to the thought that standard English is a kind of commodity fetish.

**Chapter 2: An Approach To Style**
**Rule: 1. Place yourself in the background**

" *Write in a way that draws the reader's attention to the sense and substance of the writing, rather than to the*
*mood and temper of the author. If the writing is solid and good, the mood and temper of the writer will*
*eventually be revealed and not at the expense of the work. Therefore, the first piece of advice is this: to achieve*
*style, begin by affecting none- that is, place yourself in the background. A careful and honest writer does not*
*need to worry about style.*(Strunk and White, 97)

**This section of *The Elements of Style* made me think of those**
**commercials that leave you with the memory of the hip song they**
**feature…. and nothing else…**

*Screenshot from Group 4's Wiki page, illustrating how a student responded (bottom) to The*
*Elements of Style.*

This selection, "Rule 1" from *TEOS*[21] is one of forty-three numbered pre-
scriptives in the book, and is taken from the section that White himself
wrote, titled: "An Approach To Style (With A List Of Reminders)." It was
annotated by Tracy, a senior English major, and member of Group 4.[22] Tracy's intuitive reference to a sales pitch contains the seeds of a multifaceted

critique of Carmen Kynard's "unquestioned and un(der)theorized dominant center" of academic discourse.[23] White affectionately endorsed the "sharp commands" of "Sergeant Strunk." [24] In the first edition, he set out to respond to American education's post GI Bill move away from the traditional rhetoric of his youth and toward a more inclusive mode of teaching writing to a newly diverse student population [25].

Class discussion around Rule 1 and its accompanying annotation focused on Tracy's reference to commodification and what might be for sale. What does standard English "buy" you? In exchange for what? What agendas are being served by the "selling" of standard English as access to the status quo? And what ways of knowing and seeing are hidden in the production of this desired discourse– a move that seems to reference commodity fetishism?[26] Tracy's choice of image as discussed below brought some of those questions to the foreground, including the surprising notion that standard English could qualify as a sort of commodity fetish, with all the associations of hidden identities that come with that term. Students were vocal about their perceived necessities for this exchange: the English majors wanted acceptance into a professional discourse community. Good grades come from good writing. In another move toward acceptance, Lane, an ROTC student, went on to write his final paper about the ways Strunk & White help him to write clearly and forcefully for his future career as an Army officer. He talked about family members coming to him to do their important correspondence because of the way he uses language.

Once the class read White's famous essay, "Once More To The Lake," originally published in 1942 for the readership of *Harper's Magazine*, students started to get a clearer picture of the social and historical context that gave rise to such vocabulary: dominant American culture, with values of individualism and privilege, an orderly hierarchy of affluent and educated summer vacationers and poorer, less educated local workers in the camp. The stillness of the lake mirrored the stillness of language promoted in *TEOS*, with nothing to break the sense of order—literally—until the end of your life. In this group discussion about "Once More To The Lake," one student insightfully remarked that the essay was a "this is how we do things" description. Another student noticed, coming back to White and *TEOS*:

this way of writing, too, is how WE (Strunk, White and their sociocultural milieu) do things.

Tracy further developed her response to Rule 1 by including an illustration from the 1999 film version of Frank McCourt's book *Angela's Ashes.* In her annotation she pointed out that, in the memoir, the author's "I" is fused to a foreground of "poverty and despair and hope and escape"[27] and the visual impact of two rain-soaked boys on an empty unpaved street makes a powerful and embodied counterimage to the slick car commercial leaving a song as its impression. Tracy's response that Rule 1 reminds her of the advertiser's disembodied soundtrack reflects that Strunk & White ask some writers literally to leave their bodies out of their writing, to separate from deep ways of knowing and adopt deceptively neutral ones instead. From creative assemblages students formed a nuanced context in which to situate their discussion of standard English, and their own relationships to the ideologies that go with it.

## Digital Poetics: Wearing Mine on Yours

In the screenshot below, Group 4 responds to one of Strunk's original rules: "Choose a suitable design and hold to it"[28] by disagreeing with the notion that "success" is attached to a writer's clear sense of standard forms. The dialog between page and screen is literally illustrated by the Tumblr image of the Gregson poem referencing older technologies of typewriter and paper straight out of Strunk & White's era. Gregson's poem points to many things. He seems to celebrate the agency of the writer by typing in defiance of the lines. Bending the traditional Romantic notion of individual expression, "hearts on ... sleeves" changes to the transgressive "mine on yours" instead. This movement from communication as a linear progression (author to lover/reader), when contrasted with the layered image of the poet speaking through two subjectivities, is a startlingly accurate metaphor for the networks accessible in digital writing. It could be the description of a retweet, and references the "performance self" of today's social media user. Group 4's choice of this image represented a moment in the classroom where all these many subtle and important connections could be teased out in discussion, bringing to light students' many modes of literacy, digital and material. This led to a crucial question for students to consider. *TEOS* is relatively unchanged from 1959; half of it is a text from 1918. How does the form and content of Gregson's poem suggest to you ways writing has changed and why has *TEOS* changed so little over the years?

Strunk and White believe that "the more clearly the writer perceives the shape, the better are the chances of success" (Strunk & White 31.) I don't completely agree with that because sometimes novels, poems, and other forms of writing come out of nowhere. In many cases the real genius is in the spontaneity.

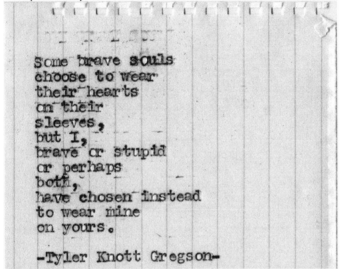

*Group 4's response to "choose a suitable design and hold to it" (TEOS, 31), which they illustrated with a poem by Tyler Knott Gregson (copyrighted by author and used here with permission).*

## Student Protest and the Power of Glitch

In his book *Noise Channels: Glitch And Error In Digital Culture*, Peter Krapp describes the embrace of glitch as an aesthetic that resists the "jitter-free" "tamper-resistant" aesthetic of digital sound production.[29] But he is really onto a much larger concern that resonated with me as a writing instructor who sometimes sees students suffering from Krapp's "agency panic of the user" [30] when they are faced with the jitter-free, tamper-resistant ground of academic discourse and standard English. Glitch, and the relationship between "noise" and "signal" in terms of language, knowledge and power is more than an aesthetic. It is a guiding image for critical engagement with the status quo: digital writing pedagogy should be a pedagogy of the glitch, identifying and recuperating whenever possible moments of breakdown in the autonomous status of standard discourse. The affordances of digital writing practices make tampering easy, and the concept of "glitch" as a digital or language byproduct "is a way of maintaining a space of playful exploration"[31] which allows for student agency and the accompanying unsettling of hierarchies.

Some student wiki annotations illustrate the productive resistance of glitch. When Lorenz, a sophomore physics major, commented on Group 1's presentation, he demonstrated the power of allowing other kinds of knowledge to change standard English, an important point I had hoped students would find their way into. In contrast to Strunk and White's call for orthodox spelling, Lorenz pointed out the importance of what he called "da VuRnAkULAR" and intuitively channeled James Joyce and the Modernist project of jamming the signals of traditional discourse. During the discussion period, Lorenz blurted out "I hate this book," and described a scene in his dorm where he and his friends had gone through *TEOS* and "laughed at it" together. This was exactly the kind of "protest" I had been curious to see evolve out of this project: the intact, neutral and autonomous writing handbook examined and protested through exposure to the experiences of the student community. Foregrounding a noisy discourse that alludes to Joyce and Irvine Welsh, and arguing for the benefits of non-standard language, Lorenz outlined that protest most eloquently when he reappropriated the whole concept of "Propa" language, and characterized "speaking/riting" as "evolving 1 minde at eh time."[32]

## Looking Forward: WikiThink and Object Oriented Writing

One place for further research lies in the ways that students find agency as they publicly publish a comment and as they negotiate between an "authentic self" and the complex subjectivity of digital performance. In *My Word! Plagiarism And College Culture*, Susan Blum cites the anxious quality of a student's "performance self" in the age of Facebook, Instagram and blogs:

> . . . the performance self must constantly worry about the judgments
> of others, must constantly wonder if a given set of actions is the most
> effective, or is even appreciated, and what the consequences will be of
> her or his actions.[33]

This "constantly groomed version"[34] of the self complicates critical engagement with issues and ideas that might involve staking claims and challenging group norms. In this way, social annotation can complicate the critical pedagogy I would like to practice. During the open review of this essay, a related point was raised about individual student response to a text and how students may "feel their personal reading is being overtaken by others who got there and left comments first."[35] I believe both of these valid issues of negotiating student agency in social annotation should be part of further research into ways that we will teach digital reading and writing practices. How does the traditional cultural sense of ownership of one's reading intersect with the collaborative and communal potential of the digital? Tracy and the students of Group 4 shared material and insights that exposed fascinating networks of knowledge needing to be brought to the surface through discussion, suggesting that digital pedagogy includes developing student reading of non-linear, multimodal connections in sophisticated critical ways, as I expand on below. Lorenz found a way to speak to authenticity while exploiting a digital public forum in a way that challenged and delighted the others in the class. What led to his creative and substantial challenging of *TEOS*'s standard English that effectively served both individual and communal interests?

In broad terms, "The Elements of Styl(in')" reflection profits from recent work in the areas of collaboration and object oriented theories that propose reconfigurations of academic writing.[36] These fields offer exciting thought for digital writing pedagogy, particularly as web writing continues to evolve and gain acceptance as rigorous academic discourse. A recent article by William Duffy sees collaborative writing as better configured outside of Composition's long-held "conversation imperative"[37]; He looks instead to "something that a social turn theory of collaboration lacks: a third character at work in the equation, those objects that collaborators discourse about."[38] What Duffy points to as interaction with "discursive ecologies" of human and non-human "actors"[39] describes how the class went about composing and receiving the bricolaged wiki. Building again on Duffy, we "triangulated" thinking around TEOS and other discourse objects: its history and authors plus pictures, videos, text blocks, ideas, questions and opinions. The surprising combination of objects such as a car commercial, standard English and a film still from Angela's Ashes turned our focus on tracing the links between them. It is in the tracing of those links that new knowledge is made in the realm of the "adjacent possible…the range of discourse available to us at any particular moment."[40] Expanding the idea of collaboration in the writing classroom to include objects of discourse as equal interlocutors along with the humans makes sense in our post-human world, Duffy suggests. I think it also opens new avenues of inquiry for students via still emerging digital reading and writing and thinking. Students are not always comfortable with the "risky Utopian leaps"[41] they are asked to take in Shor's empowered classroom. I remember Lorenz' nervous body language as he said to me: "I hate this book," in a public group of peers and professor, some of whom had voiced support for *TEOS* as a handbook. That moment contributes to my belief that these emergent practices and the less easily defined practice of "wikithink" must be developed as critical "protest" tools and rigorous ways to "question the answers" through non-hierarchical collaborative knowledge-making.

*About the author: Laura Lisabeth (@lauralhny) is a doctoral candidate at St. Johns University in Queens, NY, where she currently teaches literature and composition.*

## How to cite:

Laura Lisabeth, "Empowering Education with Social Annotation and Wikis," in *Web Writing: Why and How for Liberal Arts Teaching and Learning*, ed. Jack Dougherty and Tennyson O'Donnell (University of Michigan Press/Trinity College ePress edition, 2014), http://epress.trincoll.edu/webwriting/chapter/lisabeth.

*See an earlier version of this essay with open peer review comments.*[42]

# Notes

1. "Sample student excerpts from Group 1 Wiki, ENG 2200: Introduction to English Studies, St. Johns University, Queens, New York, Spring 2013, http://introtoenglishstudies.pbworks.com/w/page/68417145/Group%201%20Wiki%20Page.

2. Ira Shor, *Empowering Education: Critical Teaching For Social Change* (Chicago: The University of Chicago Press, 1992).

3. William J. Strunk and E.B. White, *The Elements of Style (TEOS)*, illustrated by Maira Kalman (New York: Penguin Books, 2000).

4. "'Amplified Marginalia': Social Reading, Listening, and Writing," HASTAC forum, May 9, 2013, http://www.hastac.org/forums/amplified-marginalia.

5. Billy Collins, "Marginalia" poem, 2005, http://www.billy-collins.com/2005/06/marginalia.html.

6. Derek N. Mueller, ENGL 328 "Writing, Style and Technology" syllabus, Winter 2012, http://www.derekmueller.net/rc/teaching/archive/engl328wi12/syllabus.html.

7. Richard Mook, MUS 362 "Rap Music and Hip Hop Culture" syllabus, Summer 2013, https://herbergeronline.asu.edu/hiphop/syllabus.pdf.

8. Kate Vieira, "On the Social Consequences of Literacy," *Literacy in Composition Studies* 1 (March 2013): 29, http://licsjournal.org/OJS/index.php/LiCS/article/view/7/.

9. Bruce Horner, "Ideologies of Literacy, 'Academic Literacies,' and Composition Studies," *Literacy in Composition Studies* 1 (2013): 1-9, paragraph 2.

10. Carmen Kynard, "Literacy/Literacies Studies and the Still-Dominant White Center," *Literacy in Composition Studies* 1 (2013): 63-65, paragraph 5.

11. Shor, 34-35.

12. ibid.

13. Editors' Mission Statement, *Literacy in Composition Studies* 1 (2013), p. v, paragraph 2.

14. Jesse Stommel, "Decoding Digital Pedagogy, Pt. 2: (Un)Mapping the Terrain," *Hybrid Pedagogy: A Digital Journal of Learning, Teaching, and Technology* March 05, 2013, paragraph 3, http://www.hybridpedagogy.com/Journal/decoding-digital-pedagogy-pt-2-unmapping-the-terrain/.

15. N. Katherine Hayles, *How We Think: Digital Media and Contemporary Technogenesis* (Chicago: The University of Chicago Press, 2012), 32.

16. Mark Sample, "Difficult Thinking about the Digital Humanities," *Sample Reality*, May 12, 2014, http://www.samplereality.com/2014/05/12/difficult-thinking-about-the-digital-humanities/.

17. "Sample student excerpts from Group 1," ENG 2200, Spring 2013, http://introtoenglishstudies.pbworks.com/w/page/68417145/Group 1 Wiki Page.

18. Laura Lisabeth, "The Elements of Styl(in) Group Project Assignment," Google Document, ENG 2200: Introduction to English Studies, St. Johns University, Queens, New York,

Spring 2013, https://docs.google.com/document/d/1TL6DU1c-UvkqbzYxV-ZwN6VDAOkRFg-mfQwfaz0bi9A/edit?usp=sharing.

19. Katherine Hayles, *How We Think*, 13.

20. Sean Michael Morris, Pete Rorabaugh and Jesse Stommel, "Beyond Rigor," *Hybrid Pedagogy*, Oct. 9, 2013, http://www.hybridpedagogy.com/journal/beyond-rigor/.

21. Strunk and White, 97.

22. "Sample student excerpts from Group 4 wiki," ENG 2200, Spring 2013, http://introtoenglishstudies.pbworks.com/w/page/68678680/Group 4 Wiki Page.

23. Kyndard, *Literacy/Literacies*, para. 5.

24. Strunk and White, xiii.

25. Catherine Prendergast, "The Fighting Style: Reading the Unabomber's Strunk and White" *College English* 72:1 (2009): 13.

26. "The Spectacle of the Other," *Representation*, second edition, edited by Stuart Hall, Jessica Evans and Sean Nixon (Sage Publications, New York, 2013), p. 256.

27. Tracy, comment on Group 4 wiki presentation, April 1, 2013.

28. Strunk and White, 31.

29. Peter Krapp, *Noise Channels: Glitch And Error In Digital Culture* (Minneapolis: University of Minnesota Press, 2011), xx.

30. Krapp, 54.

31. Ibid.

32. Lorenz, comment on Group 1 Wiki Page, http://introtoenglishstudies.pbworks.com/w/page/68417145/Group%201%20Wiki%20Page.

33. Susan D. Blum, *My Word! Plagiarism And College Culture* (Ithaca: Cornell University Press, 2009), 64.

34. Blum, 70

35. Barbara Fister, comment on open peer review version of this essay, *Web Writing*, Fall 2013 edition, http://webwriting2013.trincoll.edu/citation-annotation/lisabeth-2013/#comment-8323.

36. Ian Bogost, *Alien Phenomenology or What It's Like To Be A Thing* (University of Minnesota Press, 2012).

37. William Duffy, "Collaboration (in) Theory: Reworking the Social Turn's Conversational Imperative," *College English* 76 (2014): 416-435.

38. Duffy, 7.

39. Ibid., 10.

40. Ibid., 7.

41. Joe Marshall Hardin, "Review of *When Students Have Power* by Ira Shor," *Journal of Rhetoric, Culture and Politics* 17 (1997): 525-529, http://jaconlinejournal.com/archives/vol17.3/hardin-when.pdf.

42. Lisabeth, "Empowering Education with Social Annotation and Wikis," in *Web Writing* (Open peer review edition, Fall 2013), http://webwriting2013.trincoll.edu/citation-annotation/lisabeth-2013/.

# There Are No New Directions in Annotations

*Jason B. Jones*

## Annotations Are the Original Web Writing

The fact that more or less anyone can publish to the web often makes people think that self-publication is its main use. And maybe that is its most common use. But the propleptic visions of Vannevar Bush and Douglas Engelbart, writing in the 1940s and 1960s respectively, remind us of the primary importance of annotations.[1]

In these early imagined futures of computing, Bush and Engelbart focus on the ability to mark up a document of some sort, the ability to formally instantiate that marked-up document, and the ability to share that with others—each of these three abilities are still fundamental to the way we interact online with text, images, sound, and video. They can also be invaluable aspects of web writing for the liberal arts.

Annotation is of course far older than the web. For as long as there has been writing, there have been readers who follow along and "write back." Medieval marginalia is so well-known that amusing or disconcerting instances of it are fodder for viral aggregators such as Buzzfeed and Brainpickings, and the fascination with other readers' reading is manifest in sites such as Melville's Marginalia Online or Harvard's online exhibit of marginalia from six personal libraries.[2] When I was a graduate student, one of my favorite moments was visiting the collections at UC Santa Cruz, and looking at Thomas Carlyle's alternatively-metered edition of Robert Browning's poems. What has become distinctive now is the extreme rapidity of searching one's own marginalia, as well the ability to see how others read. For these purposes, the web has proved ideal.

Even before there was a web, there were dreams of annotations. Vannevar Bush's hypothetical "memex," described in "As We May Think", reaches its apotheosis in imagining the future utility of annotations:

Wholly new forms of encyclopedias will appear, ready made with a mesh of associative trails running through them, ready to be dropped into the memex and there amplified. The lawyer has at his touch the associated opinions and decisions of his whole experience, and of the experience of friends and authorities. The patent attorney has on call the millions of issued patents, with familiar trails to every point of his client's interest. The physician, puzzled by a patient's reactions, strikes the trail established in studying an earlier similar case, and runs rapidly through analogous case histories, with side references to the classics for the pertinent anatomy and histology. The chemist, struggling with the synthesis of an organic compound, has all the chemical literature before him in his laboratory, with trails following the analogies of compounds, and side trails to their physical and chemical behavior. The historian, with a vast chronological account of a people, parallels it with a skip trail which stops only on the salient items, and can follow at any time contemporary trails which lead him all over civilization at a particular epoch. There is a new profession of trail blazers, those who find delight in the task of establishing useful trails through the enormous mass of the common record. The inheritance from the master becomes, not only his additions to the world's record, but for his disciples the entire scaffolding by which they were erected.

The "associative trails" blazed by the expert poring over the record of human invention and creation would, Bush foresaw, soon be themselves available for ready searching. In addition to making repeated research much quicker, such a scheme would also allow for the serendipitous discovery of new ideas. As Steven Johnson has pointed out, systems like DEVONThink, which automatically suggest just associative trails as Bush imagined, facilitate "finding documents that I've forgotten about altogether, finding documents that I didn't know I was looking for," and "can create almost lyrical connections between ideas." The power and limit of an individual memex such as DEVONThink, according to Johnson, is that "I have curated all these passages myself, which makes each individual connection far more likely to be useful in some way."[3] By contrast, the open architecture of the World-Wide Web, which posits "a global distributed medium in which anyone can be a publisher, and a hypertext document structure in which it is trivial to jump from a newspaper article to an academic essay to an encyclopedia entry in a matter of seconds," makes for a far more open system of annotation and discovery.[4]

Douglas Engelbart's 1962 essay "Augmenting Human Intellect: A Conceptual Framework" already recognized that "It would actually seem quite feasible to develop a unit record system around cards and mechanical sorting, with automatic trail establishment and trail-following facility, and with associated means for selective copying or data transfer, that would enable development of some very powerful methodology for everyday intellectual work."[5] Recognizing that a mechanical card-based system would be obsolete at the moment it was delivered, Engelbart stretches out just a little, and imagines a situation not unlike our own (the speaker is a hypothetical "friendly fellow" named Joe):

> I'm sure that you've had the experience of working over a journal article to get comprehension and perhaps some special-purpose conclusions that you can integrate into your own work. Well, when you ever get handy at roaming over the type of symbol structure which we have been showing here, and you turn for this purpose to another person's work that is structured in this way, you will find a terrific difference there in the ease of gaining comprehension as to what he has done and why he has done it, and of isolating what you want to use and making sure of the conditions under which you can use it. This is true even if you find his structure left in the condition in which he has been working on it—that is, with no special provisions for helping an outsider find his way around. But we have learned quite a few simple tricks for leaving appended road signs, supplementary information, questions, and auxiliary links on our working structures—in such a manner that they never get in our way as we work—so that the visitor to our structure can gain his comprehension and isolate what he wants in marvelously short order. Some of these techniques are quite closely related to those used in automated-instruction programming—perhaps you know about 'teaching machines?'[6]

As Engelbart's example makes clear, the work of annotation is already a thing all students and scholars do: we work over other people's texts in order to better understand it. Being able to draw on the experiences of others is also surely helpful. After all, that is why things such as footnotes and endnotes exist in teaching editions of books, or in anthologies. Bush and Engelbart add to this already well-known formula the ability to easily share this experience. Lurking behind their imaginative essays is an ideal of full comprehension–that we might be able to truly understand one another if we could just track down all the relevant influences and contexts and motives. We can also see how such a vision becomes oddly depersonalizing. In Bush's memes, for example, the thoughts and expertise of a colleague might be perfectly captured so that we don't even need that person's flash of insight.

While I don't think we need to subscribe fully to an ethics of full understanding, I do think that the notion of better understanding a text through others' experience of it is arguably the foundational experience of most liberal arts classrooms. Students read or watch things, they think and write about them, and they come together to share how they have come to understand the text. What Bush and Engelbart dramatize is a world in which that experience is made vivid and accessible. When contemplating incorporating web writing into one's own courses, it can be helpful to remember that annotation has a long and honorable tradition at the heart of web writing.

## Annotating in the Liberal Arts Classroom

When thinking about annotation in the liberal arts classroom, the model that is probably the most familiar is that of a scholarly edition or teaching edition: some sort of primary document, marked up with the commentary of an editor or editors. As Laura Lisabeth shows in "Empowering Education with Social Annotation and Wikis" (in this volume), this model can be quite powerful when extended to include students. Annotations in this situation need not be restricted to clarifying factual, contextual, or textual conundrums, but can indeed be as interpretative as one wishes. Indeed, it would be possible to have classes construct their own self-edited anthologies of source materials—at least as long as the material is out of copyright.

We need not be restricted to remediating online already-existing experiences. Indeed, as Bush and Engelbart's examples suggest, when viewed in a certain light, the entire web can seem driven by a massive will-to-annotate. Tim Carmody has argued that the fundamentals of blogging are essentially annotative in the most generous sense: "I have seen something that I feel strongly enough to think and write about, and what would make me happiest is if you look at it, then think and write about it too."[7] Social bookmarking tools, such as Pinboard.in or Diigo or Delicious, or socially-aware reference systems, such as Mendeley, or Zotero, can also be opportunities for students to mark up and share items that they feel strongly about.[8]

But there are other forms, too. Adrianne Wadewitz, Anne Ellen Geller, and Jon Beasley-Murray have described the ways in which having students write for Wikipedia, which demands citations, turns into a remarkably reflexive process of research, writing, and revision.[9] Although many academics (still!) reflexively mistrust Wikipedia's flexible epistemology, exposing students to the process of needing to document all claims can be helpful.

Beyond the world of pure text, Mark Sample and Kelly Schrum have described the possibilities of collating multimedia and multimodal forms online. As Sample explains:

> In addition to making student writing public, I've also begun taking the words out of writing. Why must writing, especially writing that captures critical thinking, be composed of words? Why not images? Why not sound? Why not objects? The word text, after all, derives from the Latin textus, meaning that which is woven, strands of different material intertwined together. Let the warp be words and the weft be something else entirely.[10]

There are an increasing number of tools that allow one to think more expansively about annotation, such as Pinterest or even meme generators and GIF tools.[11]

More substantial weaving can be done with tools such as Scalar or Omeka, each of which lend themselves well to juxtaposing text with digital objects of all sorts. Omeka is a tool for building online exhibitions, and is commonly used by librarians and museums. Julie Meloni has written an excellent introduction to it, but the "What is Omeka?" video is also helpful.[12] Jeff McClurken has outlined some ways to use Omeka in the classroom, and the Center for History and New Media has recently assembled a more comprehensive list of examples.[13]

Scalar is a more comprehensive multimodal publishing platform, but is still very much rooted in Bush's and Engelbardt's vision of annotation. The Scalar project aims to "enabl[e] scholars to work more organically with archival materials, creating interpretive pathways through the materials and enabling new forms of analysis. In particular, we aim to draw out more general lessons about the relationship of scholarly analysis to emerging digital typologies or genres; about how best to organize the digital archive to facilitate scholarly analysis; and about efficient and meaningful work flows between primary evidence, research and publication."[14] Indeed, Scalar's Annotations feature allows the direct markup of video, images, and more–essentially anything that can be captured in a digital repository. The best way to come to grips with Scalar's classroom potential is by working through this Scalar exhibit on "Teaching and Learning Multimodal Communications".[15]

## New Tools for Old Models: CommentPress, Highbrow, and Hypothes.is

In this last section, I want to highlight three tools for annotation that indicate both the potential of new tools and also how radically familiar they should be to anyone in a liberal arts environment.

CommentPress will of course already be familiar to anyone who read the open peer-review edition of this book, because it is the publication platform. CommentPress was developed at the Institute for the Future of the Book as a way to permit "readers to comment paragraph-by-paragraph, line-by-line or block-by-block in the margins of a text. Annotate, gloss, workshop, debate: with CommentPress you can do all of these things on a finer-grained level, turning a document into a conversation."[16] CommentPress is a plugin and theme for the blogging platform (WordPress) which facilitates more focused conversation than a typical blog site. Typically, documents created in CommentPress are chunked into paragraphs, allowing readers to comment on a text paragraph by paragraph.

As Fitzpatrick has pointed out, the visibility of this annotative action is both a gift and a problem. Did most people comment on paragraph 1 because it was the best? The worst? The only one they read? And what does the lack of comments mean? Does that indicate readerly assent, indifference, or worse? An assignment built on CommentPress would want to think explicitly about the distribution of comments.[17]

LINK            BLEAK HOUSE BY CHARLES DICKENS        [ LOGIN TO EDIT ]
SEARCH TEXT       < LEFT | + ZOOM IN | ZOOM OUT - | RIGHT >       COMMENTARIES

**Section**                      **Notes**

Click on a section above to inspect it here.

*Welcome to the Highbrow Commentary Browser version 0.14*

*Click on a note in the text on the right to inspect it here.*

*Annotation of "Bleak House" by Charles Dickens on HighBrow, created by Jason B. Jones.*

Highbrow is a "textual annotation browser" developed by Reinhard Engels at Harvard. Pictured above is a Highbrow-enabled version of Charles Dickens's *Bleak House* that my students used last fall.[18] What is nice about it from a teaching point of view is captured in the screenshot: The tool gives you a heatmap, as it were, of where students are commenting in a particular text, providing information which could then be used to guide discussion.

Engels has explained how to use Highbrow (It's still early days for the tool, so some of this might have changed.) My students found the tool very easy-to-use, and I liked being able to browse annotations before class. Similarly, Augusta Rohrbach and David Tagnani report great satisfaction in using Highbrow for cross-institution collaborations.[19]

CommentPress and Highbrow are obviously similar in that they are focused on a collective reading of a single document. The priority is always on the main text, then the comments are important, but still secondary. And the comments remain attached, in some sense, to the primary document. It is possible to imagine other visions of social reading, however. Amazon's Kindle e-readers, and the related apps for other platforms, will make passages visible that other readers have highlighted. Kindle users can even access their notes, using tools such as Bookcision, for repurposing into other contexts.[20] While CommentPress and especially Highbrow imagine a deliberately collective reading of a text–as in a class or research group–the Kindle lets us imagine other forms of accessing the common reading experiences of individuals.

For a quite different approach to annotation it is worth paying attention to Hypothes.is, an annotation tool that is just in its alpha stages. What's powerful about Hypothes.is is that in principle it allows *anything* online to be annotated, without special tools beyond a browser plug-in. (I highly recommend Dan Whaley's talk, "The Revolution Will Be Annotated" as a defense of annotating.[21]) Hypothes.is lets you read other people's annotations, and it also gives you control over your own annotations so that you're able to collect them elsewhere. Hypothes.is is even trying to address problems in cross-format annotation, which occurs when the same document appears in multiple formats, or in multiple places.[22] Hypothes.is's ultimate goal is to allow the same annotation to appear in the same place on all of those formats, and in all of those places, which will truly bring Vannevar Bush's memex to life.

Because Hypothes.is is still in an alpha stage of development, it is difficult to anticipate exactly how the service will develop. But Ryan Brazell has described some of the appeal:

> Whether you are using the browser plugin or viewing a permanent link, all of the pertinent data and metadata is maintained: the full original source, the specific section of the text referred to by the annotator, and any comments that refer to that specific section of text.[23]

Hypothes.is is one of the fruits of the Open Annotation project that has been working on metadata standards that will allow different annotation and reference systems to work together.[24] One of the things that this work implies is that, in a few years, there will be less pressure about which tool one chooses, because (in principle) all of them should be able to work together.

What's striking about annotation at the present time is how ubiquitous it is—indeed it is so common that it is almost becoming invisible. Social media platforms such as Facebook encourage annotating photos by identifying people's faces; YouTube videos allow for the easy insertion of brief comments about a video; photo platforms such as Flickr allow for free-form notes that allow people to share tips for taking better pictures, as well as to admire particularly well-composed shots; SoundCloud lets music and podcast fans comment directly on moments in a song or other digital recording. Annotation is so popular at the present time that one site, Genius.com (formerly RapGenius) has gotten into the business of annotating all documents whatsoever, and tens of thousands of users have participated in the collaborative marking-up of a wide variety of texts.

(As this example makes clear, at least in the United States, copyright will be a concern. Although it goes beyond the scope of this essay, it does seem clear that annotation works best when the original document is in the public domain, has been licensed for public use, or is otherwise made available by the rights owners. Having said that, what is convenient about annotation is that it often leaves the source material in place and inserts comments as metadata. Hopefully this approach will be understood as fair use, although that will remain to be seen.)

Not all web writing can be, or ought to be, primarily annotative in nature. Ultimately, students in a liberal arts classroom need to go beyond glossing the perspectives of others, and move toward formulating their own distinctive voice. Having said that, the kinds of annotation practices available today offer a remarkable set of tools for students to begin that work, and in a more collaborative, connected way than has been previously possible.

*About the author: Jason B. Jones is director of educational technology at Trinity College (Hartford). With George Williams, he is the co-founding editor of ProfHacker, currently hosted at the Chronicle of Higher Education. Follow him on Twitter at @jbj.*

### How to cite:

Jason B. Jones, "There Are No New Directions in Annotations," in *Web Writing: Why and How for Liberal Arts Teaching and Learning*, ed. Jack Dougherty and Tennyson O'Donnell (University of Michigan Press/Trinity College ePress edition, 2014), http://epress.trincoll.edu/webwriting/chapter/jones.

*See an earlier version of this essay with open peer review comments.*[25]

# Notes

1. Vannevar Bush, "As We May Think," *The Atlantic,* July 1945, http://www.theatlantic.com/magazine/archive/1945/07/as-we-may-think/303881/; Douglas C. Engelbart, "Augmenting Human Intellect: A Conceptual Framework," SRI Summary Report AFOSR-3223, October 1962, http://www.dougengelbart.org/pubs/augment-3906.html.

2. "20 Bizarre Examples Of Medieval Marginalia," *BuzzFeed Community,* September 28, 2012, http://www.buzzfeed.com/babymantis/20-bizarre-examples-of-medieval-marginalia-1opu; Maria Popova, "Oh, My Hand: Complaints Medieval Monks Scribbled in the Margins of Illuminated Manuscripts," *Brainpickings,* March 21, 2012, http://www.brainpickings.org/index.php/2012/03/21/monk-complaints-manuscripts/; Steven Olsen-Smith, Peter Norberg, and Dennis C. Marnon, eds., *Melville's Marginalia Online,* http://melvillesmarginalia.org/front.php; "Marginalia: Six Personal Libraries," Harvard University Library Open Collections Program, http://ocp.hul.harvard.edu/reading/marginalia.html.

3. Steven Johnson, *Where Good Ideas Come From: The Natural History of Innovation* (New York: Riverhead, 2010), pp. 114, 116. Johnson has also discussed his use of DEVONthink online: http://www.stevenberlinjohnson.com/movabletype/archives/000230.html.

4. For the latest in web-enabled serendipitous discovery, see the new tool by the Center for History and New Media, Serendip-o-matic: http://serendipomatic.org/.

5. Engelbart, "Augmenting Human Intellect."

6. Ibid.

7. Tim Carmody, "Three-step Dance," *Kottke.org,* May 6, 2011, http://kottke.org/11/05/three-step-dance.

8. These resources can be accessed at: Pinboard (http://pinboard.in); Diigo (http://www.diigo.com); Delicious (http://www.delicious.com); Mendeley (http://www.mendeley.com); Zotero (http://www.zotero.org).

9. Adrianne Wadewitz, Anne Ellen Geller, and Jon Beasley-Murray, "Opening up the Academy with Wikipedia," *Wikipedia.org,* http://en.wikipedia.org/wiki/User:Awadewit/TeachingEssay. This essay is also available as "Opening up the Academy with *Wikipedia*" in the print edition of *Hacking the Academy: New Approaches to Scholarship and Teaching from Digital Humanities* (Ann Arbor: University of Michigan Press, 2013), p. 84-86.

10. This is also available as "What's Wrong with Writing Essays: A Conversation" by Mark Sample and Kelly Schrum in the print edition of *Hacking the Academy: New Approaches to Scholarship and Teaching from Digital Humanities* (Ann Arbor: University of Michigan Press, 2013), p.87-97.

11. Pinterest is available at http://www.pinterest.com. For an exemplary assignment drawing on the annotative power of popular memes, see Bill Wolf's "WRTS10 Assignment 2: Memes and Remixes," *williamwolff.org,* http://williamwolff.org/courses/wrt-spring-2010/wrt-assignments-s10/wrts10-assignment-2-memes-and-remixes/. And for a representative collection of assignments using animated GIF files, see the DS106: Digital Storytelling assignment bank, University of Mary Washington, http://assignments.ds106.us/types/animatedgifassignments/.

12. Julie Meloni, "A Brief Introduction to Omeka," *ProfHacker*, August 9, 2010, http://chronicle.com/blogs/profhacker/a-brief-introduction-to-omeka/26079; "What is Omeka?" video, http://vimeo.com/6401343.

13. Jeffrey McClurken, "Teaching with Omeka," *ProfHacker*, August 9, 2010, http://chronicle.com/blogs/profhacker/teaching-with-omeka/26078; "Back to School Edition, Use Omeka in Your Class," Center for History and New Media, August 20, 2013, http://omeka.org/blog/tag/teaching-and-learning/.

14. "About the Alliance," The Alliance for Networking Visual Culture, http://scalar.usc.edu/about/.

15. Alyssa Arbuckle, Alison Hedley, Shaun Macpherson, Alyssa McLeod, Jana Millar Usiskin, Daniel Powell, Jentery Sayers, Emily Smith, Michael Stevens, *Teaching and Learning Multimodal Communication*, version 58, http://scalar.usc.edu/maker/english-507/index.

16. "Welcome to CommentPress," Institute for the Future of the Book, http://futureofthebook.org/commentpress/. For a discussion of CommentPress in the context of academic publishing, see Kathleen Fitzpatrick's *Planned Obsolescence: Publishing, Technology, and the Future of the Academy* (New York University Press, 2011), or watch her video, "Tulane Digital Trends: Kathleen Fitzpatrick and CommentPress," 2008, https://www.youtube.com/watch?v=295_rd1W720.

17. For a fascinating discussion of pedagogy and CommentPress, see Matt K. Gold's interview with Bob Stein, "Becoming Book-Like," *Kairos* 15:2 (2010), http://kairos.technorhetoric.net/15.2/interviews/?page_id=33.

18. Reinhard Engels, "Highbrow: A Textual Annotation Browser," https://osc.hul.harvard.edu/highbrow/.

19. Augusta Rohrbach and David Tagnani, "Reading with the Stars: Teaching with the Highbrow Annotation Browser," *ProfHacker*, December 6, 2011, http://chronicle.com/blogs/profhacker/reading-with-the-stars-teaching-with-the-highbrow-annotation-browser/37591.

20. Bookcision is available at http://www.norbauer.com/bookcision/.

21. Dan Whaley, "The Revolution Will Be Annotated," Youtube.com, July 2, 2013, https://www.youtube.com/watch?v=2jTctBbX_kw.

22. Ed Summers, "Cross Format Annotation," Hypothes.is, May 13, 2013, http://hypothes.is/blog/cross-format-annotation/.

23. Ryan Brazell, "Hypothes.is Just Might Make The Web Relevant Again," *RyanBrazell.net*, August 16, 2013, http://ryanbrazell.net/hypothesis-just-might-make-the-web-relevant-again/.

24. The Open Annotation Project's website is http://www.openannotation.org/. You can watch Robert Sanderson and Herbert Van de Sompel, both of Los Alamos National Laboratory, discuss "Interoperable Annotation," video, http://vimeo.com/8481040.

25. Jones, "There Are No New Directions in Annotations," in *Web Writing* (Open peer review edition, Fall 2013), http://webwriting2013.trincoll.edu/citations/jones-2013/.